William Porcher Dubose

The Ecumenical Councils

William Porcher Dubose

The Ecumenical Councils

ISBN/EAN: 9783337301675

Printed in Europe, USA, Canada, Australia, Japan

Cover: Foto ©Lupo / pixelio.de

More available books at **www.hansebooks.com**

Library of The Theological Seminary

PRINCETON · NEW JERSEY

⇶⃪

PRESENTED BY

Mrs. Kennedy History Fund

'*By a bright, attractive appearance, by a very comfortable typography, by the participation of dignified scholars and experienced writers, this Series is likely to enjoy a deserved popularity.*'—THE NEW WORLD.

Eras

of

The Christian Church.

EDITED BY

JOHN FULTON, D.D., LL.D.,

AUTHOR OF 'INDEX CANONUM,' 'CHALCEDONIAN DECREE,' ETC.

MESSRS. T. & T. CLARK have pleasure in announcing the Serial Publication of 'ERAS OF THE CHRISTIAN CHURCH.'

Christians of all denominations have begun to understand that many of the existing divisions of Christendom had their origin partly in misapprehensions and partly in causes which have long since passed away, and that the cause of unity will be most surely promoted by a calm and impartial study of the history of the Church in its long and varied experience under the guidance of the Holy Spirit.

It is impossible, however, for persons of ordinary leisure and opportunity to make a profound study of ecclesiastical history. It has therefore been suggested that a series of popular monographs, giving, so to speak, a bird's-eye view of the most important epochs in the life of the Church, would supply a real want, and this Series is intended to furnish such monographs.

The Series will be completed in Ten Volumes,

Price Six Shillings each.

† [P.T.O.

ERAS OF THE CHRISTIAN CHURCH.

Three Volumes are now ready, price 6s. each.

I.
The Age of Hildebrand.

BY PROFESSOR M. R. VINCENT, D.D.,
PROFESSOR OF NEW TESTAMENT EXEGESIS, UNION THEOLOGICAL SEMINARY, NEW YORK.

The magnificent scheme of ecclesiastical supremacy projected by Hildebrand; the bold attempt of Boniface VIII. to absorb the power of the Empire into the papacy, which led at last to the temporary extinction of papal power, though not of papal claims, at the Council of Constance; the rise of the Franciscan and Dominican Orders; the conditions of monastic and clerical life; the beginnings of the modern national spirit; the establishment and progress of universities.

II.
The Age of the Great Western Schism.

BY REV. CLINTON LOCKE, D.D.,
CHICAGO.

The Great Schism, dividing European Christendom for generations into two hostile camps, which was terminated by a supreme humiliation of the papacy; the Popes at Avignon; the persecution of the Templars; the rival Popes, and the Councils of Pisa, Constance, and Basle.

III.
The Age of the Crusaders.

BY J. M. LUDLOW, D.D.,
AUTHOR OF
'CAPTAIN OF THE JANIZARIES,' 'A KING OF TYRE,' ETC.

The Crusades, with their heroic personalities, their dramatic, tragic, and romantic histories; the real religiousness out of which the crusading movement grew, and its unconscious preparation for intellectual and spiritual movements which no man could then have imagined.

ERAS OF THE CHRISTIAN CHURCH.

The following Volumes are in Preparation—

The Apostolic Age.
By the Right Rev. A. C. COXE, D.D., LL.D.

The death of Bishop Coxe makes it necessary to place this Volume in the hands of a new Author, whose name will be announced later. The four chapters completed by the Bishop prior to his death (his last literary work), will be published either as an Appendix or Supplement to this Volume.

The constitution, the fundamental polity, the doctrine, the worship, and the social and the spiritual life of the Apostolic Church.

The Post-Apostolic Age.
By the Right Rev. H. C. POTTER, D.D., LL.D.,
BISHOP OF NEW YORK;
and Archdeacon C. C. TIFFANY, D.D.

The development of doctrine in the Second and Third Centuries, and the influence of Greek thought in suggesting questions which rose into paramount importance in the Fourth; the growth of liturgical forms, and the gradual self-adjustment of the Episcopal and Conciliar Constitution of the Church; the ascetic and monastic tendencies in which there was so much good purpose and the beginning of so much evil practice; and the universal evidence of a genuinely new power working in humanity.

The Ecumenical Councils.
By Professor W. P. DUBOSE, D.D.,
DEAN AND PROFESSOR OF EXEGESIS AND MORAL SCIENCE, UNIVERSITY OF THE SOUTH, TENNESSEE.

The age of the Ecumenical Councils, with its tragic importance and its incidental comedies, with its majestic figures and its incomparable saintliness in contrast with contemptible intrigue; and, above all, the ultimate and authoritative definition of the essentials of the Christian faith.

The Age of Charlemagne.
By Professor CHARLES L. WELLS, Ph.D.,
UNIVERSITY OF MINNESOTA.

The formative period of the Ninth Century, with its picturesque figures and stirring events, and the laying of the foundations of the mediæval system, ecclesiastical and civil.

ERAS OF THE CHRISTIAN CHURCH.

Volumes in Preparation—*continued.*

The Age of the Renaissance.

By HENRY VAN DYKE, D.D., AND PAUL VAN DYKE.

The intellectual and political movements which preceded and anticipated the Reformation, including the Italian Renaissance, with the extravagances and sanities of the Humanists; the general growth of universities and great cities; the fuller development of a national spirit, especially in France and Germany; the religious fervour and the awakened spirituality which appeared most conspicuously in such tragedies as that of John Huss and Jerome of Prague, in the Lollard movement in England, and in many abortive attempts at reformation elsewhere.

The Protestant Reformation.

By PROFESSOR WILLISTON WALKER, PH.D., D.D.,
HARTFORD THEOLOGICAL SEMINARY.

The Protestant Reformation in Germany, Scandinavia, Holland, Switzerland, and Scotland, in which the life and labours of Luther, Calvin, Melancthon, Erasmus, John Knox, and other worthies, will be appreciatively described.

The Anglican Reformation.

By WILLIAM R. CLARK, LL.D., D.C.L., ETC.,
PROFESSOR OF PHILOSOPHY IN TRINITY COLLEGE, TORONTO, TRANSLATOR OF BISHOP HEFELE'S 'HISTORY OF THE COUNCILS OF THE CHURCH.'

A graphic survey of the Anglican Reformation which had so much in common with the Continental and Scottish movements, and yet was differentiated from them by peculiarities of principle and action which remain to the present time.

Such are the topics of the 'ERAS OF THE CHRISTIAN CHURCH.' Their perennial interest to Christian people is unquestionable, and no pains will be spared, either by the writers or by the publishers, to make the volumes worthy of their several themes.

EDINBURGH: T. & T. CLARK, 38 GEORGE STREET.
LONDON: SIMPKIN, MARSHALL, HAMILTON, KENT, & CO. LIMITED.

Eras of the Christian Church

☩

Edited by

John Fulton, D.D., LL.D.

☩

The Ecumenical Councils

William P. Du Bose, S.T.D.

Eras of the Christian Church

THE ECUMENICAL COUNCILS

BY

WILLIAM P. DU BOSE, S.T.D.

AUTHOR OF "THE SOTERIOLOGY OF THE NEW TESTAMENT"

WITH AN INTRODUCTION

BY

THE RT. REV. THOMAS F. GAILOR, D.D.

BISHOP COADJUTOR OF TENNESSEE

SECOND EDITION

Edinburgh

T. & T. Clark, 38, George Street

MDCCCXCVII

Press of J. J. Little & Co.
New York, U.S.A.

CONTENTS.

	PAGE
PREFACE TO SECOND EDITION	ix
PREFACE	xi

CHAP. I.—THE CHRISTOLOGY OF THE NEW TESTAMENT.—Qualification for Interpreting Christ.—Christ as Ethical and Religious Ideal.—Christ more than an Ideal of Humanity.—Relation of Christ to Old Testament.—The Primitive Gospel.—Christ's Authority.—The Divine and the Human in Christ.—Divinely Human and Humanly Divine.—The Law and the Gospel.—Truth is Polar.—Duality of Our Lord's Person.—The Organic Age of Christianity 1

CHAP. II.—THE NATURAL BASIS OF A SCRIPTURAL AND CATHOLIC CHRISTOLOGY.—Harmony of the Early Fathers.—Incarnation and Generation.—Human Knowledge of God.—Truth and Reason.—Incarnation and Atonement Necessary.—Meaning of Inspiration.—Particular and Universal Truth.—The Increment of Truth.—The Church and the Council.—Authority and Experience.................... 27

CHAP. III.—EBIONISM AND DOCETISM.—Jewish and Gentile Christians.—The Mission of Judaism.—Heathenism, Judaism, Christianity.—Ebionism.—Artemon and Paul of Samosata.—Samosatenism and Arianism.—Dualism.—Gnosticism.—Docetism.—Apollinarianism and Eutychianism.... 48

CHAP. IV.—SABELLIANISM AND THE BEGINNING OF THE TRINITARIAN DISCUSSION.—Patripassian Monarchianism.—The Immanence of God.—Relation of God and the World.—The Truth of the Trinity.—Piety versus Speculation.—Primitive Thought of the Trinity.—Primitive Thought of the Logos.—Nature and the Supernatural.—Absoluteness of Our Lord's Humanity.—Christian Pantheism... 69

CHAP. V.—THE ORIGIN AND RISE OF ARIANISM.—Theological Motive of Arianism.—Need of an Exact Terminology.—

Outbreak of the Heresy.—Tenets of Arianism.—Denies both Godhead and Manhood.—The Catholic Doctrine.—Logos and Son.—Constantine the Great.—Sincerity of his Policy. —Gradual Approach to Christianity.—His zeal for Unity and Uniformity.—Failure of Constantine's Policy......... 90

CHAP. VI.—THE COUNCIL OF NICÆA.—Note of Ecumenicity. —The Emperor and the Council.—The Arians in the Council.—Conservatives in the Council.—Athanasius and the Catholics.—Arius and Athanasius.—The Creed of Nicæa.— Necessity of Definitions.—The Arguments of Athanasius.— Result of the Council 114

CHAP. VII.—ARIANISM AFTER THE COUNCIL OF NICÆA.— Testimony Prior to Reflection.—Doubt and Reaction.— Action of the Different Parties.—The Conservatives.—Objections to the "Homoöusion."—Force of the "Homoöusion." —Meaning of "Substance."—Policy of the Arians.—Attempt to Destroy Athanasius.—Athanasius in Exile.—Violence of Constantius.—Julian, Jovian, and Valens.—Disintegration of Arianism.—Triumph of Nicenism............ 134

CHAP. VIII.—THE FIRST GENERAL COUNCIL OF CONSTANTINOPLE.—Continuation of Nicene Theology.—Meaning of "Hypostasis" or "Person."—Review of Trinitarian Thought.—Distinctions within the Godhead.—Growth of a Religious Philosophy.—Lights and Shadows of the Period.—Faithfulness of the Common People.—The Creed of Constantinople.—Practical Legislation 162

CHAP. IX.—APOLLINARIANISM.—Opening of Christological Discussion.—The End of the Incarnation.—The Eternal Humanity of the Son.—Christ the Realization of Humanity. —Significance of Redemption.—Christ's Humanity Ours.— Opposition to Nestorianism.—Tendency to Monophysitism. —The Humanity not yet Defined.—Christianity more than a Revelation.. 180

CHAP. X.—NESTORIANISM.—The School of Antioch.—Theodore of Mopsuestia.—Our Lord's Dual Personality.—A Gnomic Unity.—St. John Chrysostom.—Nestorius.—The Counter-school of Alexandria.—Opposite Points of View.— St. Cyril of Alexandria.—Attitude of the Roman Bishop... 201

CHAP. XI.—THE COUNCIL OF EPHESUS.—Conservative Temper of Antioch.—Division in the Council.—Movement toward Reconciliation.—Obstacles to Reconciliation.—Net Result of

	PAGE
the Council.—Doctrine of the "One Incarnate Nature."—Alexandrian Christology Defective.—Character of Cyril.—Renewal of the Issue	223
CHAP. XII.—EUTYCHIANISM AND THE COUNCIL OF CHALCEDON.—Character and Views of Eutyches.—The "Robber Synod."—Leo's Letter to Flavian.—The Synod Sustained by the Emperor.—Council of Chalcedon.—The Chalcedonian Decrees.—The Chalcedonian Symbol.—Criticism of the Tome.—Its Insufficiency.—Defects of Leo's Christology.—Political Schemes of Leo.—Primacy of Rome	242
CHAP. XIII.—THE MONOPHYSITES AND THE SECOND COUNCIL OF CONSTANTINOPLE.—Revolt against Decrees of Chalcedon.—Monophysite Propaganda.—Justinian as Mediator.—Edict of the Three Chapters.—The Fifth General Council.—Principal of Monophysitism.—The Scientific Difficulty.—The Religious Difficulty	267
CHAP. XIV.—THE MONOTHELITES AND THE THIRD COUNCIL OF CONSTANTINOPLE.—One Will or Two?—Maximus Confessor.—Sequence of Events.—Sergius of Constantinople.—Honorius Originator of Monothelitism.—Excuse for the Monothelitic Revolt.—The Sixth General Council.—John of Damascus	284
CHAP. XV.—ADOPTIONISM.—Meaning of Adoptionism.—Nature of Our Lord's "Sonship."—Human Sonship by Nature and by Grace.—Appeal to Scripture.—Sonship and the Resurrection.—Error of Adoptionism.—Christ Universal Humanity.—God the Essence of Our Personality.—Fate of Adoptionism	301
CHAP. XVI.—THE CHRISTOLOGICAL GOAL.—Christ Truer than Our Science of Him.—The Inductive Method.—Christ the Way to God.—The Proper Deity of the Human Jesus.—The Logos the True Personality of Men.—The Kenosis.—The Incarnation Spiritual not Physical.—Theory of Self-depotentiation.—Theory of Progressive Incarnation.—Soteriology Dependent on Christology.—The Sum of Spiritual Science	320

PREFACE TO SECOND EDITION.

N the original preface to this volume the reader was forewarned that the work was to be not so much a history of the outward events of the period of the councils as rather an historical study of the great subject that occupied its inner life and thought. The admission was made with a misgiving that this was more the case than was quite justifiable in one of a series professing to be "popular monographs, giving a bird's-eye view of the most important events in the history of the church." When, therefore, it was suggested that this very reasonable ground for criticism might be partially removed by prefixing an historical and chronological outline of the outward course of events, of which the text might be charged with being rather the interpretation than the narration, the author was prepared to feel that such an addition was due to the claims of the general plan of the publications, while it would add to the usefulness and interest of the particular volume.

That the introduction thus prefixed to this edition has been prepared, not by the author but by one far more qualified to make it both accurate in matter and attractive in manner, is so distinct a gain as to render unnecessary either explanation or excuse. The part which Bishop Gailor thus assumes in the volume is an act of personal friendship which will prove as much a boon to the reader as it is gratification to

THE AUTHOR.

PREFACE.

HE present volume does not profess to be properly a history. In so far as it is historical it is neither critical nor original. It deals with a well-known course of events the story of which it was necessary to repeat, but only with the ulterior purpose of tracing the evolution of a process of thought. It is properly an historical study of the growth and formation of the catholic doctrine of the person of Jesus Christ,—that is to say of that personal union of the divine and human in our Lord which makes him the supreme object of our spiritual and religious interest. It has not been thought best therefore to prefix a critical historical apparatus, which as a matter of fact has not been used. References to sources of information are superfluous in this well-worn period, and those who desire such can easily find them elsewhere.

As to the proper subject-matter it is hoped that the necessary indebtedness of any work of historical Christology to the great classic of Dr. Dorner has not in this volume been anywhere disguised. But as the author's obligation has been probably even more through a long general familiarity with that high authority than from immediate use of it, it is difficult for him to measure its exact extent.

The aim of the book then is distinctly Christological, and it may be well to indicate in advance something of its point of view. If Jesus Christ is what the church believes him to be, he is and will always be very much more in himself than our science of him. Christology will therefore never be complete; but it is quite complete enough to convince us that there is a truth in it of which while it is greater than our knowledge we may yet know more and more. No human mind can grasp the unity or organic whole of nature, yet science knows that nature is such a whole and that it can forever approximate to it. So the church knows that Jesus Christ stands to us for a fact of God in nature and in humanity of which it may know the truth although it can forever only approximate the whole truth. There is no question to it about Christ, the only question is of our Christology,—to what extent our science truly represents and expresses him.

There is everywhere a manifest revival of Christological interest and discussion, and there are signs of a still deeper renewal of Christological thought and science. A religious activity more earnest as well as more varied and conflicting than the world has known for a long time presses upon us with questions which demand both historical and scientific treatment. Especially is there serious and longstanding confusion with regard to the union and relation of the divine and human natures and functions in the person of our Lord. Partial, defective views of his human activities, knowledge and power, —a higher or psychical Docetism,—characterize our current theology. If we are to study these questions anew we must begin by going back to the past; but we must not expect to find a completed and satisfactory solution of them in past thought, because the mind of Christendom has not yet fully thought them out. We must accept the genuine results of a former science, but we have something of our own to add to those results, as each succeeding age will have something to add to ours.

W. P. DU BOSE.

UNIVERSITY OF THE SOUTH,
June 18, 1896.

CHRONOLOGICAL TABLE.

Birth of Arius, A.D. 256.
Birth of Constantine, 274.
Death of Constantius Chlorus, 306.
Battle of the Milvian Bridge, 312.
Edict of Milan, 313.
Council of Arles, 314.
Outbreak of Arianism, 319.
Council at Alexandria, 321.
Battle of Chrysopolis, 323.
Council of Nicæa, June 19, 325.
Athanasius consecrated, 326.
Council of Tyre, 335.
First exile of Athanasius, 335.
Death of Arius, 336.
Death of Constantine, 337.
Restoration of Athanasius, 338.
Second exile of Athanasius, 340.
Council of Antioch, 341.
Councils of Sardica and Philippopolis, 343.
Council of Milan (Makrostichos), 345.
Restoration of Athanasius, 349.
Death of Constans, 350.
First Council of Sirmium, 351.
Council of Arles (Second), 353.
Council of Milan (Second), 355.
Third exile of Athanasius, 356.
Second Council of Sirmium, 357.
Council of Ancyra, 358.
Third Council of Sirmium, 358.
Beginning of Macedonianism, 359.
Council of Ariminum, 359.
Council of Constantinople, 360.
Restoration of Athanasius, 362.
Outbreak of Apollinarianism, 362.
Council of Alexandria, 362.
Fourth exile of Athanasius, 363.
Death of the Emperor Julian, 363.
Death of Hilary of Poitiers, 368.
Death of Athanasius, 373.
Accession of Gratian, 378.
Second Ecumenical Council (Constantinople), 381.
Death of Gregory of Nazianzus, 390.
Death of Theodosius, 395.
Death of Gregory of Nyssa, 395.
Death of Chrysostom, 404.
Death of the Emperor Honorius, 417.
Death of Jerome, 420.
Death of Theodore (Mopsuestia), 428.
Outbreak of Nestorianism, 429.
Pope Celestine's council at Rome, 430.
Death of Augustine, 430.
Third Ecumenical Council (Ephesus), 431.
Death of Cyril (Alexandria), 444.
Flavian's council at Constantinople and outbreak of Eutychianism, 448.
Leo's letter to Flavian, 449.
Latrocinium, or Robbers' Council, 449.
Death of Theodoret of Kyros, 450.
Death of Theodosius II., 450.
Fourth Ecumenical Council (Chalcedon), 451.

Circular letter of Emperor Basiliscus, 476.
Fall of the Western Empire, 476.
Zeno's Henoticon, 482.
Reaction under Justin, 520.
Justinian ascends the throne, 527.
Anti-Origenistic council at Antioch, 543.
Justinian's edict against the Three Chapters, 544.
Judicatum of Pope Vigilius, 545.
Fifth Ecumenical Council (Constantinople), 553.
Justinian claims right to confirm papal election, 555.
Columba's mission to Scotland, 563.
Columbanus on the Continent, 589.

Augustine's mission to England, 596.
Rise of Monothelism, 616.
Hegira of Mohammed, July 15, 622.
Pope Honorius indorses Monothelism, 635.
The Ecthesis of Heraclius, 639.
Pope Theodore excommunicates the bishop of Constantinople, 646.
The Typos of the Emperor Constans II., 648.
First Lateran Council (Martin I.), 649.
Mutilation of Maximus, 662.
Sixth Ecumenical Council (Constantinople), 680.
The Quinisext Council (in Trullo), 692.

BIBLIOGRAPHY.

The following works should be consulted by the student of the history of the six ecumenical councils.

I. The general history of all these councils, together with their internal history, their debates and decisions, in short the sources, will be found authoritatively collected by J. HARDOUIN: Collectio maxima conciliorum generalium et provincialium; Paris, 1715, 12 vols.; and by J. DOM. MANSI: Sacrorum conciliorum nova et amplissima collectio; Florence and Venice, 1759-98, 31 vols. The mere English reader finds, however, this matter digested in accessible form in C. J. HEFELE: A History of the Christian Councils from the Original Documents; English translation, Edinburgh, T. & T. Clark, vol. i. (2d ed., 1883) to vol. v. (including the Sixth Ecumenical Council), 1896.

II. The chief contemporary writers who treat of these councils and of the matters which came before them are:

For the First Ecumenical Council, Nice, 325. EUSEBIUS: Life of Constantine, book ii., chaps. lxix.-lxxiii.; book iii., chaps. iv.-xxiii. English translation in vol. i. of the second series of Nicene and Post-Nicene Fathers, pp. 516-518, 520-526; New York, Christian Literature Co. ATHANASIUS: Select Works (in vol. iv. of the above-cited series).

For the first three ecumenical councils: Nice, 325; *Constantinople,* 381; *Ephesus,* 431. SOCRATES: Ecclesiastical History from 305 to 439 (in vol. ii. of the series cited above).

For the first two ecumenical councils: Nice, 325; *Constantinople,* 381. SOZOMEN: Ecclesiastical History from 323 to 425 (in vol. ii. of the series cited above). THEODORET: Ecclesiastical History from 323 to 440 (in vol. iii. of the series cited above). PHILOSTORGIUS, Epitome of the Ecclesiastical History of (in Bohn's Ecclesiastical Library, same vol. with Sozomen, pp. 429-528. It is an epitome by Photius and extends from 324 to 425).

For the third, fourth, and fifth ecumenical councils: Ephesus, 431; Chalcedon, 451; Constantinople, 553. EVAGRIUS: Ecclesiastical History from 431 to 594 (in Bohn's Ecclesiastical Library, same vol. with Theodoret).

For the Fourth Ecumenical Council, Chalcedon, 451. LEO THE GREAT: Select Letters and Sermons (in vol. xii. of the second series of Nicene and Post-Nicene Fathers, cited above).

For the Sixth Ecumenical Council, Constantinople, 680. See the sources in Hardouin and Mansi.

III. Of modern histories drawn from the sources may be mentioned:

J. C. L. GIESELER: A Text-book of Church History; English translation, revised by H. B. Smith; New York, Harper & Brothers, 1855–79, 5 vols. (vol. i.). Valuable for extracts in the notes.

A. P. STANLEY: Lectures on the History of the Eastern Church; London, Murray; New York, Scribner; new ed., 1884. Picturesque and yet scholarly.

W. BRIGHT: A History of the Church from the Edict of Milan, 313, to the Council of Chalcedon, 451; London, Rivington, 1860; 2d ed., 1888. The work of an exact scholar.

W. BRIGHT: Notes on the Canons of the First Four General Councils; London and New York, Macmillan, 1882; 2d ed., 1892.

PHILIP SCHAFF: History of the Christian Church, A.D. 1–1073; New York, Scribner, 1882–84, 4 vols., rev. ed.

CHRISTOPHER WORDSWORTH: A Church History to the Council of Chalcedon, 451; London, Rivington, 1881–83, 4 vols.; 2d ed., 1885. Written from the High-Church standpoint.

W. MOELLER: History of the Christian Church to the End of the Middle Ages; English translation by Andrew Rutherfurd; London, Sonnenschein; New York, Macmillan, 1892–93, 2 vols. Condensed learning; valuable for consultation.

INTRODUCTION.

THE Edict of Milan, issued jointly by Constantine and Licinius in the spring of the year 313 A.D., may properly be taken as the beginning of the epoch in church history commonly known as the period of the ecumenical councils. Constantine, born in A.D. 274 and educated at the court of Diocletian, joined his father, Constantius Chlorus, at York in Britain, in A.D. 305, and was proclaimed Augustus by the soldiers at his father's death, July 25, A.D. 306. His mother, Helena, was a Christian, and his father favored Christianity. He immediately took possession of Britain, Gaul, and Spain; and after a brilliant campaign against Maxentius, ending with the battle of the Milvian Bridge, he became master of Italy, October, A.D. 312. Before that battle, according to Eusebius ("Vita Constant.," p. 28), he had seen above the declining sun a cross in the heavens, with the inscription τούτῳ νίκα. The vision had reinforced the tendency inherited from his parents, and the victory was won under a new banner, which he himself had prepared, bearing the cross and the monogram of

Christ—the Labarum. His first official act, in conjunction with his Eastern colleague and brother-in-law, Licinius, was the framing of the Edict at Milan, proclaiming a universal and unconditional toleration of Christianity and all other religions, and adding a special order for the restoration of the confiscated property of the Christian body (*corpus Christianorum*). The affairs of the Christian church were thus brought within the recognition of the law and the official cognizance of the emperor, and he was not slow to exercise his authority.

The matter that was engaging the attention of the Roman Christians in A.D. 313 was the Donatist schism, which had originated in North Africa the year before. Cæcilianus, bishop of Carthage, had had for one of his consecrators Felix of Aptunga, who was a *persona non grata* to some of the extreme enthusiasts, because he was a restored traditor, i.e., one who had flinched in the persecution, either by surrendering his Bible or by otherwise evading the punishment for being a Christian. The protestants elected another bishop and created a schism, deriving their name "Donatists" from their greatest leader, Donatus. They were strict puritans (Cathari), and boasted of their gloomy and narrow zeal for the purity of the church. Meletius, the bishop of Lycopolis in Egypt, had organized a similar movement against Peter, the Pope of Alexandria. The Donatists appealed to Constantine, and thus were the first in Christian history to invoke the interference of the secular power. They were condemned in a council held at Rome by Melchiades, October 10, A.D. 313, and again in a council of all the Western bishops at

Arles in A.D. 314. This latter council is important chiefly as being perhaps the largest council hitherto assembled (numbering no less than four hundred bishops), and from the fact that three bishops of the church in Britain were among its members. It passed twenty-two canons, of which the first ordered that Easter should be kept by all on the same day, and that the bishop of Rome should communicate the date to the churches; and the eighth decreed that baptism in the name of the Trinity, even if conferred by heretics, should be accepted as valid.

The Donatists appealed to the emperor against the council, and he gave his final decision in favor of Cæcilianus at Milan, November 10, A.D. 316.

Meanwhile the church in the East was enjoying an interval of quiet, except that some of the provinces were vexed by the more or less direct persecution of Licinius; and in the midst of a general prosperity, marked by an enthusiasm for the building and restoration of churches, and by the rapid development of ceremonial in the conduct of worship, the publication of the Arian heresy plunged the church into a controversy that threatened the foundations of the faith and shook the empire for fifty years.

Arius, the father of Arianism, was born in Libya about the year 256 A.D. and was educated in Antioch. He was ordained deacon in Alexandria by Peter, but was afterward excommunicated for joining the Meletian schismatics, to whom reference has been made above. Early in the year 313 he recanted his errors and was received back into the communion of the church by Achillas, the successor of Peter, and was ordained to the priesthood and placed in charge of the important church of Baukalis in Alexandria. Achillas died within two months, and Alexander succeeded him, although Arius was a prominent candidate for the vacant see. The personality of Arius was such as to command attention. He was tall and dignified, of severe aspect and gracious manner, the popular preacher of the city, with a large following, including no less than seven hundred ladies. Stanley calls him a "moonstruck giant," and Neander says that he had "a contracted intellect without the intuitive faculty." His heresy, properly speaking, did not relate to the incarnation, but to the being of God. It was many years after this that his followers began to teach the imperfect humanity of Christ. The Bishop, Alexander, in the year 319 addressed his clergy on the subject of the triune Godhead, asserting the ancient faith of the equality of the Father and the Son. To this Arius took exception. His training at Antioch and the natural bent of his mind made him recoil from the mystery. His logic, he said, taught him that if the Father was God, then the Son was a creature of the Father. He was willing to worship the Son as a kind of secondary God, a middle being between God and the world, a being created before the world, before time, yet created. "There was" (he would not say "time") "when he was not (Ἦν ὅτε οὐκ ἦν)."

To this the orthodox replied that such a conception of God was undisguised polytheism and denied the first principle of the Christian faith, "We believe in *one* God."

Alexander called a meeting of his clergy, and the matter was brought up for discussion. Among the deacons present was a young man named Athanasius, twenty-three years old, who by his published writings, "Against the Gentiles" and "On the Incarnation," had already established his reputation as the most accomplished theologian in the Egyptian church. The council, after three days' deliberation, condemned Arius and his teaching, only nine out of ninety who were present voting on his side. A council of the suffragan bishops of the patriarchate of Alexandria, nearly one hundred in number, was held soon afterward (A.D. 321), and Arius, with the two bishops who adhered to him, was anathematized. Arius, however, continued to exploit his heresy from the pulpit of his church, and wrote letters to his friends, especially to his fellow-students of the school of Antioch, invoking their encouragement and assistance. His position naturally commended itself to the heathen, who liked its practical compromise with the prevailing polytheism, and also to the more rationalistic or timid among the bishops, who agreed with its "logic" or else were attracted by its apparent breadth and liberality. Of those who gave him their active support the most important was Eusebius, bishop of Nicomedia, the fifth city in the empire, who was also the favorite of Constantine. Among the timid ones was Eusebius of Cæsarea, afterward the great ecclesiastical historian, who seems to have wanted peace at any price, and preferred to be thought an abettor of Arius rather than to take a decided stand in the approaching conflict.

Arius was finally forced to leave Alexandria, and went to Palestine, and thence to Nicomedia, where he spent his time with Eusebius in writing letters to his friends and popularizing his opinions in his chief work, the "Thalia" or "Banquet," a mediocre performance, half poetry, half prose, in the style of the poet Sotades. Only fragments of this remain, in one of which he speaks of himself as being "very celebrated for the glory of God." He also wrote a letter to Alexander, setting forth more explicitly the points of his creed, and composed songs for sailors, carpenters, and travellers, so that the new doctrine of the person of Christ became the subject of violent controversy not only among the professed theologians, but with people of all classes and conditions. Constantia, the wife of Licinius and sister of Constantine, became a partisan of Arius, and Licinius himself, in his war with Constantine (A.D. 323), persecuted the Christians, but did not molest Arius or Eusebius. In fact, Arius took advantage of the oppression of the church and returned to Alexandria.

Constantine defeated Licinius at Chrysopolis, September 10, A.D. 323, and became sole emperor. His attention was immediately called to the Arian dispute, and he addressed a letter to Alexander and Arius (in which probably Eusebius of Nicomedia had a hand), urging them to stop the contention about an unimportant distinction, too subtle for the human mind to grasp and only confusing to the people. He even sent his friend and adviser Hosius, the aged bishop of Cordova in Spain, to Alexandria to reconcile them. But the question was too vital to be summarily dismissed.

The foundations of the Christian faith were involved in it—the nature of God, the value of the sacraments, the fact of the incarnation. The emperor's letter and Hosius's visit both failed, and by the advice of the bishops ("ex sacerdotum sententia") Constantine summoned all the bishops in the empire to meet in council at Nicæa (now Isnik) in Asia Minor, a place convenient to his own residence, Nicomedia. The bishops began to assemble on May 20, A.D. 325, and the council was formally opened by the emperor on June 19th. There were three hundred and eighteen bishops finally present, although the number was considerably smaller in the earlier sessions, and about two thousand clergy in attendance. The bishop of Rome was not present, but sent two priests to represent him. Alexander, the Pope of Alexandria, as he was commonly called, was directly and personally involved in the controversy. Eustathius of Antioch probably presided. There were three parties represented in the discussions as they proceeded:

(1) The Catholics; and here we notice that the word "Catholic" begins to connote orthodoxy, i.e., universality in time as well as universality in space. This party had for its principal champion Athanasius, who, while not strictly a member of the council, was in attendance with Alexander and had been conceded the leadership in the debate.

(2) The Arians proper, who held simply that the Son is a creation of God, not equal to God in any sense, being capable of change, and essentially different ($\dot{\epsilon}\tau\epsilon\rho o\dot{v}\sigma\iota o\varsigma$) from the Father; hence the name Heterousiasts,

(3) The Eusebians, afterward called Semi-Arians or Homoiousians, led by Eusebius of Nicomedia, who would have liked to arrive at the same result as Arius without using such very straightforward language. They preferred to say that the Son was ὁμοιούσιος ("of like substance") with the Father.

It soon became evident in the debates that the original Arianism would be overwhelmingly condemned, simply as a novel and strange denial of the divinity of our Lord. But the Eusebians were slippery antagonists; they professed a willingness to accept any statement in Scripture, putting their own interpretation on it, and protested against any phraseology that was metaphysically definitive. Athanasius finally insisted upon the word ὁμοούσιος ("of the same essence") as the proper description of the relation between the Father and the Son, the Son being, not the creation of the divine will, but the unfolding of the divine nature; and this definition prevailed and was inserted in the creed set forth by the council. The word had, indeed, been used before by the Sabellians, who denied the distinction of personality in the Godhead, but the council took the ground boldly that identity of essence involved no denial of differentiation of persons, and so laid the basis of the intellectual expression of the fact of the incarnation which has ever since prevailed. The council set forth a creed containing the definitive language, "One Lord Jesus Christ, the Son of God, begotten of the Father, only begotten, that is, of the essence of the Father; God of God, and Light of Light; very God of very God; begotten, not made; of one essence with the Father (ὁμοούσιον)," with an anathema added against those who say, "Once he was not," and "Before he was begotten he was not," and "He came into existence out of nothing," or who say that "the Son of God is of another substance or essence, or is created, or mutable, or changeable."

To this all the bishops present subscribed, except Arius, Eusebius of Nicomedia, and four others. Three of them, including Eusebius, changed their minds, and the other three were exiled into Illyria.

The council issued an encyclical letter and passed twenty canons.

Canon VI., after reciting the formula which was really the key-note of the council, "Let the ancient customs prevail," orders that the bishop of Alexandria shall have the same patriarchal jurisdiction in Egypt that is exercised by the bishop of Rome in Italy. This canon demonstrates the fact that the doctrine of "papal supremacy" was unknown to the members of the Council of Nicæa.

The decision of the council with reference to the Easter question coincided with that of the Council of Arles, except that the bishop of Alexandria, and not the bishop of Rome, was charged with the duty of making the annual announcement. Heretofore the Eastern Christians had commemorated our Lord's crucifixion on the 14th of Nisan (without regard to the day of the week), keeping Easter on the third day after, and were therefore called Quartodecimans. Now it was ordered that Easter must always fall on Sunday, the nearest Sunday to the actual anniversary.

In the case of Meletius, he was admitted to communion and allowed to retain the title of bishop. His clergy were to be received after the defects in their ordination were supplied.

At the close of the council the bishops were entertained at a banquet by the emperor, and were congratulated on the successful issue of their deliberations.

Eusebius of Nicomedia admitted the dishonesty of his subscription to the creed of Nicæa, and this, together with his political scheming, led to his banishment shortly after the council adjourned.

For nearly three years there was a lull in the storm. Athanasius returned to Alexandria, and on the death of Alexander in A.D. 326 was forced by the outcry of the clergy and people to accept the bishopric. He entered energetically upon the administration of the affairs of the patriarchate, visiting the Thebaid and the remoter parts of his jurisdiction. It was his high privilege to consecrate Frumentius as the first apostle of the church in Abyssinia and to see it grow in numbers and influence. It was not until A.D. 328 that Eusebius and Arius dared to renew the conflict. In the early part of that year they succeeded, partly by the influence of Constantine's widowed sister Constantia, and partly by pretended acquiescence in the Nicene formula, in being recalled from exile. Their struggle from this time forward was manifestly not for any doctrine, but for revenge. They would get rid of the bishops who stood in their way. Eustathius of Antioch and Eutropius of Hadrianople were the first victims. Then the emperor was induced to write letters to Athanasius, urging him, and finally commanding him, to admit Arius to communion in the Alexandrian church. To this order

Athanasius gave an emphatic refusal, and it does not appear that Constantine respected him any the less for it. The next year was spent by the faction in stirring up the Meletians and in concocting charges against Athanasius's official and moral character—that he had helped a rebel, that his agent had broken down an altar, that he had murdered a Meletian bishop. Eusebius represented to Constantine that such charges as these ought to be inquired into, and Athanasius was summoned to answer at a council to be held in Cæsarea (A.D. 334); but the council was never held, because he refused to attend it. However, in A.D. 335 a council was held at Tyre, and although the charges were proved to be without foundation, Athanasius was declared to be deposed. Athanasius appealed in person to the emperor and was at first successful; but a new charge against him, of stopping the transportation of corn from Alexandria, touched the emperor in his weak spot, and the bishop was banished to Treves in Gaul. Constantine soon afterward, in spite of the protests of Alexander, the nonagenarian bishop of Constantinople, ordered the public restoration of Arius; but Arius was taken suddenly ill the day before the ceremony, and died under such awful circumstances as seemed to the Catholics to justify the belief in a providential interposition. Constantine himself died on Whitsunday, A.D. 337, having received baptism at the hands of Eusebius of Nicomedia. He was succeeded by his three sons, Constantine, Constans, and Constantius, who took severally the western, middle, and eastern divisions of the empire.

For a year longer the Alexandrian church had to

endure the absence of its bishop, until on June 17, A.D. 338, Constantine II. announced that Athanasius had been restored to his see. He arrived in Alexandria in November, and the tumult of popular rejoicing that welcomed him only exasperated his enemies. Constantius raised Eusebius to the bishopric of Constantinople and put himself in his hands. Athanasius was driven from his see in Easter week, A.D. 340, and took refuge with Julius, bishop of Rome, some weeks after his friend, Constantine II., had been slain.

Arianism was now a political party devoted to the destruction of Athanasius and having no fixed theological position. Ostensibly there were three divisions of the Arians: (1) the Eusebians or Semi-Arians, who taught that the Son was similar in essence with the Father (ὁμοιούσιος); (2) the Aëtians (from Aëtius, a deacon of Antioch) and the Eunomians (from Eunomius, bishop of Cyzicus in Illyria), who taught that the Son was of a different essence (ἑτερούσιος) and unlike the Father (ἀνόμοιος), hence the names Heterousiasts and Anomœans; (3) the real Arians, who adhered to the formula, Ἦν ὅτε οὐκ ἦν ("There was when he was not"). Practically there was no agreement. No less than seventeen creeds were put forth by the party between A.D. 340 and 360; so that, although they did achieve a political supremacy, the body of the church was never formally committed to an Arian creed. The history of the period is a record of Arian and Semi-Arian councils, and of the truly marvellous labors and adventures of Athanasius. The Council of Antioch (A.D. 341), held in connection with the dedication of the " Golden Church," confirmed the decision of Tyre deposing Athanasius. In A.D. 341 Julius, bishop of Rome, invited the Eusebians to a council, and when they did not appear met with fifty Western bishops and confirmed the innocency and orthodoxy of Athanasius.

Eusebius died in Constantinople the next year (A.D. 342), and Paul, who had been forcibly deprived to make way for Eusebius, was reinstated by a popular movement, in which Hermogenes, the Arian nominee, was slain, and as a consequence Paul was banished. Macedonius was the Arian candidate for the succession, consecrated by the Eusebians, but was not installed. The Arian cause was helped a little by the rashness of Marcellus of Ancyra, who, while vehemently defending Athanasius, had laid himself so open to the charge of Sabellianism as to incur the rebuke of Athanasius himself. In 343 Julius of Rome succeeded in getting the Emperor Constans, with the consent of Constantius, to summon a council at Sardica (Sofia in Bulgaria). About one hundred and seventy bishops met, but when the Eusebians found that a majority were in favor of treating Athanasius without reference to Tyre or Antioch, they withdrew and held an opposition council at Philippopolis, just across the border. The Sardican Council proceeded to inquire into the charges against Athanasius and pronounced him innocent. There are twenty canons of the council extant in Greek, which run in the names of Hosius of Cordova and Gaudentius of Naissus in Dacia. The third, fourth, and fifth give appellate jurisdiction to Julius, bishop of Rome, in case a bishop is deposed by his comprovincials. It has always been a matter of debate as to whether this was a local provision, or a personal privilege granted to Julius, or a general concession to the Roman see. The Eusebian council issued sentences against Athanasius, Hosius, Julius, and others, and put forth another creed. Constans showed himself a firm friend to Athanasius, and Constantius was induced to be a little more complacent. During the next two years the Eusebians put forth at Antioch the Long-lined Formula (*Formula Makrostichos*), a more elaborate statement of the Homœan position ("The Son is like the Father in all things"), and condemned Marcellus and his pupil Photinus, both of whom, in their zeal for our Lord's divinity, had detracted from the reality of his manhood. This Makrostichos was presented to the Catholics in a synod at Milan in A.D. 345, which also condemned Photinus.

Athanasius had an interview with Constantius the next year, and returned the second time to Alexandria, after the death of the intruding bishop Gregory, A.D. 349. The death of Constans in A.D. 350 removed the only restraining influence upon Constantius. The first great Synod of Sirmium met in A.D. 351, condemned and deposed Photinus, and put forth a formula in which there was no explicit Arianism, but the homoöusion was avoided. The synods of Arles (A.D. 353) and Milan (A.D. 355) demanded the condemnation of Athanasius without debate, and the few bishops who refused—Paulinus, Eusebius of Vercelli, Lucifer of Cagliari, Dionysius of Milan, Hilary of Poitiers, Liberius, the successor of Julius at Rome, and the venerable Hosius of Cordova—were sent into exile. Athanasius himself, who had written some of his greatest theological treatises in the meantime, was again banished in A.D. 356, and it seemed as if the final triumph of Arianism was assured. The very success of the heresy proved, however, to be its failure. The extreme Arians immediately came to the front and threw off every mask. The Anomœans (also called Exukontians, Heterousiasts, and Eunomians) took the lead. In vain the Eusebians at the Council of Sirmium (A.D. 357) put forth the second colorless Sirmian formula, and restated the more moderate position at Ancyra (A.D. 358) and in the third Sirmian formula (A.D. 358). The extremists were not satisfied, although Hosius and Liberius were weak enough to obtain their freedom to return by subscribing to these seemingly vague, but actually uncatholic, creeds. The effort to be inclusive and reach a broad ground of union had resulted in more and more indefinite positions. At first the Semi-Arians were for the Homoiousion, i.e., that "the Son is of like substance with the Father." In the third Sirmian formula they say, "Like unto the Father in everything, according to the Scripture." This was made the text at Ariminum in May, A.D. 359, which nearly all the bishops accepted. At Seleucia, later in the year, Acacius of Cæsarea succeeded in getting the formula cut down to "Like the Father" (the word "essence" or "substance" being significantly omitted). Hence arose the Homœans or Acacians, who were triumphant in the council at Constantinople (A.D. 360), where the Aëtians (Anomœans), the old

Eusebians (Homoiousians), and the Catholics were alike condemned. This had the effect of opening the eyes of the more moderate Semi-Arians and drew them nearer to Athanasius; so that by the accession of Julian, whose policy it was to recall all the discordant elements in Christendom, the Catholic cause was materially strengthened. Athanasius returned the third time to Alexandria, February 22, A.D. 362, where for four years the intruder George had ruled with brutal irreverence and cruelty, and had finally been murdered by a pagan mob, December 24, A.D. 361.

Athanasius was quick to see the opportunity, and immediately addressed himself to the work of reconciliation. There were three chief difficulties to contend with:

(1) The older Nicæans had used the words "ousia" and "hypostasis" interchangeably, as meaning substance or essence. To men, therefore, who understood by "hypostasis" something more than nature, a *personal* subsistence, the statement of "one hypostasis in the Godhead" sounded like a Sabellian denial of the Trinity.

(2) The second difficulty was the condition of the church in Antioch. There Eustathius, the eminent defender of Nicæa, had been deposed, and Meletius had succeeded; and when Meletius showed himself too orthodox to suit the Arians he was deposed by the emperor and replaced by Euzoius. There were thus three parties in Antioch, viz., the Eustathians, the Meletians, and the followers of Euzoius; but the Eustathians had no bishop, and Meletius was ready

to subscribe to the homoöusion and unite the Semi-Arians and the Catholics.

(3) The third difficulty was involved in the fact that in the discussions about the Son the doctrine as to the personality and divinity of the Holy Ghost had been involved. Many who were ready now to subscribe to the homoöusion were unprepared to apply it to the Holy Spirit. In fact, Macedonius, the turbulent bishop of Constantinople (A.D. 343–360), had made himself conspicuous by his denial of the divine personality of the Holy Ghost.

Athanasius held a synod at Alexandria (A.D. 362), in which these matters were carefully and wisely considered. (1) The real meaning of the terms "ousia" and "hypostasis" was explained; and the Semi-Arian use of "hypostasis," as they understood it, was justified. Both parties expressed their condemnation of Sabellianism, and the terms "ousia," "hypostasis," "prosopa," and "persona" were properly distinguished. (2) The Holy Ghost was declared to be of the same substance and divinity as the Father and the Son. (3) The perfect humanity of Christ was asserted as against the opinion into which Apollinaris, one of Athanasius's friends, had fallen. (4) The greatest leniency was exercised toward those who, having been in the attitude of Arians, desired to return to the faith of the church.

It is an immortal honor to Athanasius that he showed the temper and spirit of Christ in dealing with men who had so bitterly opposed him. The schism of Antioch was not healed by the council, for the reason that Lucifer of Cagliari, with hot-headed precipitancy, had hurried away from Alexandria and had supplied the defective organization of the Eustathians by consecrating a bishop for them in the person of Paullinus. Athanasius had to flee from Alexandria a fourth time by order of Julian, but that emperor's death (June 26, A.D. 363) permitted his return. The Emperor Valens expelled him for four months (October, A.D. 365), but restored him in fear of a popular tumult, and he was not again molested. As he approached the end of his career he was blessed with the knowledge that since A.D. 330 the church had never been so united, nor the faith so secure. Another generation of men had been raised up to do their battle for the creed of Christendom, who were well able to succeed him. The great Hilary of Poitiers was dead (January 13, A.D. 368), but Basil of Cæsarea, Gregory of Nazianzus, and Gregory of Nyssa, with many others of the younger generation, had already proved themselves to be men and theologians to whom the burden of the future might, under God, be confidently transmitted.

Athanasius, well surnamed "the Great," died peacefully on Thursday, May 2, A.D. 373. Möhler says of him that "the narrative of his life is a panegyric which words can only enfeeble," and Canon Bright, "Looking at the whole man, we shall not be extravagant if we pronounce his name to be the greatest in the church's post-apostolic history."

The Emperor Valens openly favored the Arians, and after the death of Athanasius endeavored by force of arms, in the East at least, to make the heresy supreme. Ambrose, the great bishop of Milan (A.D. 374–

397), and the Cappadocians (Basil and the Gregories) strove successfully, however, "in the interest of a real theological conviction in the ways of Athanasius, by seeking to set aside the old objections, by prudent definition of dogmatic terminology, and by proceeding in their championship of the Godhead of the Spirit with great prudence and regard to the ideas that had hitherto been so fluctuating." This applies especially to Basil, whose negotiation for the universal peace of the church would have more readily succeeded if the bishop of Rome, Damasus (succeeded Liberius A.D. 366), had given him more loyal assistance. The death of Valens (A.D. 378) ended the hopes of the Arians, for Gratian was from the first a devoted friend to Ambrose and Nicæa, and his associate in the East, Theodosius, showed himself of like disposition.

The cessation of hostility on the part of the civil power gave the church an opportunity to consider prevailing opinions, and to declare what theories, even among the orthodox, had transcended the limits of tolerated speculation. Doubtless, if the literature remained to us, we would find a vast variety of interpretation in the writings of the fifty years preceding. The Arians had, with great ingenuity, from time to time entertained almost every possible conjecture as to the essential relation of the Father and the Son, and in their statements of the incarnation had come to deny the completeness of our Lord's human nature. But Apollinaris, bishop of Laodicea (A.D. 362), seems to have arrived at his peculiar views from another direction. He was a man of many-sided literary activity (note application of Greek poetic art to Christian matter), and at one time a devoted friend of Athanasius. His adherence to the homoöusion was undoubtedly sincere, but he fell into three notable errors: (1) While deserving credit for his deeper appreciation of the difficulties involved in the incarnation, he seems to have thought that the mystery could be explained in detail by the methods of finite reasoning. (2) It seemed to him, with his human logic, that to ascribe a perfect humanity to the Logos meant a human person in Christ; but if Christ had a human personality, then there could be no complete union (ἄκρα ἕνωσις), but only a conjunction of two perfect wholes (cf. Nestorianism), i.e., no incarnation. (3) He assumed that the νοῦς is the seat of personality and is by its very nature sinful (cf. Calvin). On these grounds Apollinaris denied the νοῦς in the humanity of our Lord, while at first admitting the ψυχή and σῶμα, and set forth the theory of a composite mixture of Godhead and manhood. It was only another step to say that, as the flesh had God for its soul, there was no real flesh, but only an appearance. And this was the position of the later Apollinarians.

Athanasius, Basil, Gregory of Nyssa, and others pointed out the utter ruin to the idea of the incarnation wrought by this teaching, and in the year that Athanasius died Pope Damasus held a council at Rome, in which the completeness of the human nature in our Lord and the personal divinity of the Holy Ghost were strongly asserted as against the Apollinarians and the Macedonians (Pneumatomachi, " Fighters against the Spirit "). In the condemnation of the Apollinarians is included the anathema of those "who say that the Virgin Mary is not Theotocos (Mother of God)," this being a consequence of one form of Apollinarianism. To settle these questions and to regulate the affairs of the church in Constantinople, the Second Ecumenical Council was convoked by the Emperor Theodosius, and met in Constantinople, May, A.D. 381. Among its one hundred and fifty members was Meletius, the aged bishop of Antioch, who had come to an agreement with Paullinus (the bishop so unadvisedly consecrated by Lucifer of Cagliari) that the schism should be healed at the death of either of them by the submission of all to the survivor. Gregory of Nazianzus, Gregory of Nyssa, and the aged Cyril of Jerusalem were also present. There was no Western bishop in attendance, for, indeed, the decision of the West had been expressed in the Roman Council eight years before. Gregory of Nazianzus had been for some time stirring the hearts of the people of Constantinople by his wonderful eloquence, and had made the private house which he had fitted up for a church a real *anastasia*, as he himself called it, a place of "resurrection" for the Nicene faith. The first act of the synod was to declare the title of Maximus to the see of Constantinople (he had been secretly consecrated without election) void, and to elect Gregory to the see. Gregory most reluctantly accepted the burden,—for such it was,—and on the death of Meletius, a few days afterward, became president of the council. Unfortunately, the younger bishops present objected to the recognition of the compact between Meletius and Paullinus, and succeeded in having another bishop —Flavian—elected to succeed Meletius, thus perpetuating the schism in Antioch. This grieved Gregory so that he absented himself from the council, and when he heard that some of the newly arrived Egyptian bishops objected to his occupancy of the see of Constantinople on canonical grounds, he immediately returned to the council, resigned his see, and took his farewell in a speech magnificent alike for eloquence and truth. His resignation was accepted, and Nectarius, a much less learned and less desirable man, was elected in his place. An effort was made to open negotiations with the Macedonians, but it failed. The council put forth a decree of faith embodying an enlarged form of the Nicene Creed as we now have it, without the Filioque. This creed is said by some to have been from the pen of Gregory of Nazianzus, by others of Gregory of Nyssa. The most probable opinion is that it was a creed that had been used for about ten years by the church and was thus naturally incorporated in the conciliar decree.

The slight variations in this Nicæno-Constantinopolitan Creed from the Nicene original consist of verbal changes to meet the heresies of Apollinaris and Macedonius, viz.: *Before all ages; from heaven;* he was incarnate *by the Holy Ghost of the Virgin Mary; and was crucified for us under Pontius Pilate; and was buried; and sitteth on the right hand of the Father; again, with glory; whose kingdom shall have no end;* and all the words after "I believe in the Holy Ghost." The Greek codices contain seven canons of this council, the last three of which are generally regarded as spurious. Canon I. condemns all forms of Arianism, Apollinarianism, and Sabellianism. Canon II. prescribes the limits of episcopal jurisdiction in dioceses and provinces. Canon III. raises the see of Constantinople to precedency of rank above Alexandria and Antioch, " because it is New Rome," implying that the precedency of Rome itself was based simply on the political importance of the place. This canon was never accepted by the West. The council is ranked as an ecumenical council, however, because its decrees of faith were afterward accepted by the whole church, although they were not formally ratified until the Council of Chalcedon, A.D. 451.

Of the many synods which were held in the East and West just before and after the Second Ecumenical Council, probably the most important was the Council of Laodicea (*circ.* A.D. 370) in Phrygia, attended by thirty-two bishops and passing sixty canons. This legislation is mainly disciplinary and liturgical, and the sixtieth canon gives a list of the books of the Old and New Testaments that " may be read aloud." The list includes the Book of Baruch in the Old Testament and omits the Apocalypse from the New Testament. A similar list appears in the thirty-sixth canon of the Council of Hippo (A.D. 393), which, however, gives Judith, Esdras, and the Maccabees in the Old Testament and the Apocalypse in the New. Athanasius in his festal epistle (xxxix.) (A.D. 367) had given the received list of the canonical books exactly as we now have them.

The last years of the fourth century and the first

of the fifth were years of great mental and spiritual activity and development for the church, although they mark the beginning of the rapid decadence of the empire. About A.D. 370 the Huns began their movement westward from their settlements north of the Caspian, conquered the Ostrogoths, and forced the Visigoths (who had been converted by Ulphilas to an Arian form of Christianity) to appeal to the Emperor Valens for permission to cross the Danube. This request was granted, and they settled in Moesia. In their subsequent revolt Valens lost his life. Theodosius stopped the progress of the Goths, but in A.D. 386 admitted no less than forty thousand of them into the imperial service. Theodosius died in A.D. 395, and divided the empire between his two sons, Arcadius and Honorius. During the next fifty years Italy was invaded by Alaric and the Visigoths, by Radagaisus and the Suevi, by Genseric and the Vandals, and by Attila and the Huns. By A.D. 410 most of the outlying provinces in the North, including Gaul and Britain, were permanently severed from the empire. Honorius died in A.D. 417 and was nominally succeeded by his nephew, Valentinian III., a boy six years old; and for twenty-five years his unworthy mother, Placidia, with two able generals, Aëtius and Boniface, held the reins of power. Arcadius in the East died in A.D. 408, and was succeeded by Theodosius II., whose sister Pulcheria managed the affairs of government for forty-two years. The interest of the ecclesiastical historian centres, during the period, in Ambrose of Milan (A.D. 374–397), Augustine of Hippo (A.D. 395–430), Jerome (A.D. 346–420), Chrysostom (A.D. 398–404). Gregory of Nazianzus died A.D. 390, and Gregory of Nyssa, A.D. 395.

Ambrose is the wise, practical statesman of the episcopate: a theologian drawing his material largely from Greek sources; a spiritual ruler asserting his authority over the Emperor Theodosius and successfully resisting the expiring political effort of Arianism in the person of Justina; a grave and far-sighted man of affairs, revising and enriching the worship and hymnology of the church; commanding a respect and confidence far and wide, that made Milan for twenty years superior to Rome itself in ecclesiastical importance.

Augustine is the master mind of Western theology; in fact, the greatest philosophical theologian of the church, East or West, since Origen. Against the Donatists, who amid all the controversy of the Arian times had maintained and increased their influence in North Africa, he developed and formulated the idea of the church, her nature and authority, with a clearness and force that have made it a precious heritage to Christendom. His own conversion, a profound and real spiritual experience, taught him the meaning of sin and redemption, and sharpened the arguments he used against the Pelagians, who denied the necessity of grace and trusted in the natural sufficiency of man for his own salvation. Augustine believed in the necessity of regeneration for each individual; and this was historically dependent upon the incarnation of God in Christ; and this incarnation is conveyed to men by and through the church; and this church, founded by the divine counsel "before the foundation of the world," is the actual though gradually progressive realization in time of the history of humanity in the "City of God" (*Civitas Dei*). Augustine's "Confessions," the history of his conversion from heathenism and Manicheism to Christianity, is the greatest religious autobiography the church has yet produced.

Jerome (Sophronius Eusebius Hieronymus) is the representative of the monastic and ascetic tendencies of the age, and is also in breadth and variety of literary activity the man of culture, "the first ancestor of the humanists." Born at Stridon in Dalmatia in A.D. 346, an anchorite in Chalcis (A.D. 375), a disputatious presbyter at Antioch (A.D. 380), an ascetic critic and preacher in Rome (A.D. 381–383), a founder of a monastic establishment in Palestine (A.D. 386), his life was a continuous conflict. A man extremely sensitive, intolerant of opposition, incapable of "seeing the other side," he was born for controversy. His immortal fame rests upon his incomparable labors as biblical critic and commentator, and his contributions to ecclesiastical history, more especially in his letters and his "De viris illustribus." His quarrel with Rufinus opens up the Origenistic controversy, which, inextricably allied with monasticism, had much to do with the Christological disputes of the fifth century.

Origen was the father of two apparently opposite statements with regard to the Logos, viz., the "subordination of the Son" and the "eternal generation of the Son." Athanasius saw no difficulty in reconciling the two truths, and never faltered in his warm regard for Origen. The Arians, however, took the doctrine of "subordination" and pressed it into service on their side, referring to Origen as authority for denial of the consubstantiality of the Son. The wide use of Origen's name by Arians, together with his really harmless speculations as to the resurrection, created a deep distrust for him in the minds more especially of the Egyptian monks, who were becoming a power in Christendom. Jerome's quarrel with his old friend Rufinus and his vehement recantation of his earlier regard for Origen are the most unpleasant revelations of the weakness of his character.

John, surnamed Chrysostom, was bishop of Constantinople for only nine years, three of which he spent in exile. He was the most celebrated orator of the Eastern Church, and the largeness of his mind and the sanity of his interpretation have made his scriptural homilies a storehouse of practical religion for the students of every age. The contrast of his strict asceticism with the worldliness of his predecessor Nestorius; his courageous refusal to respect the person of the Empress Eudoxia in his denunciation of evil; his strict discipline of the bishops and clergy under him; his defiance of the growing Arian-Gothic influence—these things made his episcopate a practical confessorship for the truth. To him in A.D. 401 came three Origenistic monks, "the Long Brothers," and asked for refuge from the persecution of the fanatical Theophilus of Alexandria, who had deposed and exiled all Origenists. Because Chrysostom received these men, without restoring them to communion, and pleaded on their behalf, Theophilus came to Constantinople (A.D. 403), and held a synod at the imperial estate called "The Oak," and with incredible insolence pronounced Chrysostom deposed. Through the subsequent machinations of Theophilus and the active coöperation of the vindictive Eudoxia, Chrysostom was banished, then recalled, and finally exiled to Cucusus, and died under the hand of his persecutors of sickness and fatigue, with the words, "God be thanked for everything." Henceforth there would be little love lost between Constantinople and Alexandria. The rift was permanent.

The school of Antioch, which produced Arius and Eusebius, was destined to bring forth another heresy quite as destructive of the Christian faith as Arianism and yet more consistent and insidious. This school reached its highest point in the first quarter of the fifth century, in the persons of two men. The greater of these was Theodore, born at Antioch, a fellow-pupil with Chrysostom of the rhetorician Libanius and the theologian Diodorus, and bishop of Mopsuestia (A.D. 392–428). His fame as a theologian was for centuries practically unrivalled in the East. His view of the incarnation is based upon a strong antagonism to the "imperfect humanity" of Apollinaris, and he emphasizes the human side of our Lord's life, endeavoring, by an attractive and highly speculative philosophy, to grasp and elucidate the mystery of the union between God and man. He takes man as the predestined bond between the universe and God, now under limitations in a mortal state, and argues the necessity of the incarnation to complete the universe and reveal the higher stage (κατάστασις) of ordinary human life. Christ is man, surpassing all other men in moral strength and perception, and winning his way by his foreseen virtue to perfect and entire union with God, which was consummated by the resurrection and ascension.

The core of Theodore's teaching is stated in his own words: "The two natures, united together, make only one person, as man and wife are only one flesh. . . . If we consider the natures in their distinction, we should define the nature of the Logos as perfect and complete, and so also his person, and, again, the nature and the person of the man as perfect and complete. If, on the other hand, we have regard to the union (συνάφεια), we say it is one person."

There seems to be little doubt that Theodore held the view of the natural sinlessness of man, his freedom from the guilt of Adam's fall, that was known as Pelagianism in the West. This would affect his views of salvation and fit in with his theory of the incarnation, which is necessary only if man is insufficient for himself. There are passages in Theodore's writings that seem to conflict with this view, especially his use of the word "Theotocos," but evidently he applied it in a peculiar sense.

The other name closely associated with the school of Antioch at this period is that of Theodoret, bishop of Cyrus or Cyrrhus (A.D. 423–453), a man of wide learning and brilliant ability and deep piety, strong in his likes and dislikes, intolerant of opposition, a controversialist whose invective knew no limit of fairness or good taste. He never wavered from his personal allegiance to the Nicene faith, although he permitted his feelings for Nestorius to make him venomous in his antipathy to Cyril of Alexandria.

The schism of the church in Antioch was at last healed in the episcopate of Alexander, whose gentleness and goodness persuaded the Eustathians and brought about the union (A.D. 414). Alexander was succeeded by Theodotus (A.D. 418), and Theodotus by John (A.D. 429), who became prominent in the controversies of that period.

It was on April 10, A.D. 428, that Nestorius of Antioch, the friend and disciple of Theodore, who had just died, was consecrated bishop of Constantinople. His first acts for the repression of heresy showed him to be of a harsh and peremptory disposition. His private chaplain entered heartily into his plans and seems himself to have been a pretentious theologian. This presbyter, Anastasius, preaching before Nestorius in December of that year, said: "Let no one call Mary Theotocos ('Bringer-forth of God'); for Mary was but a woman, and it is impossible that God should be born of a woman." This emphatic denial of a term which had been used by the greatest fathers, from Tertullian to Origen and Athanasius and Basil, created great disturbance, and was publicly resented by many, especially by Eusebius, a layman, afterward bishop of Dorylæum. Nestorius immediately took the matter in hand, and preached a course of sermons to defend and reinforce Anastasius's position. These sermons are extant. They show curious confusion of thought at times and a strange determination to misunderstand the orthodox position. So vehement was Nestorius that he had Eusebius and many others of his critics flogged and imprisoned. When Proclus, bishop of Cyzicus, preaching by his invitation at St. Sophia, surprised him by a clear and emphatic statement of the fact that if our Lord is God, and if he was born of the Virgin, then the Virgin was certainly the Theotocos, Nestorius undertook to answer him then and there before the congregation left the church, lest the people should be injured by the doctrine they had heard.

The fact was that Nestorius had his mind saturated with Theodore's teaching, that an impersonal human nature was no human nature, and that, to assert the completeness of Christ's humanity against Apollinaris, one must believe that the human person was united in a moral union with the divine Person. "We will separate the natures," he says, "and unite the honor; we will acknowledge a *double* person and worship it as *one*." Thus, as in the case of the Arians, he would use any language to describe that union, Theodochos or Christotocos, except the one word that defined the hypostatic (i.e., personal) union of the two natures in our Lord. To the mind of Nestorius, therefore, the Theotocos meant nothing less than that Deity originated in a mortal woman; and to say that God suffered was to assert the passibility of the divine nature; and he would not see it any other way, although he was again and again assured, as he might have discovered in the writings of any of the great fathers, that no Catholic theologian had ever entertained such monstrous absurdities.

Nestorius and his friends were not on the defence. They were aggressive propagators of a doctrine which they maintained was the only reasonable faith, and they scattered their writings far and wide. Thus the matter came to the notice of Cyril, bishop of Alexandria (A.D. 412–444), who was the successor of his uncle Theophilus in that see—a man of strong will and resolute nature, imperious and exacting, but learned and exceedingly able, gifted with the Athanasian grasp of theological questions. Hearing that the opinions of Nestorius were being circulated in his patriarchate, he took occasion in his annual paschal letter (A.D. 429), without any personal reference to Nestorius, to state the doctrine of the incarnation in the clearest and simplest terms, that the real, true, and perfect manhood in Christ was joined to the divine nature in one divine Person. Again, four months later, he wrote another letter to the monks on the same subject. These letters coming to the notice of Nestorius stirred him to great wrath, and he engaged one Photius to answer them. Meanwhile Celestine, bishop of Rome, had inquired of Cyril as to the genuineness of the sermons said to have been preached by Nestorius, and that began Cyril's correspondence with the bishop of Constantinople, in which unquestionably Cyril appears better, as to both matter and form, than his antagonist. The second letter of Cyril was incorporated in the acts of the general council and is a luminous statement of the faith. On August 11, A.D. 430, Celestine held a council at Rome, decided against Nestorius, and notified Cyril that he must proceed at once against Nestorius and give him only ten days to retract or be deposed and excommunicated. Cyril did not act hastily. He assembled a council and drew up a serious and elaborate letter, with twelve chapters affixed, anathematizing certain errors, and this was sent to Nestorius with the demand that he sign them. At this point Theodoret enters the lists with little credit to his mind or temper.

In November, A.D. 430, the Emperor Theodosius issued a summons to a general council at Ephesus. Cyril arrived there with fifty bishops, June 2, A.D. 431. The great Augustine had died on August 22, A.D. 430, before the respectful letter of the emperor, requesting his attendance, could reach him. Juvenal of Jerusalem, Flavian of Thessalonica, and Memnon of Ephesus arrived with about one hundred other bishops soon after Cyril. They waited sixteen days beyond the appointed time for John of Antioch and his suffragans. Two of the metropolitans of the patriarchate of Antioch arrived and said that it was the wish of John for the council to proceed with its business without him, as he was delayed on the way. Nestorius refused to attend until " the other bishops were present." Cyril and his friends could not restrain their impatience, and the synod was opened without further delay (June 22, A.D. 431) in the cathedral at Ephesus, named Theotocos. The proceedings of the council were quiet, dignified, and most solemn. The records show the most exhaustive examination of evidence, extending to the reading aloud of extracts from the writings of many of the fathers. The sentence was finally passed upon Nestorius as follows: "We discovered that he held and published impious doctrines in his letters and treatises, as well as in discourses which he delivered in this city, and which have been testified to. Urged by the canons and in accordance with the letter of our most holy father and fellow-servant, Celestine, the Roman bishop, we have come with many tears to this sorrowful sentence against him, namely, that our Lord Jesus Christ, whom he has blasphemed, decrees, by the holy synod, that Nestorius be excluded from the episcopal dignity and from all priestly communion." More than two hundred bishops signed this sentence, and thus concluded the first session of the council. Five days afterward, John of Antioch arrived, and, refusing the invitation of the delegation sent by Cyril, held a *conciliabulum* of his own, with thirty-nine other bishops, and, without mentioning Nestorius or his opinions, pronounced Cyril and Memnon to be deposed and excommunicated. The papal legates from Rome reached Ephesus a few days later, and with them Cyril held six sessions of the council. The council issued a decree of faith (comprising the Nicene Creed without the Constantinopolitan additions) repeating the judgment against Nestorius's doctrine, deposed John of Antioch, and passed six canons, in one of which Pelagianism is condemned by implication.

The last session of the council was on July 31st. Count John then arrived with a message from the emperor, who was ignorant of the whole proceedings, saying that he acquiesced in the deposition of Cyril, Memnon, and Nestorius. These three bishops were thereupon arrested and put in prison. After much consultation and petitioning, the emperor finally acquiesced in the action of the council, and Cyril returned to Alexandria, October 30th. About eighteen months afterward John of Antioch was fully reconciled to Cyril, and the council was generally accepted as ecumenical. Nestorius was deposed and exiled by order of Theodosius, and lived until about A.D. 450. He was a man whose errors were due more to weakness of intellect than to intentional wrong-doing. He was not a leader of men either in mind or character. His friends fell away from him, and subsequent events showed that the Antiochian school and its great teachers were more responsible for the heresy called Nestorianism than he was.

Nestorianism continued in vigorous life under Ibas, the devoted disciple of Theodore, head of the Persian school, and afterward (A.D. 435) bishop of Edessa. Barsumas, bishop of Nisibis (A.D. 435–489), became the founder of Persian Nestorianism, and his celebrated school at Nisibis the fountain of its teachings. Nestorian missionaries made their way to India, China, and Japan. Their chief dogma was revived in the West in a modified form by the Adoptionists in Spain (A.D. 792).

Cyril died at Alexandria in the year A.D. 444. His character has been a favorite object of attack by those who despise a man that will fight for a theological definition, even if it involve a fundamental principle of faith. His enemies have even charged him with the murder of the philosopher Hypatia, although with that crime he had absolutely nothing to do, except in so far as a bishop may be held responsible for the sins of a people whose lawlessness he had once before encouraged. His was a strong personality, peremptory, vehement, impatient, and sometimes harsh. His earlier letters to Nestorius and his deliberation in entering upon the struggle are evidences of his desire to be just; for to him from the first the denial of the Theotocos meant, and rightly so, the utter destruction of the truth of Christ, which he had sworn to defend. The universal mind of Christendom has entirely justified him in this contention. For Nestorianism was and is the most subtle and dangerous of all the heresies with regard to the incarnation. Arianism, after all, was an inconsistent, uncertain compromise with polytheism, and without the aid of mere political influence and personal animosities would have had no history. Apollinarianism was a frank denial of the human side of Christ's life, and was too nearly allied to outworn theories of Gnosticism to enjoy any great or wide-spread popularity. But Nestorianism had its roots in a seemingly profound and original philosophy of man and God, that gave a new and fresh interpretation of the universe, with suggestions of larger and richer meaning in human life, and a more natural and intelligible account of the gradual growth into the perfection of Sonship through the perfection of manhood in Jesus Christ. There is a real appeal to many men in the language of Theodore, that "Christ strove against the psychic passions of his body and mastered pleasure," "mortifying sin in the flesh and taming his lusts." But, in spite of the beauty of his subtle and mystic pantheism and the ingenuity of his modifying phrases, our instinctive feeling of distrust is justified by the result. There was no union (ἕνωσις) of God and man in Christ, but a mere conjunction (συνάφεια). No verbal declamation upon the glories of the resurrection and ascension, in perfecting that union, can veil the naked fact that there was no incarnation after all, but only a good man in whom God dwelt; and no good man, though he were the best of all the race from the beginning to the end of time, is sufficient to satisfy the language of the New Testament or save the world. The whole fabric of Christianity—the nature of the church, the reality of the sacraments, the meaning of the atonement—rests upon this unique and transcendent truth: that the Son of God, of the same substance with the Father, very God of very God, did in his own person take upon himself our human nature and live a human life. It was God himself who loved us, who gave himself for us. It was God who, in his human nature, was tempted, hungered, suffered, died. Anything less than this may be an interesting philosophy, but it is not a gospel.

The Nestorian controversy gave permanence to three phrases in the language of Christian theology, viz.:

(1) The "hypostatic union," i.e., the union of two complete natures in one person. The single person is the basis and bond of the union.

(2) "Communicatio idiomatum," i.e., communication of properties. Whatever may be predicated of either nature may be predicated of the person, e.g.:

"God suffered," i.e., "He who was God suffered" (in his human nature). Cf. Acts xx. 28: "The church of God, which he hath purchased with his own blood."

(3) Θεοτόκος, a title of the Blessed Virgin; though originally used, not to give honor to her, but to preserve the glory of her Son. It was in common use among Christian writers from the end of the second century. The later history of the word is significant. Θεοτόκος (Θεός and τίκτω) may be literally translated "Bringer-forth of God," i.e., of him who was God. So the earlier Latin translation of it was "Deipara." Gradually this became "Genetrix Dei," and this "Mater Dei." The Greeks then adopted the Latin form and spoke of Μήτηρ Θεοῦ. There can be no question that this phrase, "Mother of God," carries with it a little more than is meant by Theotocos, but it accords more definitely with the mediæval reverence for the Blessed Virgin.

The Nestorian controversy had evoked bitter vituperation on the side of both Antioch and Alexandria, and the feeling was only intensified by the great ability and popularity of the respective leaders. If the sympathizers with Antioch could not forget the persistence and success of Cyril's antagonism, neither could Alexandria forget the harsh and sneering things that had been said by Theodoret and others against Cyril. The flame was ready to burst forth when Flavian, archbishop of Constantinople, assembled the bishops then present in Constantinople in a council, November 8, A.D. 448. As soon as the special business of the synod was concluded, Eusebius, bishop of Dorylæum (the same who had accused Nestorius), presented a written accusation against the foremost champion of Alexandrian theology in Constantinople, and demanded that it be read. It was read, and created a great sensation. Eutyches, who was thus accused of heresy, was seventy years old, in priest's orders, the archimandrite (*mandra* = monastery) of a convent outside the walls of Constantinople, a devoted friend of Cyril of Alexandria, the godfather of the influential minister Chrysaphius, a conspicuous opponent of Nestorianism and Antioch. To accuse him seemed almost like accusing Cyril himself. The charge against him was a denial of the two natures in our Lord, a relapse into Apollinarianism, a Docetic and unreal conception of Christ's humanity. The old man was summoned before the council, and, after repeated evasion, admitted that he held and taught "that before the union Christ had two natures, but after the union he had only one nature." This was a clear denial of the human side of our Lord's life, and represented the exaggeration of the position of Cyril against Nestorianism. Flavian was evidently much averse to entering into the strife, but there was nothing else to do. The council condemned and deposed Eutyches.

Soon the whole church was involved in the controversy. Dioscorus, the successor of Cyril in the see of Alexandria (A.D. 444–454), a violent and headstrong partisan, immediately threw himself upon the side of Eutyches. Leo I., bishop of Rome (A.D. 440–461), the first great theologian in that see and the real founder of the papal monarchy, at first inclined to listen to the statements of Eutyches and the emperor; but when he had received the acts of the council from Flavian and realized the issue, he gave his emphatic judgment against Eutyches. His letter to Flavian (June 13, A.D. 449) (Ep. 28) was a complete theological statement of the Catholic doctrine of the incarnation, and was afterward formally adopted by the Council of Chalcedon as the expression of the faith of the universal church.

Eutyches and Dioscorus demanded the calling of an ecumenical council, and, the court being on their side, the imperial summons was issued in the names of Theodosius II. and Valentinian III., May 30, A.D. 449. The synod met at Ephesus on August 8th. There were one hundred and thirty-five bishops present. Dioscorus presided by the emperor's decree, which also provided that Theodoret should not be permitted to attend, and that the bishops who had voted against Eutyches in Flavian's council might be present, but could not vote. Three legates represented Leo, bringing with them several letters, among them the Tome to Flavian. Two high officers and a guard of soldiers were on hand to prevent disturbance. Immediately upon the opening of the synod the Roman legates presented Leo's letter and asked that it might be read, but Dioscorus refused. Eutyches came forward and gave an account of his faith, denouncing Flavian as a heretic. Flavian in vain begged that the accusation of Eusebius might be heard. Dioscorus pronounced Eutyches innocent, and called on the bishops to agree. "If you cannot shout," he said, "hold up your hands." He hectored them into submission; their hands went up. "Eutyches is innocent." "I pronounce Flavian and Eusebius deposed." The Romans called for Leo's Tome. Flavian said, "I decline your jurisdiction." Hilary, the Roman legate, uttered one emphatic word in his own tongue— "*Contradicitur.*" Onesiphorus threw himself on his knees before Dioscorus and begged him to forego this outrage. Dioscorus exclaimed, "He that will not sign this sentence has to deal with *me*. If my tongue were to be cut out for it, I would say, 'Depose Flavian.' Call in the Counts." The soldiers, monks, and rabble rushed in, and there was wild work. Hilary fled for his life and made his way to Rome by unfrequented paths. Flavian was beaten and kicked so that he died on his way to exile a short while afterward.

The Eutychians now had the Eastern churches in their hands, and during Theodosius's lifetime there was little hope of change. The orthodox bishops looked to Leo for support, but his letters and denunciation of the Latrocinium (Robbers' Council), as he called it, were of no avail.

On July 29, A.D. 450, Theodosius died, and his sister Pulcheria at once "made the senator Marcian her husband and colleague." Marcian was ready to hold a full council of all the bishops, and if possible give peace to the church. Leo wanted the council held in Italy, and he also urged that the doctrinal question should not be reopened, thinking most likely that he had already settled it in his Tome. But Marcian was firm in deciding that the whole matter should be discussed *de novo*. The summons was issued on May 17th for a council to meet September 1, A.D. 451. On that day five hundred and twenty bishops met at

Nicæa, but the emperor was prevented from joining them. Finally, when many began to be attacked with sickness and all were impatient, the emperor called them to meet at Chalcedon, where, he said, it would be convenient for him to despatch public business at Constantinople and attend the council also. The sessions of the council opened October 8, A.D. 451, and the discussions occupied fifteen days. The proceedings were remarkable for soberness and dignity. The whole question between Eutyches, Dioscorus, and Flavian, with the acts of the Robber Synod, was gone over carefully. Many bishops asserted that they had been terrorized into agreeing to the acts of that council. The Latrocinium was condemned. At the third session Dioscorus was tried and deposed. The Roman legates insisted that Leo's Tome should be adopted as it stood, but the council preferred to discuss it point by point. At the fifth session, October 21st, the council appointed twenty-one bishops as a commission to meet separately and draw up a decree of faith and present it to the council. All parties were represented in this commission, and its report was unanimously adopted. The formula begins with a reverent recognition of the acts of the three preceding ecumenical councils, and the Constantinopolitan form of the Nicene Creed, and then proceeds with an elaborate exposition of the doctrine of the incarnation. "This one and the same Christ is recognized in two natures, which indeed are united without intermingling ($ἀσυγχύτως$), without change ($ἀτρέπτως$), indissolubly ($ἀδιαιρέτως$), inseparably ($ἀχωρίστως$), inasmuch as the distinction of the natures is by no means abolished by their union, but much rather the peculiar properties of the two natures are retained, and only combine in the unity of the person or hypostasis."

Theodoret and Ibas came before the council, declared their adhesion to the Ephesine Decrees, and were reinstated.

The acts of the council contain an allocution to the Emperor Marcian, giving a statement of the faith, in which Leo and his Tome are eulogized, and to which a catena of extracts from eminent fathers is appended.

The council enacted thirty canons, of which the twenty-eighth was passed over the protest of the Roman legates, reënacting the third canon of the Council of Constantinople, raising Constantinople to a place of preëminence next to Rome, for the reason that Old Rome was granted its privileges on account of its character as the imperial city.

In spite of its size and character, the Council of Chalcedon did not satisfy the extreme Monophysites, as the followers of Eutyches began to be called. Theodosius, a monk, in Palestine, Timotheus Ælurus in Egypt, and Peter the Fuller in Antioch succeeded in stirring up strife and opposition to the Chalcedonian Decrees. This was increased in A.D. 476 by the circular letter of the Emperor Basiliscus, who depended for his throne on the support of the Monophysites. In this letter he repudiated the Council of Chalcedon, and got five hundred bishops to subscribe. Zeno, however, soon overthrew Basiliscus and declared for Chalcedon. His Henoticon, published in the interest of harmony, appeared in A.D. 482. As a compromise it pleased no one, except the Monophysite patriarch of Egypt, Peter Mongus. It was emphatically rejected by Felix III., bishop of Rome, who was the acknowledged leader of the orthodox bishops in the East and West. Another Monophysite came to the throne in the person of Anastasius, Zeno's successor (A.D. 491), and Jerusalem, Constantinople, and Antioch continued to be the scenes of violent discord. The Pope Hormisdas (A.D. 514–523) followed so firmly in the footsteps of Felix that in the reaction under Justin (A.D. 518–527) his severe measures in Constantinople alienated many who had hitherto been orthodox. The Emperor Justinian (A.D. 527–567) was a Catholic, but his wife Theodora was an active Monophysite. The Roman bishop Agapetus died in Constantinople in A.D. 536, and his deacon, Vigilius, who was in attendance upon him, was induced by Theodora to promise that if he became Pope he would give the influence of the Roman see for her party and against Chalcedon. Vigilius was made Pope, and tried to "play a double game," but failed. Meanwhile the old Origenistic disputes broke out again among the monks in Palestine, and the opinions of Origen were condemned at Antioch (A.D. 543) and at Constantinople (A.D. 544). At this an Origenistic monk, Theodorus Askidas, finding that Antioch was the real seat of the opposition to Origen, and also desiring to divert the emperor from that discussion, suggested to Justinian that a repudiation of the Nestorianism of the Antiochian school would satisfy all parties. Justinian agreed to this and issued an edict (A.D. 544) repudiating the Three

Chapters, viz.: (1) the person and writings of Theodore of Mopsuestia; (2) the writings of Theodoret against Cyril; (3) the letter of Ibas of Edessa to Maris the Persian. Most of the Eastern bishops agreed to this, but in the West, especially in North Africa, it was violently opposed as a practical surrender of Chalcedon. Vigilius, alarmed at the attitude of his own bishops and clergy, vacillated and finally refused to sign. For this he was taken to Constantinople by the emperor, and there signed a secret compact to condemn the Three Chapters. He tried to influence his bishops in a synod in Constantinople (A.D. 545), but failed. He then undertook to get the individual assents of the bishops, and sent forth a document called the Judicatum, which condemned the Three Chapters, but reserved the authority of Chalcedon. He tried to keep the authorship of this document a secret, but it was spread far and wide, and Vigilius was condemned throughout the West, one of the Carthaginian councils pronouncing him deposed.

At last Justinian summoned a general council to meet in Constantinople, May, A.D. 553, after making Vigilius take a solemn oath to condemn the Chapters. The council met, attended by one hundred and sixty-five bishops, including all the Eastern patriarchates, but by only five Western bishops. Vigilius was afraid to be present, but sent a paper called Constitutum, in which he, with sixteen other bishops, condemned some passages from the writings of Theodore, but protested against the condemnation of the Three Chapters. Justinian then declared to the council the secret promises and oaths of Vigilius, and asked it to strike his name from the diptychs, which the council did. After confirming the decrees of the four earlier councils and condemning the Three Chapters, as above described, the council adjourned. It is still a matter of debate whether the opinions of Origen were noticed, except by implication.

As for Vigilius, he changed his mind, and made his subscription to the decrees of the council, and was allowed to return home. He died on the way, June 7, A.D. 555, and in the appointment of his successor, Pelagius, Justinian, emboldened by the submissiveness of Vigilius, marked an epoch in the history of the Papacy by assuming for the first time for the imperial crown the privilege of confirming the election.

The Monophysites in the latter half of the fifth century had begun to be disturbed by the inevitable divisions among themselves. The Severians (from Severus, bishop of Antioch, A.D. 512–519) represented the original Eutychians, who held one nature after the union, but did not deny the ordinary human conditions of our Lord's earthly life. Julian of Halicarnassus, on the other hand, asserts the indestructibility of Christ's body (Ἀφθάρσια); hence Aphthartodocetics and Phantasiasts. Again the more conservative Severians endeavored to get right on our Lord's human nature, and asserted the limitation of his knowledge; hence Agnoëtæ. On the contrary, others denied any distinction between the human and divine natures in Christ; hence Adiaphorites.

Jacobus Baradæus (from his beggar's cloak) became the hero of the Monophysites in Syria and

Mesopotamia; hence the Jacobites of that region. The Fifth General Council did not satisfy the Monophysites in Egypt, and that unhappy church was the scene of indescribable riot and confusion until its people became an easy prey to the Mohammedans (A.D. 640). The Copts of to-day, so called from their pure Egyptian blood, are the descendants of the Monophysites, and Abyssinia has been always under the same influence. The Melchites (*melek* = king), who continued loyal to the Council of Chalcedon and the regular patriarch, were a feeble remnant against whom the Mohammedans directed their fiercest persecutions. The Armenian Church (founded by Gregory the Illuminator and King Tiridates in the fifth century), the first national church in history, became Monophysite through ignorance of the Decrees of Chalcedon. Under stress of persecution by the Persians in A.D. 491, the Armenian bishops in synod signed the Henoticon of the Emperor Zeno and thus repudiated Chalcedon; and in spite of the efforts of the Catholicos Kyrion (A.D. 594) and the Emperor Maurice (A.D. 597) only a small part of the church has ever been reconciled.

From the sixth century the real interest of ecclesiastical history centres in the West. Here we note especially the conversion of the West Gothic kingdom of Spain from Arianism to the Catholic faith, under Reccared, the son of Leovigild, A.D. 586. This conversion was destined to produce unique results, both in the political history of the Gothic monarchy and in the faith of the church. The Third Council of Toledo, the most important of Spanish councils, assembled by King Reccared's command, May, A.D. 589, the decrees of which were signed by sixty-seven bishops and five metropolitans, emphatically anathematized Arianism and recognized the authority of the ecumenical councils of Nicæa, Constantinople, Ephesus, and Chalcedon, and adopted twenty-three canons, which throw interesting light upon the conditions of the time. In the version of the creed (Nicæno-Constantinopolitan) recited at this council, the Filioque clause appears for the first time: "Proceedeth from the Father *and the Son.*" It became the popular use in Spain, and thence made its way to Gaul. Its permanent place in the Western form of the Nicene Creed is due, more than to any one else, to Charlemagne. During his reign (A.D. 768–814) Pope Leo III. and his synod at Rome (A.D. 810) protested against the innovation; but Charlemagne's influence was strong enough to establish the use, which became in after years (cf. Council of Florence, A.D. 1438) one of the most serious subjects of controversy between the Eastern and the Western Church. The fact is that the Filioque was interpolated in the creed without authority, but the *doctrine* expressed by the Filioque has never been denied by the East or the West. After it had come into general use it seemed inexpedient to expunge it, as such action would have been misunderstood.

The impulse given by Justinian to the study of law shows itself not only in the Collection of Canons and Decrees (Dionysius Exiguus, A.D. 500; cf. also Johannes Scholasticus of Antioch, A.D. 578), but in the gradual tendency to fixity and rigidity of doctrinal formulas and the unquestioning submission to the authority of ancient writings. One good result of this decline of speculation was the development of practical activity in missionary work among the now ubiquitous and all-conquering barbarians. The greatest name in this connection is Gregory I. the Great of Rome (A.D. 590–604), by whom the mission of Augustine to the Anglo-Saxons was begun (A.D. 597), and who succeeded in reconciling the queen of the Lombards, Theodelinda, to the bishop of Milan and advancing the church among that people. Gregory took the ground that, while he accepted the judgment of the Fifth Council on the Three Chapters, yet that that council dealt rather with personal matters and did not stand upon the same level with the first great four.

Benedict had founded the Benedictine order at Monte Cassino (A.D. 528), and monasticism at its very best did its noblest work in that and the following century. Columba began his mission to Scotland (A.D. 563), founded the monastic college at Hy (Iona), and for thirty-four years did the work of a missionary. Columbanus (A.D. 560–615), from the great Irish monastery of Bangor, began his wonderful labors on the Continent in A.D. 589, establishing monastic missions at Anegray, Luxeuil, and Fontaines, and finally at Bobbio, where he died (A.D. 615). His friend and follower, Gall, went northward into Switzerland in A.D. 614, where he also founded the monastery that bears his name.

The Eastern Church made its last effort for the solution of the Christological problem in the Monothelite controversy, which began in the reign of Heraclius, with Sergius, the patriarch of Constantinople, about A.D. 616. Heraclius was raising his army for what proved to be his brilliant war against Khosroes, King of Persia—the expiring effort of the Eastern Empire. Mohammed was beginning to proclaim the doctrines of his "heavenly vision" in Arabia. Sergius, in consultation with Theodore, bishop of Pharan in Arabia, and reinforced by an expression he had found in the writings of one of his predecessors, Mennas (contemporary of Vigilius), began to publish abroad the doctrine of one theandric (divine-human) operation in Christ: that Jesus had but *one will;* that whatever may be said of him, as God or as man, it is the one single operation of God the Word. This was pleasing to the emperor as a possible ground of reconciliation of the Monophysites; and at the instance of Heraclius and by the assurance of Sergius, Cyrus, patriarch of Alexandria, reunited the Severians of that place (A.D. 633) to the Catholic Church on this platform. The first opposition to it came from Sophronius, a monk of Palestine, afterward patriarch of Jerusalem (A.D. 634). He contended that it was a distinct injury to the human nature of our Lord and involved ultimately a repudiation of Chalcedon. Sergius wrote to the bishop of Rome, Honorius, giving the history of the matter and requesting his formal opinion. To his delight, Honorius wrote (A.D. 635), giving his unconditional indorsement to the formula of one will and one theandric operation, and declared Monothelism to be part of the Catholic faith. Sophronius replied to this with great ability and spirit, and at his death (A.D. 637) made his suffragans promise to resist the innovation. Heraclius vainly tried to quiet the trouble by putting forth a decree (A.D. 639) called the Ecthesis, which was written by Sergius. It was repudiated by the West, although accepted by Constantinople and Alexandria. The invasion of the Mohammedans rendered Antioch and Jerusalem unable to oppose it. Theodore of Rome (A.D. 646) excommunicated Paul, the new bishop of Constantinople. The Emperor Constans II. (A.D. 648) issued another edict, called Typos, recommending silence on the subject; but Martin I. of Rome, in the First Lateran Synod (A.D. 649), anathematized the doctrine of one will, and for this was deposed and taken to Constantinople, where he was treated with great severity and died in exile. Finally Constantine IV., Pogonatus (the Bearded), summoned a general council, which met November 7, A.D. 680, in the room of the palace at Constantinople called Trullus, and lasted thirty-nine days. There were two hundred bishops present, the sees of Alexandria and Jerusalem being represented by two presbyters. Agatho, bishop of Rome, was present by his legates and in full sympathy with the proceedings. The council was notable for the order and impartiality of its deliberations. The patriarch of Constantinople professed his agreement with Agatho and the Roman synod, but Macarius of Antioch persisted in affirming only one will, and was condemned. In the fifteenth session a diversion was created by a Monothelite monk, who asked permission to vitalize a corpse as an argument for his doctrine. The request was granted, but the test failed. The council finally issued a decree of faith asserting the coexistence of the two wills in the one Lord Christ. The Monothelites were condemned, and Honorius, bishop of Rome, was judged by his written statements, and declared by the council to be included in the anathema. This anathema of the name of Honorius was included in the profession of faith subscribed by the popes of Rome for centuries, and gave great trouble to the ultramontane party at the Vatican Council of A.D. 1870 in their efforts to frame the decree of the official infallibility of the Pope. But if posterity has awarded to Honorius the place of the conventional "villain" in the Monothelite controversy, its real and great hero is Maximus.

Maximus was born in Constantinople in A.D. 580. At first, being small and feeble in body, he devoted himself to study, and became private secretary to the Emperor Heraclius. For some reason he gave up this position (A.D. 615) and became a monk in the monastery of Chrysopolis, near Constantinople. When the Monothelite controversy broke out he was soon recognized as the leader of the opposition, and rallied the whole of northern Africa to his side. There his disputation with the exiled Pyrrhus of Constantinople (held in Carthage, July, A.D. 645) marks an epoch in the controversy. His adversary was vanquished in argument, and, strange to say, gave hearty assent to the doctrine of Maximus. Maximus went to Rome (A.D. 646) as a member of a deputation from North Africa, and succeeded in binding the Roman bishop to the faith. When Constantine's Typos appeared in A.D. 648, it was Maximus who persuaded Pope Martin to hold a council and repudiate the imperial decrees of faith. Like Martin, he was arrested and taken to Constantinople. In A.D. 662 he was tried and anathematized by a Monothelite synod, his tongue and right hand were cut off, he was whipped through the streets, and finally shut up in the castle of Shemari. He was the author of many books, and, as Wagemann says, "forms a most interesting transition from Dionysius Areopagitica to Scotus Erigena. The mysticism of the Greek theology he carries from the former to the latter." His most important works are his treatises "On the Two Natures of Christ," "On Behalf of Chalcedon," and "Against the Monothelites." These writings are really "the chief monuments of the whole Monothelite controversy."

One more supplementary council has had its legal enactments accepted in the code of the universal church. The councils of Constantinople (A.D. 553–680) paid no attention to laws affecting the constitution of the church, so that Justinian II. (A.D. 685–695) convened a council in the Trullus at Constantinople in A.D. 692, which passed one hundred and two canons.

Canon I. declares adherence to the faith as defined in the six general councils.

Canon II. confirms eighty-five "apostolic canons" and those of Ancyra, Neocæsarea, Gangra, Antioch, and Laodicea, and the canonical epistles of various fathers. This canon displeased the Romans because the papal decrees were not included.

Canon XIII. allows clerical marriage and censures those who oppose it.

Canon XXIX. disallows the African practice of receiving the holy communion on Maundy Thursday without fasting.

Canon XXXII. orders the use of the mixed chalice.

Canon XXXVI. repeats the ordinance giving honor to the see of Constantinople.

Two hundred and eleven bishops signed these canons, but many of them were afterward rejected by Rome. This concludes the record of the definitive action taken by the Catholic Church on the greatest, the most difficult, the most important, of all subjects of inquiry, the mode and manner of the incarnation of the Lord Jesus Christ. The first lesson of this history is the fact that the church shrank from definition, which was only forced from her by the erroneous opinions of those who claimed to hold the true faith. That the mind of the church rested with the Monothelite decision as the final expression of dogma in human language is plain. It is not so plain that by this definition all further thought and speculation, within the lines laid down, are forbidden to her people. The promulgation of dogma is the exercise of a solemn and tremendous authority, given by Christ to the whole church for the purpose, not of restricting freedom, but of protecting liberty—the liberty wherewith Christ hath made us free. For any individual to formulate dogma by inference from the writings of men, however pious and learned,—or, worse, for a part of the church, however large and powerful, to promulge dogma and attempt to narrow the lines of Christian thinking,—is to injure the freedom of the gospel. The church as a whole has authoritatively spoken in the Christological definitions of the councils that we have reviewed, and nowhere else. Whatever opinion or teaching can be clearly shown to traverse these definitions ought to be disallowed. But there are many earnest minds in our time who do not believe that the depths of spiritual appreciation of the great mystery of love were exhausted in the controversies of the conciliar period, and who, knowing indeed that the incarnation of God in Christ is an ocean without shore, yet find their highest spiritual employment and reward in reverently seeking more and more, from day to day, his " wonders in the deep." To forbid such search, such speculation, is both uncatholic and futile. So long as the historic and actual Christ is not lost sight of in dreams about the Logos; so long as the two inevitable poles of error present at Chalcedon are avoided, and the human and divine natures kept distinct, entire, and unconfused; so long, finally, as the church's positive and emphatic definition, that the fulcrum, the $\pi o\hat{v}\ \sigma\tau\hat{\omega}$, of union of the natures is the divine Person, is loyally accepted,—we need fear no injury to the faith, but may rather look for enrichment, from those thinkers, who reverently and religiously strive to find new meaning and comfort in the intellectual expression of the great and saving truth that hath filled the world.

CHAPTER I.

THE CHRISTOLOGY OF THE NEW TESTAMENT.

STUDY of the period of the great councils must be chiefly a study of the great fact or truth to the understanding and interpreting of which the mind and life of the period was devoted. Its interest must centre in the task that was undertaken and in the results that were attained. Anything else, such as the personality of the actors, the picturesqueness of the situations, the dramatic movement and effect of the incidents and events, must be kept strictly subordinate and secondary to the absorbing interest and importance of the truth involved. For this truth, if it be what it claims to be, holds in it the life and the destiny of mankind.

The question at issue was, primarily, simply that of the person of Jesus Christ. But because Jesus Christ is at once the most divine and the most human fact and factor in the history and experience of our race, the problem of his person became at once the impulse and starting-point of an entire science of God, of man, and of the essential and final relation between God and man.

If the subject-matter upon which the councils were

engaged were only a matter of human speculation, if the person of Jesus Christ, human and divine, were a creation of the ethical and religious idealizing faculty of humanity, the period would still possess, in many ways, a very real interest for us; but it would be an interest so infinitely below that by which the age believed itself to be actuated that in comparison it dwindles into nothing. The thought and life of the time felt itself engaged not in evolving dreams and speculations of its own but in striving to receive and interpret a truth which was true before, above, and wholly independently of it. And in recalling now its interest, its labors, and its attainments, we must remember that the subject-matter of all these preceded them, and was in itself all and very much more than all that they were able to see or reveal of it. It is necessary therefore that we should not enter upon the labors of our period without first contemplating the fact which it felt itself called to interpret, and tracing down to it the interpretation that had gone before.

It were perhaps to be wished that we could go back behind all records or impressions upon others of the person of Jesus Christ, and form from himself a judgment of him for ourselves. The effort is constantly being made to do something like this, and perhaps not wholly without results. What was he who produced not this or that particular impression but the resultant of actual and permanent impressions which he has made upon the world? But even if we could make for ourselves such a point of view, the criticism which should be able to judge of Jesus, when thus seen, must combine in itself all the qualifications necessary for seeing and understanding all that he really was. There is a possibility of that prepossession or prejudice which disqualifies for seeing the truth, not from one side only, but from the other no less. Supposing that Jesus were a personal manifestation or revelation of God, visible as such, and intended to be visible in the sphere not of the natural but of the spiritual, then this divine in him, if it was to be seen and heard and touched and handled, as St. John said it was, manifestly could not be so by the organs of sense but only by some faculty of spiritual perception or apprehension. To say that we have no such faculty, and that either there is no such divine to be apprehended or that the divine cannot be so apprehended by us, is to come to the inquiry with a prepossession which disqualifies for seeing the divine in Jesus if it is there. No mere natural science, no matter how complete, can ever demonstrate that it is impossible there may be a personal God, or that he may manifest himself in the measure of their developed capacities to personal spirits, along lines other than those of the senses and by methods different from those of natural observation and experience. Christianity holds that it carries with it proofs and evidences of itself which are sufficient for itself, and which in no wise come into conflict with any science save that which carries in it the prepossession that such a manifestation of the divine in the human is impossible. It cannot be denied that, if there be in Jesus Christ such a divine as the church holds there is, it must appeal for recognition to such a divine in us, or organ of the divine, as—not contradicting nature, but on the contrary completing and transfiguring it—yet lies outside of any science of nature which on principle limits itself to the information of the senses. If therefore such a science ignores the existence, that is no proof of the non-existence, of such a divine in our Lord and in ourselves. The proof of it must in the very nature of it lie in criteria which are extrascientific, and to such we make our appeal, trusting that the definiteness and certainty of the response will testify to its truth.

It will be seen that the validity and the value of such reflections will depend upon the success with which we apply to the question of the person of our Lord such not merely natural but spiritual criteria and tests as we maintain *have* more or less both implicitly and explicitly been applied to it and have with more or less completeness determined and settled it.

In reviewing the question of the person of Christ, we too will endeavor to get behind the records and see him as he must have been in himself.

The actual or historical Jesus of Nazareth, in view of what he has become in the world, has never been seriously appraised lower than as the one who has in its history best realized in himself the ethical and spiritual ideal of human nature, life, and destiny. He is not less but more human than others, by how much more than others he has sounded all the depths and heights of humanity, and brought to actuality in himself all that is potential but incomplete in others. The actual Jesus was indeed the most human of

men; and we get farther and farther away from him,
as well as from any real and saving hold upon the
divine realized in him, the farther we get in any
direction from the reality of his humanity.

In the first place, the moral ideal which the world
has recognized in Jesus Christ it has found primarily
not in his teaching but in himself. And that ideal is
not different in him from what it is in others except
in degree. In even the heathen world, Zeno and
Epictetus and Marcus Aurelius were at work upon a
practical theory of life and conduct not different in
principle or kind from his. And the moral maxims
of our Lord were not a revelation, or ought not to
have been such, to those who had been trained for
centuries under the law which he came not to destroy
but to fulfil. The principle of the cross itself was not
a novelty. It had its truth for him only as it has,
and has always had, its truth for all. If he has made
it the necessary and universal and everlasting symbol of all highest human motive and action, it is only
because in itself and everywhere self-sacrificing love
is the sole highest motive and action, not only for
human but for all possible spiritual and free beings,
including God himself. And as the actual Jesus had
no other morality than that of men, so he attained its
heights by no other path than theirs. If he became
the perfect man, he was made perfect by the things
he suffered. He was tempted in all points like as we
are, and his endurance, his courage, his faith, his victory, his peace and joy in overcoming, have nothing
in them that we cannot know and understand.

If we see in Jesus not merely the ethical but

the religious ideal of humanity, just as little was his religion as his morality essentially different from that of all men. It was nothing more nor less than the religion of a perfect faith, a perfect hope, and a perfect love toward God and toward man. All that was different from others was that in him it was *perfect* in all these. And not only was his faith ours, but it was a faith which had fought and conquered our doubts, difficulties, and fears; it had known the " conflict with despair," and had overcome through the laying hold upon him who alone was able to save him as well as us. There is no spiritual aspiration in any religion of any race, no feeling anywhere after God if haply it might find him, that has not in it the essential principle of the perfect religion of him who has felt in himself all human want and aspiration, and found in God all human satisfaction and fulfilment.

In Jesus Christ religion and morality are not two things but one. It is the nature of man to fulfil himself not by conformity to abstract laws but by union with living persons. In our earthly relations it is not the father's authority and law enforced and obeyed, but his personal spirit communicated and received, that informs and shapes the character and personality of the son. And in the larger home and life of our universal and eternal relationships it is not obedience to natural or divine laws that perfects us, but the personal Spirit of God filling us and fulfilling himself in us, and so enabling us to fulfil ourselves in him. Not by works of the law, but by the Spirit that works through a holy faith, love and obedience wrought in us, are we saved.

But there is nothing more certain than that whatever was the human ethical or religious character attained and manifested by our Lord, it is not to that that we can attribute the immediate origin or the permanent success of Christianity as a *gospel*, or rather as the gospel; for from its first proclamation it never called or considered itself anything less than this. It was just its unqualified and unhesitating claim to absoluteness and universality as such that gave it its indestructible vitality and success. If it had faltered for one moment in the completeness of its claim, and consented to be an ethical system, a philosophy, or even a religion, it would never have become what it is. It was necessary that it should be everything or nothing. And all this needs something more to account for it than the personal virtue or piety of even a Jesus of Nazareth. No matter how truly and perfectly he thought and taught and lived, it is impossible to find in that anything to make his life and person a gospel to the world in the sense in which it claimed to be, and actually became, such.

As a matter of fact it was not the perfection merely of our Lord's teaching or character that was the primitive gospel. Christianity came with a burst of joy and gladness and hope and power, all of which betokened that something had come to pass which no saint or sage could have accomplished. What it was, was no less than this: that Jesus Christ had abolished sin and death, and that in him was to be preached to all the world the remission of sin and resurrection from death. Such a gospel, in the nature of it, could not be from man, but only of God; and that nothing less than this could have been its original proclamation is proof that there must have been in Jesus the claim of something higher than truth in his teaching, or holiness in his life. What this something higher was will only gradually appear, but it may be seen already that it must consist in some unique relation as well to God as to man, in consequence of which we are able to recognize in him not only a work of God wrought in man, but—potentially at least and virtually, if not yet actually—an entirely new relation of all men to God. In other words, what is involved in the claim of the gospel from the beginning, and what makes it the gospel, is that in the person of Jesus Christ there is manifested the essential truth, and the whole truth, of God to man and man to God. The one aspect requires his Godhead, and the other his manhood—both in a sense and to an extent which it has been, and will be forever, the occupation and the joy of the church to endeavor to receive and to define. This much, and no less, we claim for the Christ of whom Christianity is the product and the expression. We may have no direct means now of judging him, but we can judge it, and from only such a source can have come such a stream.

When we pass from such a priori considerations of the person of our Lord to the impressions actually produced by him and the records that remain of him, it may be well to dwell for a moment upon the part which the Old Testament writings played in predetermining these impressions and giving form to their expression. Christianity is quite able and ready to rest its claims upon itself, and its truth is not necessarily bound up with that of any antecedent history or historical records. But it is a part of its claim to truth in the natural as well as in the spiritual order, that it came not without preparation throughout all the previous course of the world. Indeed, if Christianity is the truest, it must also be the most natural thing in the world, and only truest because most natural. Its claim is not to be a spiritual instead of a natural, but a spiritual which is the truth and the fulfilment of the natural order. "There is a spiritual, and there is a natural. Howbeit that is not first which is spiritual, but that which is natural; and afterward that which is spiritual." Each in its order, and the higher not the contradiction and destruction, but the realization and completion, of the lower: "I am not come to destroy, but to fulfil." The natural creation itself has passed through the successive stages or orders of the mineral, the vegetable, the animal, and the human. And human history, in entering into personal relation and union with the personal divine, and so becoming spiritual, in contradistinction from its merely immanent relation to God in nature, is not thereby contradicting either nature or its own nature, but only fulfilling both. So in reality the truth of Christianity is not only true for all time to come, but it was true in all time before. It is part, and highest part, of the truth not only of the world but of the universe. It makes no difference for our present purpose what we think of the Bible, or how we define prophecy. After all that has been or can be said, the fact remains that the Old Testament history did prepare the way for Christ and the gospel. The New Testament was latent in the Old, and the Old became patent in the New. All that was essential was that the preparation should prepare and that the fulfilment should fulfil. Both did so; the end was attained; we may let the rest go. But to us it is of no little interest and profit to possess and to study the records of how, by the natural method of a progressive spiritual evolution, the needs and wants, the hopes and expectations, were formed and trained in the old order under the law, that were to be filled and satisfied in the new under the gospel; just as we recognize now in every true natural human life, not a negation or contradiction of the spiritual, but a thousand incompletenesses, wants, dissatisfactions, and aspirations, which will find their satisfaction only in the spiritual. Divine redemption from sin and death was as much the hope and promise of the first as it was the realization of the final dispensation. And we may add that it is as much the fundamental need and longing of the truly natural as it is the fulfilment and satisfaction of the truly spiritual man. The Old Testament was the divine preparation of the natural for the spiritual, and it is nothing against the divine origin and character of Christianity that only Jews, with heads and hearts full of Messianic ideas and hopes, were prepared first to recognize the Christ and welcome the gospel.

When we come to the question of what were the earliest and most authentic records of our Lord which have come down to us, what was the first gospel or written description of his person and work, here again, while the question can never be answered to the satisfaction of all the literary and critical interests involved in it, quite enough may be well known for our present purpose. It is impossible to reduce the primitive gospel to any minimum of what is contained in our synoptic gospels which will not include all that is sufficient to make that minimum *the gospel*. And to call anything the primitive gospel which did not contain in it implicitly and in germ all that has entitled the later gospel to be called a gospel at all is an historical contradiction. To say that the sum of what was in our Lord, and in the first impressions that he made upon his followers, and in their first records of him, was that he was a good man and a great teacher, through whom the world learned more clearly than before what virtue and godliness are, is simply to disconnect the origin of Christianity, and Christianity itself, from Christ and his original disciples and the original documents. That was not the Christianity that burst upon the world with an initial force and truth which was the secret of its final and permanent success. That Christianity included in it indeed the conviction of the human spiritual and moral perfection of Jesus; but it saw in that human virtue and godliness nothing less than man's atonement with God, redemption from sin, and resurrection from death. This divine and universal significance of himself, and of what he was and accomplished as a man, was a part and an inseparable part of the consciousness of Jesus himself. It is not only that St. John says, " He was manifested to take away sins; and in him is no sin. Whosoever abideth in him sinneth not." It is not only that St. Paul says everywhere that in him God has abolished sin, and with it death. It is not only that the apostles went out at the very first to preach in him remission of sin and resurrection from death. It is not only that baptism into him meant all this or meant nothing at all. It is that you cannot separate from the personal consciousness of Jesus Christ himself the sense and the knowledge that he was come to be something from God to the world, which the church after him might insufficiently receive and understand, but can never overestimate or exaggerate. Any most primitive representation of Jesus includes in it, beyond the evidences of his sweet reasonableness and humanness, an element of power and authority to which there is no natural limit, and which must be recognized in its full extent by one who would wholly know him. The developed Gospel of St. John carries this ἐξουσία to the point of quickening the dead, conferring the divine life, and being the final Judge and Saviour of men. St. Paul regards him as the second Adam in whom humanity comes to spiritual or divine life, as in the first Adam it came to earthly and natural life. The Epistle to the Hebrews sees in him the high priest in whom humanity has through death consummated its relation to God and entered within the veil. The synoptics themselves bring their story to the point at which all power is given to him in heaven and earth, and all the nations of the earth are to be baptized into his name. But if we go back behind all these to the indisputable spiritual attitude and claim of Jesus, we too shall find all that was subsequently developed out of it already contained in it. When he taught it was with the authority of the law itself, and not merely of one under the law. He himself indeed humanly obeyed and fulfilled the law, but he did it in a way to appear more the law fulfilling itself in a human obedience than a merely human obedience fulfilling the law. The church sees in him, indeed, both the divine law and the human obedience—the divine will incarnate in human life; and our Lord's own attitude sustains both. He *is* the law which he obeys.

When we turn from the authority of his teaching to that of his working, there is a point of view from which it almost seems a lowering of our Lord's spiritual and moral attitude that he should have descended to work what are called " miracles." Was he not higher as himself embodying the law—the eternal nature and truth of things—than as seemingly violating its sanctity and consistency? But, without attempting at this time an explanation, how plain it is that our Lord himself regarded the miracles as accidental and subordinate to the real and permanent purpose of his mission and ministry! In the first place, the works of healing are with him always not so much acts of power as of compassion; the explanation given of them is that " himself bore our sorrows and carried our griefs." And in the second place the real object of his compassion is conspicuously not the fruit of suffering in the body, but the root of sin in the soul. He says to the sick of the palsy, " Son, thy sins be forgiven thee." The bodily healings were with him but as parables or signs of that spiritual healing which was to be his real and permanent work in the world. They were wrought that through them we might "know that the Son of man hath power on earth to forgive and to heal sin." The blind saw, the deaf heard, the lame walked, the lepers were cleansed, the dead arose, all as illustrations of a redemption, a resurrection, which is preached to every human being in him. All this he wrought, indeed, as Son of man. He preaches and imparts nothing to us as men which he was not himself as man. But he was the man he was, and we shall be the men we shall be in him, because it was God who was incarnate in him in order that through him he may become incarnate in us. There is no primitive gospel according to which Jesus Christ is himself personally *dead*. In all he is alive, to be himself personally present in every man—the personal principle in him of his own communicated holiness and his own imparted life.

What theory of the nature and of the person of Jesus Christ is necessarily involved in such an original conception of the effects produced by him, and the abiding and influential relations borne by him to the whole human race, may not yet be present in the minds or apparent in the testimony of the first evangelists. But there is one remarkable assertion that may certainly be ventured upon without fear of controversy. If we take our gospels as they stand, it cannot be denied that the synoptics on one side and St. John on the other regard the person of our Lord from opposite points of view. The one see him primarily as human, and the other sees him as divine; and the human of the former is as thoroughgoing and complete as the divine of the latter; the Jesus of the synoptics is as simply, naturally, tragically human as the incarnate Word of St. John is divine. But there is absolutely nothing in the synoptical representation of the human character and consciousness of Jesus which unfits it or renders it inadequate for St. John's conception of it as a divine incarnation; and equally there is nothing in St. John's representation of an incarnation of the eternal Word in the person of Jesus which contradicts or impairs the reality or the completeness of his humanity as portrayed by the synoptics. On the contrary, the humanity is the wholly adequate and congruous expression and manifestation of the divinity, and the divinity is the necessary and the only explanation and account of the humanity. The divinity of Jesus Christ is not revealed outside of but in and by his humanity. The very truth and design of the incarnation is the realization and revelation of God in man; and the Godhead is manifest not in the non-naturalness but in the higher and truer naturalness of the manhood. God incarnate, that is to say, Godhead in manhood, would not and could not assume any other form than that of the divinely human and humanly divine personality and personal life of Jesus Christ. Any other would have been either less human or less divine, and therefore less both. The constant disposition and effort to make our Lord more divine by making him less human tends only to reduce the incarnation to a semblance and an unreality. On the other hand, when it is attempted to make him less divine by making him more human, we need not fear, but may even welcome, the result of the experiment. When even with hostile intent criticism emphasizes the very and entire humanness of the Jesus of the synoptics, not merely of his body and its natural affections but also of his mind and consciousness, and of his will and character and life—when it represents his virtue as consisting, like ours, of a free human will and a sweet human reasonableness, and even his godliness as being, like ours, the gift to him of the divine grace through his human faith—let us remember that these things cannot be too much emphasized, that by how much he lacked any part of them he fell short of being a man, and his humanity of being a real and a complete incarnation. Jesus Christ wholly revealed God in that he was and not otherwise than as he was the divine revelation of the whole nature, life, and destiny of man. As such he is the divine and the whole, as well of every man as of all humanity. And all this is not only expressed explicitly in the developed doctrinal or theological system of St. Paul or St. John; it is contained implicitly in the constitution of his own divine-human personality, as in the impression he made upon others and in the earliest records others have left of him.

The certain and indisputable first recorded impression of Jesus Christ was thus that of one who indeed was man, but such a man as that humanity was become in him a new thing; and new, not in the sense of ceasing to be itself or human but in the sense of now for the first time truly becoming itself or divine. For it was just the truth of humanity that it was constituted for and so predestined to what

St. Paul afterward called υἱοθεσία, or divine sonship. That is to say, it was its nature to be taken into participation with the divine nature and life; it was made for God, and could complete itself or be completed only in personal fellowship of nature and life with the personal God. If the first religious consciousness saw in Jesus rather a manhood which realizes and attains itself in the Godhead, while the later is disposed to reverse the process, and see in him God who fulfils himself in humanity, and so in individual men, this is but as it should be. The truth of either side does not contradict that of the other, but on the contrary the impairing of either truth impairs the other. The fact of the case was that the human of the earlier consciousness was such as not merely to truly and adequately embody and express the divine of the later, but to be only by it truly and adequately explained and accounted for. Out of this inevitably arose the question, Was this a divine become human or a human become divine? And if the answer was, as it must be, that it was both, then follows the further question, Which of the two was first and cause of the other? The decision of the church was that in Jesus Christ man was become divine because God was become man. If in reaching this decision there was a wavering or a temporary lingering on the way, and if even within the New Testament Scriptures there can be found at any point evidence of such halting, there is nothing in this inconsistent with the character either of the Scriptures or of the truth.

The gospel of Antioch and that of Jerusalem, to the Gentiles and to the Jews, of St. Paul and of the original apostles, have been contrasted and opposed, even to the point of making them two gospels. St. Paul does indeed say "*my* gospel," and that as against a narrower and exclusive gospel which would place or magnify barriers in the way of the universal extension of the free gift and impartation of God to humanity in Jesus Christ. There was in the nature of things an inevitable strain and conflict involved in the transition from the exclusiveness of Judaism to the universality of Christianity. To wipe out distinctions and make Jew and Gentile one body in Christ was a task of which it would be difficult to exaggerate the practical and actual difficulties. We may concede the existence through it of strained relations among the apostles themselves. But the strain was endured, and the catholic church embraced in its one bosom both parties, without the sacrifice of anything vital in the faith or practice of either. That the controversy did not involve any distinctive or essential point of Christianity itself, but turned upon issues wholly outside of it, became clear enough as soon as it was all over. Upon what constitutes the gospel there is neither in Scripture nor in tradition the slightest charge or suspicion of difference or contradiction. The apostles from Jerusalem preached a risen and living Christ, present by his Spirit in the church, and taking men up into the grace and power of his redemption from sin and his resurrection from death. They were too much as yet taken up with the fact and their experience of it to go on into any rationale of their divine salvation. And, dealing with Jews, the inevitable question did not come up with them of the relation of their new faith to their old principles and habits of thought and life. Absorbed in the former, the latter continued along with it without any thought on their part of incongruity or inconsistency. Yet there is no question that Christianity, while in one sense it fulfils and completes, in another sense supplants and displaces Judaism by a distinct change of principle. To St. Paul as apostle to the Gentiles fell the painful task of cutting Christianity loose from all trammels of Judaism and of exposing their irreconcilable difference and contrast. He resisted to the death the claim for the continuance of the rite of circumcision because he saw in it a principle of legalism which he deemed it of the essence of Christianity not merely to leave behind but to exchange for a directly opposite principle. The other apostles may very well not have so seen it or so clearly seen it; and to the Jewish Christians generally his radical and revolutionary attitude to the ancient law would amply justify all that he suffered at their hands.

St. Paul did not suffer too much, nor did he attach too much consequence to the principle at stake, since—although he alone at the time may have seen it—the principle was indeed the essential and vital one of Christianity, and to his sufferings for it we are indebted for his thorough analysis and exposition of it. The law and the gospel represent two aspects or relations of human life that are neither more nor less mutually exclusive or contradictory than the world and God or nature and grace. It was necessary in human history as in human life that each in its order should be developed into consciousness, that they should then be contrasted and opposed, and that finally they should be reconciled and combined. The principle of the law is that man cannot be fulfilled otherwise than by himself; the principle of the gospel is that man is fulfilled only in and through God. The question indeed does not end there; given that man cannot be free or complete in himself alone but only in God, does he complete himself in God or does God alone complete him? At every point the answer is that both sides are true.

It was the genius of Hebrew culture because it was its divine mission to develop the principle of moral obedience. Its contribution to the thought and life of the world was its conception of personal, national, human righteousness. Its God has been defined as "the power, not ourselves, that makes for righteousness." Its dream and prophecy of the future was a new heaven and a new earth wherein should be realized its moral ideal of a universal righteousness. Doubtless this is the first of truths for the free spirit. Kant did not emphasize too strongly either the fact of the moral law or the autonomy of the human will. Man can only be himself by himself fulfilling his law—and his whole law. Righteousness is his sole end, his only redemption, completion and salvation; and only he can be or do his own righteousness, for righteousness is essentially a personal act or habit and cannot in the nature of it be merely natural or impersonal or passive. It has been well said that the truth of the Old Testament is, No salvation but righteousness; of the New, No righteousness but Christ. If the last and greatest of the prophets just before the coming of our Lord repeated the cry of the old dispensation, it was given to St. Paul after his coming, at least most clearly and decisively of all, to utter the voice of the new. It is only one who can see and combine the truth expressed in opposites who can understand that the declaration that man can only be saved by his own obedience is not contradicted by the other declaration that man cannot be saved by his own obedience. We shall not understand all the meaning of salvation in Christ until we have learned the whole of two truths, each of which has opposite sides which must equally and wholly be held. The first is that Jesus Christ is equally God who by a divine incarnation fulfils himself in man, and man who by a human faith and obedience realizes himself in God. The second is that Jesus Christ is equally an objective human righteousness or self-realization or salvation, presented to our faith and made ours by the divine grace, and a subjective human righteousness appropriated, made our own, and wrought in us through our own obedience. We have only to reflect for a moment to see that if the divine becoming in us is to be at the expense of our own becoming, if we are to have God at the expense of losing instead of truly finding and completing ourselves, the salvation will not be that of Christ and Christianity.

St. Paul then no more than our Lord himself was set for the destruction but rather for the true and only fulfilling of the law. But his mission was to stand for righteousness or salvation not as it is through obedience or the law but as it is not through these; not as we work it but as God has wrought it for us and works it in us. Just as one might stand for the divine in Christ and not the human and yet not deny the human but if need be stand for it too, as it might seem to some, against the divine; so one might be set for the denial of the possibility of righteousness through human obedience alone without denying that a righteousness from God and by grace can only exist for us and in us as a true and free human obedience. It is as true in its place to say that God alone without us cannot make us righteous as it is to say that we ourselves without God cannot be righteous. But St. Paul was standing for the second and if to many he seems to contradict the first it is only seeming. In reality he knows as much that the material cause and condition of our righteousness is our own being righteous and doing righteously as he knows that the efficient and producing cause of our righteousness is the grace and power and new creation of God in Christ working through our faith. His so-called one-sidedness exists only for those who do not know the whole of him and it contradicted neither the other-sidedness of the apostles who were before him nor the both-sidedness of the catholic church which came after him.

When we pass on to the Christ and the Gospel according to St. John it is impossible to deny or ignore the difference of point of view or representation. If acknowledging this and not venturing to account for it we still affirm, underneath all the differences, the identity of the person and work described with those of the accounts of St. Paul, St. Peter and the synoptics, and with the actual person and work of Jesus himself, it will of course seem daring and unjustifiable to a merely natural criticism, but it is true nevertheless.

The Jesus of St. John is incontrovertibly the incarnation of a divine person; but it is never so at the expense of his being just as truly and wholly and consistently a human person. I need not add, save for those who ignorantly or wilfully misunderstand, that this does not mean that he is two persons but one who if he is as truly divine as he is human is also as truly human as he is divine. In St. John however it is only the second that needs to be made apparent. The Jesus, for example, of the fifth chapter, who feels himself one with the Father and not only works the Father's work but as it were works the Father's working ("My Father worketh and I work," as though it were not only to one result but even by one operation); who judges the divine judgment and saves with the divine salvation, yet claims do to all this humanly and accounts for doing it not on the ground of being divine but on the ground that, being human, he is wholly surrendered to God and does not oppose himself to God's being and willing and working in him. He is what he is and does what he does because he wholly seeks not himself or his own will but only and wholly the will of him who had sent him. It is as Son of man that he is sole and supreme Saviour and Judge, a savor of life unto life and of death unto death. His attitude to his own miracles is the same as that in the synoptics. They are all merely figures of his one complete and perfect work of raising humanity out of death and quickening or regenerating it with the life of God. He is the way, the truth and the life for men because he, as representing and embodying humanity, has by the one way for men—the way of self-sacrificing love and obedience, the way of the cross—attained the whole truth and lived the whole life of humanity. In consequence, power is his over all flesh to give eternal life to those who believe in and receive and love him.

The above very general outline will serve to illustrate and justify the conclusions which we wish to make the starting-point of our further studies. When we take the Christian Scriptures as a whole, leaving aside all questions of criticism, the following points become clearer and clearer to the Christian consciousness in proportion as it more and more enters into and is more and more qualified to judge them. There is no essential part of the New Testament that is not instinct and vital with the primitive impulse and life of the Christianity of Jesus Christ. All the parts are not the same but they are coördinate and supplementary parts of an organic whole which has become the faith and the life of the catholic church. The conclusions that represent the teaching of the New Testament writers as inconsistent and made up of different and contradictory impulses and directions of thought are drawn from incomplete assumptions of what the initial and essential principle and fact of Christianity is. Assume that the actual Christ is not and cannot have been what the church has received him to be, and all that flows from him must become instantly and from the beginning confusion, self-contradiction and incomprehensibility. Assume him to be what the church believes him, and the Scriptures, the thought and life of the church, the faith and formative principle of Christendom, become one, harmonious and comprehensible.

The first movement, manifestation and self-embodiment of Christianity, as destined to be not merely an idea but a realization and an institution in the world, was certainly its most living, plastic and creative act. When this stage was at an end it was found to have formed for itself an outward expression of worship and life, an organization for discipline and government, and a body of sacred books that embodied its teaching. Confining ourselves to the latter we might say that the action of the church in accepting a canon of Scripture need not have been more than the instinctive and practical wisdom of receiving as highest, truest and best Christianity's own first, living and creative expression of itself, and making this the norm and measure of all subsequent self-expressions of it. It is self-evident to the mind that takes it in as a whole that the New Testament is a single movement of spiritual and Christian thought and life and that it is complete and sufficient in itself. It is equally certain that neither the succeeding nor any subsequent age had in it either the plastic capacity or the creative power to take for itself a living form such as Christianity easily, freely and naturally assumed in its initiative stage. And therefore it was, to say no more, an act of practical wisdom to accept that first embodiment and expression of itself as in principle at least and in substance final and irreformable. In this way actually the church did adopt its primitive liturgical norm, its episcopal organization and its canon of Scripture. And since then experience has proved that neither in worship, in government nor in doctrine has the church ever well or wisely tampered with its primitive constitution or form. On the contrary experience ever brings it back to these as certainly humanly best if not indeed divinely ordered and appointed.

Returning then to the Scriptures as the source and rule of the further thinking and defining of the church's mind upon the essential doctrine of the person and work of Christ, what may we in recapitulation sum up as the essential elements of the problem? We may say first that if Christianity is to remain true to its own original claim upon the church and to the church's original impression and acceptance of it, it must continue to present in its Head and in itself not only the ideal but the reality of a personal presence and operation of God in humanity. Christianity must be primarily and essentially a divine fact and a divine act. It can never be anything less than an atonement of God with man and a redemption and completion of man in God. And in the second place since the Christ of the Scriptures represents and fills man's part as well as God's in the great act of the divine-human atonement; since as the great High Priest appointed for man in things pertaining to God he is we to Godward as truly as he is God to usward; therefore he must be really man and there must not be any more limitation in his manhood than there is in his Godhead.

CHAPTER II.

THE NATURAL BASIS OF A SCRIPTURAL AND CATHOLIC CHRISTOLOGY.

HE claim thus far made we may restate as follows: the writings that passed into the permanent acceptance of the church as its canon of Scripture belong to a single and complete movement of thought and life in which Christianity expressed its first and whole impression and conception of the person and work of Jesus Christ. Only then and there was such an expression and record of the original and originating facts of Christianity possible. No later age could either make it or materially add to it. Whatever Christ had been or had done in himself, Christianity did not originate or enter into the world until his person and his work had passed into the mind, the life and the experience of the first believers. When the Scriptures were completed they had so passed and were become the possession of the church. There was much still and would be always for Christian thought and science to occupy itself with in the Christian faith and life, but so far as the materials were concerned for all this future occupation, they

were complete in the primitive experience as recorded in the Scriptures; or if they were not there was no means or possibility of future addition to them.

What the church had to do afterward as we shall see—and it was an inevitable and necessary task—was to form out of the materials in its possession a common or catholic faith over against the incomplete, variable and conflicting faiths of its individual members. But it was more than two centuries before the church was in condition or circumstance to think and express itself again as a whole. In the meantime we have only here and there individual voices, speaking each for itself and yet testifying by their agreement to the wide-spread and unbroken certainty of the common truth and life. They of course were not infallible; some of them lived and thought only in the light of the general tradition before and without the guidance of an accepted Scripture, while all as yet were without that of an authoritative catholic consensus or agreement. A complete and all-sided faith or life is not promised or given to any individual man, and no single man even with the aid of the Scriptures holds such except as the gift to him in whole or for the most part of the common thought and knowledge of the church. The very elevation and intensity of individual attention and experience in one direction withdraws it from other directions of quite equal truth and importance. Only such a complex resultant of the operation of many minds and lives as we have in the Scriptures or in the church can combine the whole truth or express the sum of Christian experience. The earliest fathers were separated in some respects further than are we who have Scripture and catholic consent from the primitive and formative impulse and life of Christianity. We may expect to find in no one of them therefore the whole developed round of truth and life as it is in Christ. Yet on the other hand it may be claimed that in no one of them do we not find one at least or some of those truths in Christ that are essential parts of the truth as it is whole in him, and each of which is only true in the common truth of all the others. And so at the close of the second century Irenæus in Gaul, Tertullian in Africa and Clement in Alexandria, representing the Christian world of the time, are substantially and sufficiently agreed upon the essential fact and doctrine of the person and work of Jesus Christ. But that from the first and always, even within the church, there were not only partial and incomplete conceptions but also denials and contradictions of the essential truth of Christ, it is needless to say. The founder and the first teachers of Christianity foresaw that it was not only inevitable but needful that it should be so. Truth is only made known and indeed only knows itself in conflict with error; and it is the most familiar fact in connection with the actual growth and formation of catholic doctrine that it was reached by the application on its largest historical scale of the principle of exclusion.

Before beginning however to trace the process by which the church formed for itself a catholic mind from the materials of truth committed to it—that is to say, by which the truth of Scripture, consisting mainly of facts, was converted into that of the church, composed largely also of doctrine and dogma—we must first discuss a very large and important principle that underlies the whole matter.

It is very evident that there is a double problem involved in the origin and appearance of Christianity in the world—the problem namely not only of its divine giving but also of its human receiving. A divine revelation or communication of any sort can only be adequately made through an adequate human understanding and acceptance of it. Granting a true and complete revelation of God in word and work through Jesus Christ, what is the ground of assurance of a true and complete appropriation and representation of that word and work in the Scriptures and in the mind and life of the church? Both sides of the problem are everywhere recognized and presented with sufficient plainness in the New Testament, where grace or divine communication is always conditioned upon faith or human apprehension and reception. The light could but shine in darkness if the darkness comprehended it not. When St. Peter made his famous confession of the person of the Lord and was told, " Blessed art thou, Simon Bar-Jonah, for flesh and blood hath not revealed this unto thee but my Father which is in heaven," there is recognition of the fact that an objective divine revelation of truth or life is dependent upon and of no avail without a corresponding subjective human power of apprehension and acceptance. Similarly when St. Paul says, " But when it pleased God . . . to reveal his Son in me," he refers not to the objective self-revelation of God in Christ but to the divinely given power in himself to recognize the truth revealed, without which it would or could have had no significance or truth whatsoever for him. On a larger scale, the birthday of the church is truly placed in the New Testament not on Easter day when all the conditions of its new life are objectively completed in the resurrection of its Head but on Whitsunday, when by the gift of the Holy Ghost the subjective conditions are realized by which alone the risen life could become its own.

The general principle is stated in the scriptural and church doctrine that the incarnation as a whole and in all its parts is an act of the divine Word by the divine Spirit, the Logos by the Holy Ghost. In this conjoint work, as has been elsewhere said, the Word as always is the principle or agent of the objective revelation, the Spirit that of the subjective human appropriation. In the womb of the Virgin the Holy Ghost is not the divine begetter nor the divine begotten but reveals his operation in the grace of the human conception and child-bearing. The expression "conceived by the Holy Ghost" represents the Holy Ghost as mother not of the act by which the Word became flesh but of the preparation and ability of the flesh to be assumed by the Word. The function of the Word appears in the divine impartation, that of the Spirit in the human susceptibility and reception. By the Word God begets, by the Spirit humanity conceives and bears; through both God is incarnated and humanity is regenerated and redeemed.

This may all be considered the more or less figurative or symbolical language of the Scriptures and the church; but attach what meaning or importance we may to the facts or to their expressions, there is a truth that lies behind them to which in some form or other we must do justice. If Christianity is something more than a mere humanly devised theory of conduct or humanly conceived dream of religion, if God is indeed in it and between him and us there is something really given and received, then we must form to ourselves some mode of conceiving both the giving and the receiving. The former we call a revelation, the self-manifestation and self-communication of God to men, objectively and completely given in the divine-human person and life of Jesus Christ. The latter appears in Christian thought under several different forms, all of which however are but kinds or degrees of one and the same thing.

The highest of these forms is what has been designated inspiration, a term applied exclusively to that assumed true apprehension and infallible record of Christian revelation which we have in the Scriptures. The next higher form of human reception of divine truth in Jesus Christ is to be found in church authority, which claims for itself the right to interpret the Scriptures and to give, as in the creeds, a catholic doctrine which is above any private interpretation of individual Christians. Lower in a sense than either of these and yet the basis and condition of them both is the claim of the individual human soul to be able to say at all that it knows or can know God or the things that are freely given to it of God in Jesus Christ.

Of course if it is impossible for the human spirit to know God otherwise than as it conjectures his existence and its own relation to him within the course of nature; if there is demonstrably no interrelation and communion between finite spirits and the Father of spirits of a spiritual and personal character, which is to us the essence of any real religion —that ends the matter. If however there is for the spiritual man a knowledge of spiritual things, such knowledge, while on one side it must doubtless be of God, on the other side must equally be of the man himself. All knowledge must be equally of the object and of the subject and of a relation or correspondence between the two by virtue of which the one somehow makes itself known and the other somehow knows it. If God can make himself known to us or in us it is only because there is such a correspondence between him and us by virtue of which we can know him. However God in any way or degree makes himself known to us, we may depend upon it that it is through our own way of knowing him; and if it is in any sense supernatural it is only in that in which the supernatural is the highest reach and action of the natural. God's presence and operation in anything does not replace or displace the thing but completes and fulfils it; and so through any presence and operation of God in him man does not cease to be but for the first time truly and completely becomes himself. If therefore we know God and what he has given us of himself in Jesus Christ it is by virtue of some most natural faculty and criterion within ourselves as spiritual beings, or beings constituted for such knowledge of God and of the things of God. The spiritual man is judge of spiritual things because as they are for him so in some real sense he is for them, and therefore as they "find" him so he receives, measures and verifies them. Aristotle defines that to be "rational" which is so to the rational or wise man, making "the right reason" the test or measure of what is rational as conversely he makes the objectively and truly rational the test of the right reason. And so St. Paul says—and says in perfect consonance with our Lord's own position—that that is spiritual truth which is so to the spiritual man, as conversely the spiritual man is he who understands spiritual truth. These two are for each other and each is test and measure of the other; only he who is of God can know what is of God and he only is of God who knows the things freely given him of God. It has been asserted and truly that all ultimate truth, whether of the natural or of the spiritual reason, is believed at last because it is truth and not because it is proved. Truth and the reason are mutually measures and tests of each other and only that truly stands which truly unites them.

We might illustrate this position in many ways. For example, science recognizes the fact that in human thought and life there are certain ideas or sentiments which "persist," and it admits this persistence as an argument for their truth. Among these are the ideas or sentiments of God, of immortality, of religious faith and worship. Will these continue to persist as long as human thought and life continue? It is perfectly rational to reply that that depends upon whether or not they are true in themselves. If they are not true they will certainly sooner or later disappear out of that of which they are not integral and essential parts. If they are true it is equally certain that they will never disappear but will continue to give no rest to the individual or to the race until they have received fuller—and fullest—recognition and satisfaction. If there is spiritual truth for the spiritual reason and a spiritual reason in us for the truth we need have no doubt that these will finally come together; what God has made to be joined together no man or men can forever keep asunder.

Now Christianity claims to be the fulness of divine revelations and communications to man and the completeness and limit of man's capacity of reception from God. It proclaims Christ as on the one side the sum of spiritual or divine things to be apprehended, and as on the other the perfect human apprehension of these things. He perfectly represents God in things pertaining to man as he perfectly represents man in things pertaining to God and so is the perfect expression of the perfect relation between them. If this be so it follows that as Jesus Christ is the Logos of God so is he the proper content and revelation of the spiritual reason of man; and he is received and believed by the soul primarily perhaps for other reasons also but finally and permanently because and only because he is the truth and life of the soul.

Thus the proper proof of Jesus Christ is Jesus Christ himself. It is for what he is and not for any external proofs he may have given of himself or God may have given of him that he is believed on and will be believed on in the world. The same amount of proof and ten times the same amount though it were given by God himself to anything less true or less vitally true in itself could not have produced the same faith in us, because our faith goes out not to the proof but to the truth of the thing proved. Though Jesus Christ had fulfilled all prophecy and wrought all miracles and given himself up to worse than the cross and risen with a more startling and convincing resurrection from the dead, all these things would not in themselves have made Christianity a thing for all men in all time if there were not something in itself for all men and all time, if he were not indeed the way, the truth and the life.

To illustrate this more in detail: it is not enough that Christianity with its absolute and exclusive claim should be true; it must be at every point the inevitable, only and ultimate truth. This of course will not be apparent at first in the case of each such truth; it only becomes so at last as the result of a process by which the experience gradually fits and adjusts itself to the truth and the truth gradually approves and proves itself to the experience; and so the two become one in a union from which there is afterward no possible divorce. Such a union, good for time and eternity, between the spirit and those spiritual things which are its proper object, can only prove itself by its actual existence and by experience of itself; it cannot be proved from without. For example, to the tried and developed Christian consciousness it becomes more and more an impossibility that the final act and ultimate fact of relationship between God and man should be or should be thought anything less or other than an incarnation. Religion ends inevitably in incarnation; and the more the truth is explored and understood and realized not by the speculative but by the practical and spiritual reason and experience, the more the inevitableness of its being so or the impossibility of its being otherwise becomes a conviction and is raised into a certainty.

It is the same with the truth expressed by the word "atonement." It is true that theories of atonement have so revolted the reason and conscience of man as to have created a not unnatural prejudice against the doctrine; but a doctrine of atonement is an inevitable element of any real religion. The human soul is not at one and needs to be made so with itself, the moral law, and God; and no religion serves its end that does not bring this reconciliation and peace. Its necessary function is to take away sin, to remove the separation by removing that which separates between God and man, and so consummate their union and oneness.

As much may be said of the truth or fact of redemption. A gospel for us must be a gospel of spiritual and moral freedom, of liberty to be or to become our true and complete selves; it must remove the bond of blindness from the eye, of deafness from the ear, of ignorance from the mind, of weakness from the will, of sin from the soul and of death from the life.

If we turn to see how these and all other truths necessary to a real religion or gospel were realized for us in Jesus Christ we shall find the same thing. The spiritual and moral personal human life and character of Jesus Christ is human salvation—the whole and the only salvation of which humanity is in need or is capable. It is a complete incarnation, atonement, redemption, anything else, everything else which human reason can conceive or human experience realize of necessary deliverance from evil or possible consummation in good. Man can only be saved or perfected through conformity to a final standard which it is his end or destiny to attain; and the scriptural statement on the subject is the last word upon it: "Whom he foreknew, them he predestined to be conformed to the image of his Son." If we study either the religious or the ethical type of manhood which our Lord has made current in the world we shall feel the impossibility of their ever being revised or changed. If a scientific morality should succeed in replacing that which has hitherto rested upon the faith, love and obedience of Christ it will have to accept his principles though it reject his person. But the cross of Christ will never cease to be the symbol as it is the only possible principle of the highest human life and character. There is but one way either to Godhead or to the truest manhood—the VIA CRUCIS; and none can come either to the Father or to real selfhood and personality but by it.

All these are merely illustrations, the most palpable and nearest at hand, to prove that it is only that which is true of—the truth of—the soul that is true to the soul, and that the soul that knows itself knows the things that belong to it. So it knows God and so it knows that union and oneness of God with itself which it finds in Jesus Christ. And so in Christ and his cross it knows its atonement with God, its redemption from sin, its resurrection from death.

Now it is the highest reach and form of this spiritual certitude of spiritual things, as they are found in their fulness in the person and work of Jesus Christ, which was attained and expressed in the Scriptures and which we call inspiration. As our Lord himself was in fact only found and accepted of men to be divine because he was divine, so, if not all, it is perhaps enough to say of the Scriptures that they were found and received of the church to be inspired because they were inspired. At any rate the church recognized in them that highest elevation of the human spirit to receive and understand the things of the divine Spirit which it accepted as its own measure and standard of knowledge and to which it gave the name, by excellence, of inspiration. This highest knowledge of spiritual things as they are revealed in Christ it may be true that we are but it is not necessary that we should be able to distinguish in kind from that which the church continues to possess and which every human soul may have of God and of his revelation to it of himself. All that is necessary is that those who were nearest to him in time and space should have so known our Lord as it was essential that he should be known if he was to be any revelation at all of God and of human salvation, and that they should have so recorded and transmitted their knowledge of him that it should continue to be the possession of the church after them.

When we thus endeavor to find in ourselves, in our own reason and experience the basis for spiritual knowledge and certitude, we are not ignoring the operation of the Holy Ghost, whose function it is to bring us into all truth and especially to reveal Christ in us as the fulness of truth. It is indeed only God who can reveal himself in us but even God can reveal himself in us only through the spiritual reason and experience by which alone we can know him. We may not with Pelagius confound grace with nature, the spiritual real knowledge and experience of God with mere natural speculation and conjecture about him, but we must find and exhibit the presence and operation of the divine Spirit in us in the life and activities of our own spirit, which is his only organ in us.

As the right and power of the individual soul to know God and to know the things that are freely given to it of God is thus the basis and the only necessary basis of the authority of Scripture, so equally is it that of the authority of the church in after-time to interpret the Scriptures. And not only to recognize the right of personal truth but also to recognize it as the principle and basis of all other truth is not to deny the fact and necessity of a catholic any more than that of a scriptural truth. It is the function of the individual and personal reason to apprehend rational truth and there is no such entity as a universal or common reason over and above and superior to that of particular men. Just as little is there a thought or mind of Christendom or of the Christian church as a whole superior to and possessing authority over the minds and thoughts of individual Christians. All knowledge of any sort, human or divine, comes primarily through the reason and experience of individual men. But while there is no common or general faculty or organ of either reason or faith there are conclusions or decisions of individual and personal reason and faith which in time become common, general, or even universal. There is an objective truth and reality that corresponds to and complements and completes human intelligence and desire; and while this objective reality does not "find" or is not found by every individual human soul, yet in the long run the common sense and common consent of souls does so accept it as to establish its right to be called universal. There are a great many natural truths that have long since passed through individual reasons into the universal reason of mankind—by which we mean not a separate common judgment but a common consent among all the particular judgments of men. And although individuals and even many individuals may theoretically deny such truths yet the rational world does not question their claim or right to universality. In the same way there are truths of the Spirit that can be apprehended only by individual spirits but which, just because they are truths of the Spirit, necessary to spiritual thought and life and therefore true for all spirits, are so accepted of all as to constitute a body of truth which we call catholic.

It is absurd to deny the existence and necessity of such a body of catholic truth, either in the natural or in the spiritual sphere. If it were not possible by such a principle and process as we have described of general consent or agreement to be continually accumulating an ever-increasing store of common or certain truths, there would be no such thing at all as natural or spiritual knowledge and progress. It was a foregone necessity therefore that the Christian church, claiming to hold in itself the fulness of spiritual truth and life, should as soon as it was able to do so proceed to set up over against the particular vagaries of its individual members a standard of catholic faith and practice. We remember that the promise and assurance was given not to individual believers but to the body of believers—the church —of a permanent possession of the truth. And this promise was to be made good by the presence with the church of the Holy Ghost, through whom, as God was in Christ, so Christ was to be spiritually present with the church to the end of time. But it is not enough to give this merely external account of how the church was to be kept in the truth. We may depend upon it that the only true supernatural is the truest natural and that the most divine is identical with the most human safeguard of God's truth among men. And so we shall find that as all the knowledge, wisdom and progress of men in all departments of human life and thought have passed through the experience of individuals into the acceptance and possession of communities, races and the common humanity, so God makes spiritual truth for mankind pass through the spiritual experience of mankind and by proving itself true for all to become the truth of all. The church is truly the κοινωνία τῶν ἁγίων, the community, the common experience, truth, faith, life of the individual saints—any one of whom can know himself wholly as indeed he thinks or exists at all only in it. Just as the thought or wisdom of the most original thinker of any age is in the main the thought and wisdom of the age with the very slight addition of his own original contribution to it, so the greatest genius who has risen to recognition as a Christian theologian has been independent of the common thought or of the common results of thought in the church only to the extent of some infinitesimal addition of his own to the common store of its knowledge and doctrine. In this as in every other department of human experience and knowledge no individual who really adds to or advances it begins at the beginning but only at the end of an already long and large accumulation of tested, verified and accepted truth which it is ignorance and folly to ignore and to which no one who ignores it can possibly have anything to add. Indeed all truth which appeals to the common experience for its verification must appeal to an experience which is not only wider but much larger than that of individuals; for it is not only time alone but generally only a long time that reveals the natural consequences and the real nature of things. There is a sense perhaps in which no truth ought to be considered final and irreformable. If it has been only by repeated thinking over and retesting in the past that it has become generally received, why at any particular point in the present or the future should this process cease? But spiritual knowledge would be an exception to all other results of human reason and experience if nothing in it becomes practically if not theoretically final and concluded, and he must be transcendently great who with propriety sets up in such matters himself and his brief and narrow experience against the spiritual consent of the ages. The present is indeed older and ought to be wiser than the past but it is only so as it has added its own to the wisdom of the past, and the individual who in this day thinks himself independent of the church is either only ignorant whence he derives his faith or else possesses in his faith an infinitely doubtful and uncertain factor. Christianity as we have seen is not only truth from God but is also the truth of us, and while the truth from God was complete from the first in Jesus Christ and was from the first sufficiently contained in the Scriptures, yet not God himself nor Jesus Christ nor the Scriptures could sufficiently attest to us the truth of Christianity as our truth and our life if it were not equally attested as such by the spiritual common sense and experience of men always and everywhere.

It may be asked, What does the church mean by the "all, always, and everywhere" which it sets up against the uncertainties and contradictions of private judgment? But in all departments of knowledge the "all" whose consent constitutes universality and carries authority is not literal or numerical but representative; the suffrage is necessarily limited to those who are qualified to bear testimony to the common sense and reason in the matter. The "common law" is not common in any more literal sense than this and the simplest judgments and sentiments of every-day conduct and life are not literally and numerically universal. If there is any truth in the church at all or any certainty with regard to its truth, there must be in it, at least as much as in the fields of human experience and knowledge, a body of catholic or universal truth as distinguished from the infinite varieties of private opinion.

We have thus recognized the function of the church as a whole as necessary to a complete comprehension and representation of the truth as it is in Jesus Christ. It was inevitable that the church should very soon be forced to discharge this function in the formation of a body of catholic truth. This was not its sole task; it had to form for itself, for example, a catholic order or organization and a catholic worship as well as a catholic faith; but with this latter only we are at present concerned. How it should arrive at an adequate expression of its common mind was quite a secondary matter; the essential point was that that which was expressed should be truly and really the common mind. In expressing itself as it did through representative, general or ecumenical councils as soon as it was in condition to do so, it doubtless availed itself of the best possible, perhaps the only practicable instrumentality at its command. But the council merely as such was an accident and not at all the essence of such authority as might afterward attach to its utterances. It was the voice of the church, not of the council, that was of force, and this might or might not be reached through the council. Sometimes it was not when it might well have been expected, and sometimes it was when—from being smaller and less general or for other reasons—it would hardly have been expected.

The point or principle of the whole matter is that just as the reason of humanity points on the whole to the truth and the conscience of humanity acquiesces in the right, so the common or universal spiritual consciousness and experience of the whole Christian church is the only test of what Christianity is. The question is how to get its verdict; and even when under the most favorable conditions and with the best guarantee of truth the council has assumed to render this, it can only be ascertained that the verdict is true, and will stand by a long and silent process through which the decision is referred back to the church again to say whether it has correctly expressed itself through its council. If the church thus accepts the council as its voice, by that fact it imparts to it an authority which is its own and not that of the council.

The truth of Christianity is the truth of Jesus Christ and the truth of Christ is a matter of ourselves as well as of God. If it is indeed the truth and the whole truth of ourselves, then we know that it is God's truth of us. It is impossible that we should know otherwise whether or not it is of God. The authority of the church, the authority of the Scriptures, the authority of our Lord, the authority of God, are all a very great deal along with the authority of a really universal human experience (which means not all experience, but all that truly experiences). Without the latter it would be impossible that all the former should possess for us any weight or value. We could neither prove that we really have them nor enforce upon ourselves or others their claim or demand.

CHAPTER III.

EBIONISM AND DOCETISM.

N and from the day of Pentecost upon which the Christian church took its birth, the apostles in Jerusalem preached a gospel, administered a baptism and celebrated a rite of holy communion in each of which was involved the whole truth of the person and work of Jesus Christ. But it is not necessary to believe that these apostles themselves had in their minds a developed and defined doctrine of the person and work of our Lord. The incarnate truth is ever more divinely present than it is humanly apprehended or comprehended. Present in its completeness in the beginning, it will never be understood and received in its completeness until that end when we shall come to know as all along we have been known. And whatever we may say of the apostles, very certainly the infant church of Jerusalem held no perfect and explicit doctrine of the truth completely present in its midst. It would have been pure miracle or magic if it had at once consciously held the whole truth or been wholly free from error. As a matter of fact we find that while the truth as it is in Jesus had no history after it was finished in his ascension, the know-

ledge of it had a history as human and as natural as human nature itself, and that to know human nature is all that is necessary to anticipate and explain that history.

We must remember then that while the infant church was Christian it was also still Jewish and we must endeavor to realize what this meant for its immediate further progress and development. There were certainly many in it who remained much more Jews than they had become Christians and there was probably not one who had become so Christian as to be no longer a Jew. When St. Paul through his experience with Jews and Gentiles was brought at first practically and then theoretically and as a matter of essential and vital principle to see that the church could only become wholly and truly Christian by wholly ceasing to be Jewish, there was not one of the original apostles who was prepared to go the whole length with him. A series of compromises and accommodations was necessary to keep even him and them united in the common cause, and this was not always and entirely successful. The distance between the many in Jerusalem who regarded Christianity as only a higher advance or stage of Judaism and one who like St. Paul on the other extreme had come to see in it a divine reversal of the fundamental principle of Judaism was a very wide one. But St. Paul while he saw in Christianity and Judaism the gospel and the law, a reversal of principle and therefore an irreconcilable antagonism, could nevertheless see that as successive stages both were true and divine and each in its order served its purpose—the one as neces-

I

sary contrast and preparation for the other. Nevertheless between the traditional conservative Jewish spirit and the emancipated progressive Gentile spirit there was an inevitable antagonism which could not but in both directions burst the bonds of a common unity and put itself outside of the true Christian principle.

We may anticipate that the first Christian heresy was Judaistic in its form, that the tendency to it existed from the very beginning and that it consisted in a more or less partial and incomplete acceptance of the truth as it is in Jesus. Between some sort of a faith in Jesus Christ and the acceptance of him in the fulness and reality of his divine and human person and work there is a scale that runs from nothing to everything.

The heresy which embodied this Jewish imperfect conception of the person of Christ assumed a form which under many modifications became known as Ebionism. We have called it Jewish and we shall see how naturally it originated out of and how closely it is akin to the essential principle of Judaism; but the term "Ebionism" is very convenient to designate a point of view from which it is always possible and probable that the person of our Lord will be regarded; it is on one side of almost every Christological question that has arisen or can arise and it is therefore well for us to devote a little space to its history and exposition.

When one reflects upon it it might seem that Judaism was the least likely source from which Christianity should or could have originated, unless we regard it as having done so by reaction to principles the most opposed and apparently contradictory to it. Judaism was not only the most narrow and exclusive but the most deistic and legal of religions, and Christianity is the least so. This contrast between two systems of which the first was the divine preparation for the second and the second the divine outcome of the first will not surprise us if we understand in what way they bore this reciprocal relation to each other.

In the first place the mission of Judaism was to emphasize the difference and the distance between God and the world and between God and man. Its object was to break up the pantheistic, heathen confusion of the two, and to do this as a necessary preparation for substituting for the merely natural, immanental and necessary relationship between God and the world a spiritual, moral and personal relationship between them. Judaism, coming between the heathen pantheistic or substantial identity of God and his creation and the Christian theistic or personal unity of God and his creation, was designed to pull down the former in order to prepare for the erection of the latter. It separates in order to unite, magnifies the distance in order to render possible the approach and the nearness, emphasizes the infinite difference, the duality, in order to bring about the atonement, the union and unity of God with his no longer merely natural and necessary but now spiritual, free and moral creatures.

It was part in the second place of the above divine plan that Judaism was essentially a legal or moral system, that it represented the principle of law as contradistinguished not only from mere natural and animal impulse behind it but from the principle of grace or gospel before it. It was intended to develop man in his independence of God, to educate in him the ethical or moral principle of personal autonomy and responsibility and make him a law to himself and to teach him by experience the necessity and blessedness of obedience to that law and the curse of disobedience or unrighteousness. In a word the end of the law under Judaism was to make man moral in preparation for making him spiritual, to convert his unconscious, natural and necessary relation and dependence upon God into a conscious, personal and free one, to make his will his own that he might make it God's. It is a necessary part of the evolution of a true manhood that it should learn both its independence and its dependence upon God, both that God cannot make it without itself, without the free and perfect exercise of its own will, and that it cannot make itself without God, without a free and perfect realizing in itself of the divine will. The design and result of the law was thus a double one, to teach at once the necessity and the impossibility of a personal human righteousness. Man only becomes man by asserting himself in his freedom against an environment of mere nature and necessity, but equally he only becomes himself by surrendering the freedom so asserted to the personal will and wisdom that is above nature and necessity. But it is characteristic of a system of mere divine law and not grace that it casts man off upon himself; it requires of him to become himself in and by himself and so, beginning with building him up in his independence, ends by casting him down in the discovery and consciousness of his utter dependence. It might be said that it is the method of God to unchild men by nature in order to make them his children by grace, to cast them upon themselves so as to compel them to come back to him of themselves, to want and seek him through faith, and to become anew his children by the higher personal bond of mutual love,—for so alone could the natural, necessary, immanental relation and dependence of all things alike upon God pass up into the free, filial, spiritual relation and dependence of finite personalities upon the infinite divine Person.

Judaism however, while it fully accepted and accentuated its mission as against heathenism which it displaced, perhaps not unnaturally did not equally comprehend and accept its relation to Christianity which was to displace it. It stood midway between the two with a deism that was indeed free enough from pantheism, that had separated widely enough between God and the world, but that was just as far behind that true theism which through the truths of the Trinity and the incarnation was to reconcile and reunite God and the world; and with a moral law which was no longer mere naturalism and necessity but which equally fell short of the true law of grace and love and life in Christ Jesus. And so Judaism, exclusive from behind as against heathenism, excluded itself no less from before from the Christianity of which it was itself the preparation and the precursor.

It was this spirit of partial preparation for Christianity and yet of essential unpreparedness for the distinctive principle of Christianity which in the bosom of the infant church rejected in the very act of accepting it. It was the first form of that antichristianity which under its own name contradicts and destroys Christianity. To it it was impossible that there should be a real incarnation for, standing by its very nature and position for the eternal and infinite distinction between God and the world of things and men, it was unable to see any difference between the pantheistic identification of the two of heathenism and the theistic union and unity of the two of Christianity. Both alike to it blasphemed God in making God one with his creatures or any creature one with God. Judaistic Ebionism accepted Christianity as the highest law or the highest realization and expression of the law and Christ himself as the highest man or the highest prophet,—but beyond this it would not and could not go. To recognize a personal divine, an incarnation of God, either that of the Logos in Jesus Christ himself or that of the Holy Ghost in the regenerate divine life of those who are in Christ, was above and beyond its ken.

It is not our purpose to give a full historical account of Ebionism in its various modifications and changes. After it had separated itself or been excluded from the church and become a sect in opposition to it, it took its name as was early supposed from a leader by the name of Ebion, but probably from the application to it of the Hebrew term signifying "poor," which it accepted upon the ground that Christianity is a call to that poverty to which its founder attached the first "blessedness." But as a hostile principle within the church long prior to its exclusion and separate existence we are familiar with it in the form of that deadly animosity which dogged the footsteps and hindered the labors of St. Paul and for a hundred years after his death spared no effort to damn his memory and efface his influence. It was at first purely Judaic in the sense that has been described but later, through Essene and Gnostic intermixtures, it contracted certain other features from without. Yielding to the necessity of regarding Jesus as more than a mere man no matter how high or gifted, it came to represent him as the incarnation of a higher being though still a creature, who is or is to be the prince of the world to come as Satan is the prince of this world.

Ebionism would be unworthy of even the incomplete notice we have given it in the treatment of a period that had outgrown and discarded it but for two reasons.

In the first place it has come to be assumed as established among a large class of historical students that Ebionism not only lurked as a leaven of Jewish conservatism and obstructionism in the bosom of primitive Christianity but was itself original Christianity—the Christianity of Jesus and of the real apostles. According to this view the simple human moral and religious teaching of Jesus began first in the active and fertile mind of St. Paul that process of idealistic transformation which converted it finally into the catholic religion of the world. It is not for us to enter into controversy with a position which to a mind that has once felt the inherent and inevitable truth and power of essential Christianity becomes thenceforth inconceivable and impossible. That Christianity was not the truth that outgrew and cast off Ebionism as a remnant in it of Jewish error but that Ebionism was the truth from which Christianity developed as an error; that not Jesus and his apostles but false apostles and teachers, who perverted and transformed their simple and natural doctrine, are the real founders of historical Christianity; that Christianity is not a divine incarnation, atonement, redemption and eternal salvation and life for all men but only a stupendous human creation of the imagination erected upon the slender foundation of the natural goodness and piety of a mere man—this is the modern form in which the earliest Christian heresy has been resuscitated and flourishes in our own day. If what is thus claimed had been indeed the whole of primitive Christianity the world would never have become Christian; if it be proved now to be all of it the world will soon cease to be Christian.

The other reason why we have thought it well to dwell thus much upon Ebionism is that after it had passed away under that name and in its primitive form it continued to reappear in other and higher forms which however different in appearance were identical with it in principle and connected with it in origin. The course that it ran within the period under our consideration was briefly the following:

At the close of the second and beginning of the third centuries, Theodotus and Artemon taught in Rome the doctrine of the mere manhood of our Lord and were successively excommunicated by Bishops Victor and Zephyrinus. They claimed to represent the primitive truth of the church which they alleged was now for the first time perverted from its simplicity in Rome itself. But how much value need be attached to this claim may be illustrated by the fact that Artemon distinctly charges Zephyrinus with being the first perverter of the truth in condemning his teaching, whereas the preceding bishop, Victor, had passed the same condemnation upon the same teaching by his predecessor in the heresy, Theodotus.

The one representative of the heresy who attained prominence was Paul of Samosata, metropolitan of Antioch, who was deposed and excommunicated in the year 269. Paul affirmed distinctly the mere manhood of our Lord. He held indeed that the divine Logos was incarnate in him but he denied both the personality of the Logos and the reality of the incarnation in any other sense than that in which the wisdom and grace of God may be incarnate in any man. "Wisdom dwelt in him as in no other," that is to say, in degree but not in kind. The indwelling was not that of a person but of a quality or character. Jesus Christ was divine not in the sense that he was God become man but man become as God. "The deity grew by gradual progress out of the humanity" (ἐκ προκοπῆς ἐθεοποιήθη, ἐξ ἀνθρώπων γέγονε θεός). The action of the two or three synods in Antioch that finally exposed and condemned the heresy is sufficient evidence of its novelty and strangeness in the church. Paul succeeded in veiling and concealing his real error under orthodox expressions until he was confronted by an expert dialectician, who succeeded, in the language of Dr. Neale, " in exposing the subterfuges of the heretic, pursuing him to his last shifts, and reducing his dogmas to their naked deformity."

Among the alleged followers of Paul of Samosata and for that reason involved in his condemnation and for a long time separated from the communion of the church was the famous Lucian, probably one of the first of the great teachers of that famous school of Antioch with whose part in Christological science we are hereafter to become familiar.

Beside having his name associated with that of Paul, Lucian had the additional misfortune to be afterward claimed and revered as their master by most of the great representatives of Arianism, so much so as to acquire the reputation of being its real author. It is not probable that Lucian was guilty of the errors of either Paul or Arius; he died in the full communion of the church the glorious death of a martyr. But his name links together two heresies which however otherwise different agree in this, that they represent the principle of Ebionism and succeed each other historically in the denial of the true divinity of the person and work of Jesus Christ. Dr. Newman, in his " Arians of the Fourth Century," has clearly traced the presence and influence of Judaism in both Samosatenism and Arianism. Paul's great patroness Zenobia was a Jewess, and Paul himself was more than anything else a courtier and politician. Judaism at the time was experiencing a revival and was exerting a living and potent influence on the thought and life of Syria, and that it indirectly influenced not

only the theology of Paul of Samosata but also that of
the greater heresy which was to rack the church and
the world during all the succeeding century was not
only testified to by the consciousness of the great
fathers engaged in it but will also appear in the analysis of its character and essential principles. Meantime that there was an historical connection between
Samosatenism and Arianism will appear from such
testimony as the following. Bishop Alexander,
under whom about the year 318 Arianism broke out
in the city of Alexandria—though its real origin was
not there—writes concerning it to the church of Constantinople: "You are not ignorant that this rebellious doctrine belongs to Ebion and Artemas and is
in imitation of Paul of Samosata, bishop of Antioch,
who was excommunicated by the sentence of the bishops assembled in council from all quarters. Paulus
was succeeded by Lucian, who remained in separation
for many years. Our present heretics have drunk up
the dregs of the impiety of these men and are their
secret offspring. Accordingly they have been expelled from the church as enemies of the pious catholic teaching according to St. Paul's sentence, 'If any
man preach any other gospel to you than that ye
have received, let him be anathema.'"

By a not more remote bond than that which connects Paul of Samosata and Arius we may unite Arius
and Nestorius, who are far enough apart in the general character of their heresies but are alike in this
that they are ecclesiastical successors in the practical
if not intentional denial of the true divinity of the
person of Jesus Christ. In the mediæval world the

tendency was taken up again and represented by Adoptionism. In the modern world the type has reverted to its earliest form and we begin over again with a humanitarianism which is a revival in modern scientific guise of the primitive Ebionism.

We might perhaps say that as Ebionism was the natural Jewish perversion of Christianity so its heathen or Greek-Oriental natural perversion was Docetism, and of this we must next endeavor to give an account.

The world which enveloped both Judaism and Christianity was at once Oriental and Greek in that combination of the two which appeared at its height in the great city of Alexandria. The leading characteristic of this Greek world of the East, so far as concerns our subject, is that it was vastly more intellectual and speculative than it was practical or moral; it was more concerned with thought than with conduct or life. If what had concerned the best mind of the Jews was righteousness, what concerned that of these Greeks was wisdom. We might say that this was true of the Greek mind altogether if we did not remember Socrates and the schools of some of his best successors. But the moral earnestness of these had mostly passed with Stoicism over to the Romans and even the best Greek theology of the age we are about to study is characterized by this difference from Latin theology, that while it primarily at least and predominantly treats Christianity as a revelation of truth, the latter regards it as a law of righteousness and a communication of life. The general tendency thus of the Alexandrian Greek mind was already in the direction of Docetism—to dwell more upon the manifestation of the divine in our Lord's person and life than upon the reality and significance of the human; and we shall have occasion to trace this disposition in even the most illustrious representatives of Alexandrian Christianity.

The religious speculation which Christianity found already in vogue in the active intellectual world of which Alexandria was the capital was largely devoted to questions of cosmogony and cosmology, of the relations between Creator and creation, between spirit and matter. And when we remember how soon in Christianity a cosmical significance was attached to the person and work of our Lord not only through the Logos doctrine of St. John but also in the earlier teaching of the Epistles to the Ephesians, Colossians and Hebrews, we shall not be surprised at the affinity between this aspect of Christianity and those outside philosophical speculations or that these latter should have eagerly clutched at many features of Christological doctrine as easily lending themselves to their use and promising solutions to some of their most difficult problems.

The insuperable difficulty of cosmological speculation in all time has been the coexistence in one world of good and evil. The contradiction and endless conflict of these two opposites has baffled all attempts to reduce to a single principle that universe whose very title bears witness to the fact that it is a necessity of thought to think of it as a unit, instead of which the irreconcilability of these two elements, always side by side, only throws the mind back again and again upon some form of dualism. Either there are two gods or God and matter are coeternal and conflicting sources of opposite impulses and activities or if all things come from an original single first cause they cannot all alike have proceeded immediately from it. There must have intervened a series of intermediate gradual removes and lapses in the course of which changes, declensions and even contradictions have entered into the working of things, and the immediate cause or causes of the world as it is must be very far removed from its primal cause and purpose.

This last device of successive emanations (æons) from the great first principle of the universe, ending in such variations from it as to produce confusion, contradiction and evil, is the basis of the powerful systems of Gnosticism, which were the dominant fact of external religious speculation confronting Christianity almost from the moment of its inception, and which carried a priori speculation to a point perhaps never elsewhere paralleled.

Christianity itself lays claim to the true gnosis; it affirms that all the treasures of not only faith and life but wisdom and knowledge also are contained in the true doctrine of Jesus Christ. It maintains that in him are solved all the mysteries of creation and its final destination, of evil and its uses, of redemption cosmical as well as human, of the ultimate recapitulation and reconciliation of all things in God under Jesus Christ as their head. Such suggestions could not but be eagerly seized and furnish endless fuel to the flame of Gnostic speculation. Gnosticism might almost be said to have taken Christianity and run away with it. But while Gnosticism thus in a sense became Christian, Christianity itself refused to become Gnostic. In many different forms Christologies arose so remote from the sober truth of Christ as wholly to cease to be Christian. The so-called Christian gnosis was not at all Christianity making use of outside philosophical principles or methods; it was outside philosophy of the most recklessly speculative type availing itself of Christian ideas and suggestions and perverting them to its uses and ends.

A serious obstacle stood in the way of the appropriation by Gnosticism of the real matter of Christianity. The essence of Christianity is the doctrine of a divine incarnation, and the principle of the inherent evil of nature and matter, inseparable from the dualistic character of that philosophy, rendered any real incarnation in it of the Highest an impossibility. And this was the immediate cause of Docetism. The result was in all the Gnostic Christologies a more or less unreal or Docetic theory of incarnation according to which our Lord assumed not actual flesh and blood, not an actual human nature and human experiences such as our own, but a mere semblance or outward appearance of all these.

Such a mere product or feature of Gnostic speculation as the Docetism which thus originated on the outside of Christianity we need not for its own sake have paused thus to notice; but the spirit or principle of Docetism, like that of Ebionism, very soon invaded Christianity itself. The two are, one or the other of them, at the root of all its perversions in opposite directions, and they are equally subtle, pervasive and destructive of its essential truth.

Tendencies to Docetism along with other Gnostic elements are as old as the New Testament, where—beside hints of it from St. Paul—St. John is compelled to assert and emphasize the reality of even our Lord's body or flesh. Indeed one of the earliest and strongest circumstantial evidences of the primitiveness of the catholic truth if not yet the explicit catholic doctrine of the divine-human personality of Jesus Christ is to be found in the fact that from the first, if there was a tendency on one side to deny his divinity, there was an equally strong one on the other to deny the reality of his humanity. If this tendency had remained on the outside or even on the outer side of Christianity, or if it had any more than Ebionism been really when it was apparently got rid of by the later action of the church, it would be useless now to resuscitate even the memory of it. But it crept in the early centuries into the inner heart of the church while this was intent only upon excluding from itself the opposite vice of Ebionism, and while it was denied in terms by the lips of several general councils it was never successfully exorcised, as we shall see, from sentiment and life.

We must remember how quickly Christianity passed out of Hebrew into Greek thought and expression. And so long as it continued Greek, which was during all the period of the general councils, along with many advantages as regarded its science it was more or less subject to the Greek tendency to regard itself rather as revealing God than as redeeming men. Indeed its temptation was to make redemption synonymous with enlightenment, just as even Socrates the most ethical of Greeks identified virtue with knowledge. But Christianity is, in order at least of importance, even more a communication of power and life than a revelation of truth; it is primarily a fact and an experience and only secondarily a science. It is God our life and our righteousness and only as such our wisdom and our light. It is only a personal and moral interest, a sense of ourselves, our responsibilities, weaknesses and wants, our need of God, salvation and eternal life, that enables us to know either the necessity or the meaning of a divine incarnation. God comes not to manifest only but also to communicate himself to us. If mere knowledge and enlightenment were all that is necessary to our salvation a Docetic Christ, an ideal Christ, a true representation though it be only a representation of the realization of God in man and man in God would be all we need. But we do not want only to know God; we want God. We do not want a picture of redemption; we want to be redeemed.

To the heart that so wants God and what God has to give the only incarnation is one that is as real in its humanity and in its effects and results in humanity as it is in the actuality and power and glory of its divinity. For a long time the church was so wholly taken up with exposing and excluding false or insufficient views of the divine nature of our Lord that it passed over and was unconscious of no less false and insufficient views of his human nature. It had not itself as yet realized how vitally necessary it was that the flesh of the divine incarnation, the humanity of the incarnate Lord, should be known to be—what it was—not a part and that the lowest but the whole, the totality of a complete human nature, soul and spirit as well as body. It had not yet fully felt the necessity to a real incarnation of the very humanity of our Lord, not only through his whole nature but also through his whole personal human life and experiences; that it was not only essential he should have truly hungered and thirsted, been weary and suffered and died, but that he should also have been humanly ignorant and weak, been tempted, have prayed, believed, received grace and been saved, have overcome sin and conquered death. It did not realize sufficiently that it was possible to reprobate and reject Docetism when applied to the lower and merely material parts of our Lord's humanity and yet take a Docetic position toward the higher and really essential aspects and activities of it; to recognize his humanity in the merely physical and necessary functions of his life as man and ignore or deny it in those spiritual, moral and personal acts and activities in which all the truth and use of his human life lay. For if it was what God was and did in Jesus Christ that was the cause and condition, it was what humanity was enabled to do and to become in him that was the actual matter and *res* of human salvation, viz., that through trials and suffering and death it became free from sin and alive from death. In that he as man separated humanity from sin and raised it from death all humanity was redeemed and regenerated.

After the Nicene Council had disposed of all the objections to our Lord's true divinity the church was first fully awakened to the prevalence of the opposite error by the teaching of Apollinaris, who about the year 375 enunciated the heresy that went under his name. According to Apollinaris, the humanity assumed in the incarnation was limited to that of a true human body and the natural or animal soul; the rational and spiritual parts and functions were supplied by the Logos. It will be seen at once that the life of Jesus was not then that of a man but that of a divine person in the mere form or mode of visibility of physical manhood.

Apollinarianism was condemned in the Second General Council, A. D. 381. But the higher Docetism reappeared in Eutychianism, which while asserting the integrity and completeness in all its parts, body, soul and spirit, of the humanity assumed in the incarnation, yet so subordinated the human to the divine, so absorbed the ἐνέργεια or proper activity and freedom of the lower nature into that of the higher as practically to annul the real manhood.

Eutychianism in turn was condemned in the Fourth General Council of A. D. 451, but the heresy was not dead and lived on with great vigor and ability through the Monophysite and Monothelite controversies which having occupied two more general councils and having filled more than two centuries with dissension and confusion left Oriental Christendom hopelessly and permanently divided into hostile camps.

Within the catholic church itself, after and in spite of the condemnation of general councils, the higher Docetism or practical denial of our Lord's humanity in its higher aspects and functions resumed its sway after the period of the general councils. In the undiscriminating and wholesale rejection of Adoptionism the Christianity of the middle ages crushed out the last effort before the Reformation to attach a due and proportionate and vital importance to that very and complete humanity in all its parts and functions which our Lord assumed and in which alone he was very and indeed man or accomplished a veritable redemption and completion of human nature.

We have thus endeavored to expose and trace in preliminary outline the two opposite natural tendencies that were the causes of all the deflections of Christian doctrine from the beginning to right or left of that straight course which it was the mission and the effort of catholic thought to preserve in its orderly evolution or unfolding. In the First, Third and Fifth councils it was Ebionism that the church condemned in the developed forms of Arianism and Nestorianism. In the Second, Fourth and Sixth it rejected Docetism under the subtler forms of Apollinarianism, Eutychianism, Monophysitism and Monothelitism.

Thus oscillating between tendencies in opposite directions it was enabled to maintain its true direction between them with—until modern times—a leaning rather to the side of the divinity to the detriment of the humanity than to that of the humanity at any cost of the divinity.

CHAPTER IV.

SABELLIANISM AND THE BEGINNING OF THE TRINITARIAN DISCUSSION.

IT will be easily apparent that a Christology that involves primarily the divinity of our Lord must go back into very serious questions of theology. How or in what sense can Jesus Christ be said to be God? And if we say that Jesus Christ was God can we then also say that God was Jesus Christ? St. John says that in the beginning the Logos was Θεός, God. Apart from the grammar, may we say that he was ὁ Θεός? Was the whole of God—was, for example, the eternal Father—incarnate in Jesus Christ? And if not, then in what sense was the divine Person who was incarnate one with God the Father and in what sense was he to be distinguished from him? These deep questions involved necessarily much discussion of the divine nature in itself as well as in its relation to created nature and human nature. While these questions of theology were under discussion Christology was kept temporarily in abeyance and it was not until the solution was found in the doctrine of the Trinity that, with the Apollinarian controversy, Christological discussion proper was resumed.

In the second century, as the result of the long conflict of the church with Gnosticism, there emerged the doctrine of the *monarchia* or of God as the sole principle and source of the whole universe. The term was used not only against dualism, the notion of two eternal principles of things, two gods or God and matter, but also against the multiplication of secondary and derivative principles, æons or emanations, which according to Gnosticism intervened between God and created things and were the real causes or creators of the universe. Against these in the doctrine of the monarchia, as it was originally intended, the church asserted that the one God was the sole and immediate Creator and cause of all existence.

When within the church the implicit faith that not only the invisible and eternal Father but also the incarnate Son or Word was God, and that they were so in a sense that while it identified them in nature distinguished them as persons, began to become the subject of reflection and to seek for itself exact and accurate expression, still more when the relation of the second and third persons to the first began to be expressed in terms of physical derivation that naturally recalled the emanistic principles of Gnosticism,—it was not strange that there should be those who thought the truth of the monarchia at stake again and who should assert it even against the true doctrine of the Trinity. The simplest way to do this was like the Ebionites proper to deny any divinity at all or like the Arians to deny the real and coequal divinity of the incarnate Word; and this was Ebionitic Monarchianism. But there was an alternative which gave rise to the Sabellian or Patripassian Monarchianism to which the name became more generally applied. At the time that Theodotus and Artemon were successively preaching in Rome Ebionitic Monarchianism under Victor, Zephyrinus and Callistus, Praxeas and Noetus were also successively carrying thither from Asia Minor the opposite form of Monarchianism. Among their immediate successors in the heresy was Sabellius, of whom little is known but whose name became subsequently attached to it although he was neither its founder nor probably its most prominent representative. All these writers in the interest of the monarchia denied not the divinity of the Word or of the Spirit but their distinction from the Father. Father, Son and Holy Ghost according to them are one God and not three persons or distinct principles of action within the Godhead but only different manifestations and functions of the one only divine Person, who is the sole $ἀρχή$ or principle of divine activity in the universe. The consequence was urged against them: then $ὁ\ Θεός$, the whole Godhead, the divine Father was incarnate, suffered and died. Hence the term "Patripassian," the third of the three titles by which the heresy has been known —Monarchians, Patripassians, Sabellians.

It is not our purpose here, any more than in previous cases, to give the history or describe the varieties of false opinion to which we allude on the way to the true doctrine of the incarnation. Sabellianism was not only actually or historically, it was logically and of necessity the first step in conceiving the divine or theological side of the truth as it was revealed through Jesus Christ. To the simplest and most primitive faith Christ was simply God, not Θεὸς merely but ὁ Θεός. Nothing less than God—not something, not anything, not everything from God but God himself—is what the soul wants; it was made for him and will be satisfied only with him. It wants God in its life, its suffering, its very death, to be its comfort in suffering, its life in death; it will have God suffer with us, die for us, that we may live and be blessed in him and with him. What are speculative difficulties in the presence of real experiences, when one knows the reality, the mystery of the oneness of God with the soul in its depths and of the soul with God in his heights! It is not improbable that Sabellianism in its origin as in some of its recent reproductions represented the deepest interests of religion as against the comparative shallowness and trifling of even the most eager and earnest mere intellectual speculation.

We have nevertheless to try to reconcile real speculative difficulties with religious interest and experience, and there is a difficulty revealed by the term "Patripassianism." The difficulty however, in principle at least, is not limited to this particular form or instance.

The Christian doctrine of the Trinity was perhaps before anything else an effort to express how Jesus Christ was God (Θεὸς) and yet in another sense was not God (ὁ Θεὸς); that is to say, was not the whole Godhead. Whatever the heart may say in the excess of its experience and sense of the infinite condescension of the infinite Father of spirits, the head realizes the impossibility of saying that the Godhead became man and died for men. Yet on the other hand the Christian consciousness rejected from its deepest depths as the essence of irreligion and the very principle of anti-Christianity every suggestion that he who was incarnate and died was anything or in any way less or other than the most high and the most dear God of its life and its salvation. As it had rejected all intermediaries between God and the natural creation, so a thousandfold more it repudiated all inferior mediation between God and his spiritual creation, between the infinite Spirit and his own immediate presence and life in the finite spirits which are his children. But if the doctrine of the Trinity began with the task of reconciling the reality of an incarnation of God with the difficulties expressed in one word by the term "Patripassianism" it went on to solve perhaps even greater and more difficult problems of religious thought. There is no doubt that it contains the Christian theistic refutation of the universal pantheism of heathenism.

The doctrine of the divine immanence is a necessity of thought. The idea of a creation in any moment or at any point withdrawn or separate from the active intelligence, will or word of its conscious Creator is an absurdity and springs from the habit of thinking of God as of ourselves. We must identify God with his creation in an infinitely more real and intimate way and degree than any human worker with his work, no matter how closely it may be as we say part of himself. Any human so-called production, creation or work is only a change or redisposition of things already existent. Our works therefore may live after us and be quite independent of us but God's works, which are the real products or creation of his thought, will or word, can have no existence or continue to exist after or apart from his, or himself, thinking, willing and speaking. Things are his thoughts, his speech, language or words, which are the expression of himself and have no existence apart from him.

God is therefore in his world in a sense far more intimate and essential than we can think or express. And yet on the other hand it is possible to identify God too intimately and essentially with the world of his creatures. We may make him so one as to be not merely identified but identical with it. And this is just what pantheism does.

We say truly that God is in, is immanent in the world of created things. If he were not it would not be for it has no being except in him. There is no doubt that man in his divine idea and intention was predestined to incarnate God, to be the form not only of a divine life, a life like God's, but also of the divine life, the personal life of the personal God himself. God was not merely objectively to himself to express or reveal an impersonal wisdom or goodness; he was to embody himself, in a sense to realize and fulfil himself as Father and as divine love in the personal life of his personal children. Now what we say of man as the head of the creation we may say of the creation itself, which was recapitulated in Adam as its natural head and is to be recapitulated in Jesus Christ as its spiritual and eternal Head. The whole creation is already, in its idea and intention, and is predestined to become actually as well as ideally the living body of the living God—the outward form and perfect expression of his divine Logos, his personal Reason, Wisdom and Word.

When in this way we identify God and the world and say that he is to fulfil or realize himself in the world, which is to become as it were an outward form and body of himself and not merely an external and impersonal expression of his wisdom and power, we do not mean that the world is going to become the Godhead or the Godhead the world. In one sense he will become it and it will become he but in another sense he will forever remain above it and he and it can never be identical. Christianity expresses this distinction by teaching that that which is immanent and is noumenally, not phenomenally, revealed of God in the universe is Θεὸς, not ὁ Θεός. It is his Logos, his personal Thought, Will and Word, who is himself to the extent of identifying him in person with the world but not himself to the extent of making him identical in substance with the world. By ignoring these distinctions in God and in the mode of his presence in things and in men, pantheism makes him and them identical. The world is the visible body and manifestation of him, of his divine essence and substance, and not merely of his personal thought and activity. The whole Godhead is so in and of as not to be also above and outside of the world of phenomena. While true Christian theism sees God in Christ as not only ideal humanity but also the ideal cosmos or universe, pantheism can know him only as the actual world of things and men. As Patripassianism saw the whole Godhead in the suffering and dying Christ, a thought far from repulsive to the heart and the moral sense if absurd to the reason and the understanding, so pantheism sees all of God—the divine substance as well as activity: rather indeed the mere extension or evolution of his substance without conscious or personal activity—in the world of actuality, in all that is false, ugly and evil, equally with all that is true, beautiful and good. In all the thought of the world the Christian doctrine of the Trinity is not perhaps the complete and perfect but the only solution of these great and otherwise insuperable difficulties.

It might be felt that if the doctrine of the Trinity solves any intellectual or moral difficulties it does so by introducing one quite as insoluble and incomprehensible in itself. Theological science is perhaps responsible for the fact that that which was introduced to explain has become itself most in need of explanation; that a doctrine designed and calculated to make God most comprehensible to us has ended by making him an incomprehensible metaphysical abstraction. It has come to be popularly assumed that the doctrine of the Trinity is the abstrusest of human speculations which the Greek mind at its subtlest exhausted its ingenuity in devising. On the contrary if we could return to the simplicity and intelligibility of its original meaning and intention we should find exactly the reverse. To begin with, the Trinity is primarily a fact and not a doctrine. And it is a fact which alone brings God down to our apprehension and into our experience. That God reveals himself to us in his personal divine Word and imparts himself to us by his personal divine Spirit is the basis of all Christian knowledge of God. That we are baptized into a vital relation to him as Father, Son and Holy Ghost, a threefold relationship in which he is born in us and makes us his children not only by nature or generation but also by grace or regeneration,—in which through participation in the Sonship we are brought into realization and enjoyment of the Fatherhood and fellowship of the Spirit and nature and life of God—this was the Trinity as it existed first in the church. It was not the doctrine but the living and life-giving truth in which they had their whole spiritual being as Christians. It was as we have said the meaning and reality of their baptism that—taken not by sign merely but in fact into the divine Sonship now realized for all men through the humanity of Jesus Christ—they were in relationship with the Father as the source and with the Holy Ghost as the grace and power of an actual new life from heaven. It was the meaning and reality of that sacrificial and sacramental feast in which they perpetually commemorated and celebrated their new relation to Father, Son and Holy Ghost, and converted the once-for-all union into a living and abiding communion and fellowship of life and love. It was their one confession of the common faith out of which, as the simple baptismal formula, grew up those creeds in which simple statement of fact became developed doctrine and definite dogma.

The Trinity was thus to the primitive Christians simply the form in which God had come to them and had taken them into union and fellowship with himself. It existed for them as an objective reality about which it was long before they began or were willing to reason or speculate. That Jesus Christ was God who became one with us and has made us one with himself they received without question and without scientific thought of the tremendous mystery involved. That the divine life of which they were conscious in him was the personal life of the personal Spirit of Christ and of God who now dwelt in them as the body of Christ and of his own incarnation in humanity was a fact so actual to experience that, as with all things that are matters of fact, there was no thought of explaining or justifying it to the reason or the understanding.

So long before there was anything like a rational theology in the church all Christians were simply and unreasoningly Trinitarian. It was very easy for them, if they attempted anything like definite statement or formulation of their faith, to fall into confusion and contradiction. The few that boldly speculated were apt either to go astray or at least to fall short of the whole truth, which only the most comprehensive catholic thought can embrace in all its aspects and bearings. The church at first was Trinitarian simply because the truth is Trinitarian and because it accepted the truth as it was objective to itself and had not yet converted it into subjective knowledge. That this had to be done, that there had to be formed a subjective consciousness of the church corresponding to the objective form of the truth, is manifest; and it is equally manifest that that could only be effected through manifold mistakes and corrections, through much high thought and deep experience, and not without strife and contention and stirring up of other interests and motives than those to which the gospel of God ought alone to appeal.

There is abundant evidence to prove that the Christian mind was slow and reluctant to make the truth as it is in Jesus the matter of rational explanation and interpretation. Having to do with spiritual facts and experiences it was in the beginning wholly averse to speculation. The tremendous speculative activity of the second century that went under the name of Christian gnosis was as we have seen not Christian at all but came wholly from without, having no real spiritual interest or religious experience in Christianity. But it was directed upon the facts and truths of Christianity and could not but awake and provoke Christian thought to meet and refute its misrepresentations and perversions. None of the earlier heresies that arose within the church were primarily speculative; Ebionism was the reverse and Sabellianism accepted the incarnation of God literally without appreciating the speculative difficulties that necessitated the doctrine of the Trinity. When the abler and more thoughtful minds of the church like Irenæus, Tertullian, Clement of Alexandria and Origen began to be driven toward the construction of a rational and catholic doctrine of the Trinity they had to encounter a mass of conservative piety to which the application of such methods as pertain to natural and secular knowledge to the truth of God seemed profane and irreligious. The definitions and scientific formulæ forced at last upon the church by the Arian controversies were both in and after the Council of Nicæa resisted more by conservative obstruction than by speculative disagreement. It is characteristic of every one of the councils that imperial pressure, in the interest of religious and civil peace and order, had to be exerted heavily to force the church to define herself at all or to add new definitions to those already made and accepted. That the formulation of Christian knowledge and doctrine did unquestionably elicit and employ an amount of dialectic skill and of metaphysical and scientific acumen and acuteness which the world has never seen equalled either for quantity or quality is not to be denied. But so far as it all was theological and Christological, in the sense of being religious and Christian, it was purely defensive and compulsory. So far as it was merely speculative and disputatious it was not Christian but human and Greek. Even in that age, at least until politics and heresy and controversy had perverted and corrupted the public Christian mind of the East, Christianity preferred the demonstration of the Spirit to wisdom of thought or speech. Before the First General Council all the decisions of the Christian consciousness however expressed were negative rather than positive—in condemnation of what was inconsistent with the objective truth as it knew it rather than efforts to express its own subjective knowledge of the truth. Every church had its public confession of the common faith as a necessary part of its religion and worship, but infinite and even timid caution was exercised to keep this simplest statement of Christian fact true to what it had been in the beginning and was everywhere and among all.

If now we should venture to express the primitive and objective fact of the Trinity as it existed prior to the formulation of the doctrine or to the compulsory and necessary awaking and activity of the theologizing mind of the church, we might express it or explain it somewhat as follows. To the religious mind of the church there were three great facts or processes in which and in which alone it knew or could know God: first, in the natural creation and preservation of all things; second, in the incarnation and atonement or the spiritual and moral new creation of humanity in Jesus Christ; and third, in the presence and operation of the Holy Ghost and the powers of the world to come in the church and the souls of believers.

With regard to the natural creation we have seen how instinctively Christianity preserved a straight course between a deistic separation of God on the one hand and a pantheistic identification and confusion of God with it on the other. Just as soon as in St. Paul or St. John or wherever else in the Scriptures or in catholic thought the higher or preincarnate aspect of the person of Jesus Christ is dwelt upon, he is immediately brought into relation with (1) the natural creation or origin of all things and (2) the end or consummation of all things. It is he through whom all things are and it is he in whom all things are to come to their natural and predestined end and completion. Who then is he or what, whom the church from the beginning has seen with the eyes not of sense but of faith under the human form of Jesus

Christ? We will endeavor to answer this question somewhat in the order of thought or conception in which the truth may be supposed to have originated and been developed in the mind of the church.

Perhaps the very first impression calculated to be produced by even the most natural and human study of the person of Jesus Christ is that of the universality of his humanity. He is man to every man, the manhood of every man in the world. There is no human being from highest to lowest who may not see in him the meaning, the truth, the divine idea and purpose, the true conception and end of himself. It is not merely that he bears the common nature and has lived the common life and shared the common experiences of every man. He is infinitely nearer than that; he is the true human personality and the innermost human self of every man. Every human being knows himself and becomes himself only in Jesus Christ. There are many individual human reasons but every human reason finds and fulfils itself only in union and unity with the one universal reason. There are many human wills but each one of them finds its freedom and attainment only in the one perfect will. There are many men, there is only one manhood; and he who does not find that in the divine-human love and self-sacrifice and holiness and life of Jesus Christ will not find it at all. So Jesus Christ is God's truth and word to every man of himself—not only of God's self, but of every man's self. For the true, better, higher, eternal, divine self of every man, that selfhood which it is the infinite and eternal aim of every man to realize and attain, is God.

It is in this sense that Jesus Christ may be said to be the Logos, first of all, of man. He is man as the personal Godhead is personally realized in him—reason of his reason, will of his will, the very self of his selfhood or personality; and yet so that human freedom and personality are not lost but found and fulfilled in that of God. It is an insufficient account of the incarnation to say that God assumed our nature. He became ourselves, and first in that universal human selfhood or personality of Jesus Christ who is the inner and new personal manhood of every man who finds him and finds himself in him. Nothing less but a great deal more than all this is necessarily contained in that instinctive and primitive Christian consciousness which led men to seek and find themselves "in Jesus Christ," not as instead of themselves but as their true and real self, in whom they were redeemed and fulfilled.

More than all this, the first mind of the church saw in Jesus Christ the divine Logos not only of humanity but of the whole creation also. Through him and for him were all things made; he is both first and final cause of the whole creation as a unit. The natural and what is, at least misleadingly, called the supernatural world or order are not two but one. One Logos, that is to say one divine thought and purpose, one law, one creative or self-fulfilling process runs through all. The natural creation, what we might call universal evolution, comes first to its meaning and truth in rational and spiritual humanity; the rational and spiritual in man will find and complete itself in the divine humanity of Jesus Christ.

The one only Logos of God, first in nature and then in grace, first in natural and then in spiritual creation, fulfils himself through all and in all. The Christ of the future is the goal and crown of the entire creation of God. Then and there, where Creator and creature shall be one, God shall be all and in all. He will have fulfilled himself in all things and all things in himself.

Thus the primitive and genuine Christian mind does not set itself against or above nature and the natural. The so-called supernatural means only the higher natural to which the natural is predestined to come. The time will be when the science of nature will complete itself in the science of that supernature which is only not yet nature because as yet we foreknow it only by faith and know it not by sight. When we know it by sight it will be seen to be natural and our knowledge of it will become science. He then who as incarnate is in the church and in each regenerate soul as the inner and divine self it is predestined to become, is he also who is in every human reason and conscience and who is in irrational and inanimate nature as its ideal principle and law. That there is an ideal principle—a principle of intelligence, will and purpose, of love and goodness—in all nature and natural evolution may not be demonstrable from nature itself and may have much in nature apparently to contradict it. Yet the deepest natures feel it, the highest intelligences see it, and the sinful and suffering human heart believes it in spite of its sin and suffering. To the Christian reason, conscience, experience, which sees the profoundest exhibition of the love of the divine Father in the very cross and agony of the infinitely and divinely beloved Son, there is no longer a mystery of evil. It is the cross that raiseth us; the pain of the world is the lever by which God lifts us to himself. The cross that exalted Jesus the Son of God to the right hand of the Father is the Christian assurance that God and love are at the heart of all natural so-called evil; that there is no evil but sin, whose essence is ignorance and unbelief of God and love.

Here occurs a point that may illustrate if not explain in advance much of what is to come. If there is such an ideal principle in nature as we are speaking of it is there *in* and *as* nature and not outside of and beside it. It is an ultimately true principle that there are no miracles in nature. If nature is God's work, God does not work outside of it; he works in and not upon it. If there is a Logos of natural evolution or creation it may be God's, it may be God; but it is also nature's and nature. The two must be one and not two. Faith may see it as God, science can and must see it only as nature. God is and acts in nothing whatever otherwise than in the being and acting of the thing itself. Faith is of him; science is only of the thing. There is the same unity, continuity and connection in things that there is in God and science must as much recognize it under the form of natural necessity and the universal reign of law as it is necessary to believe its existence in the divine nature.

So if we are to think of a Logos or divine personal principle of spiritual and moral creation, of human redemption and completion, if we are to think of God as incarnate in humanity, we must think not only of *him* as incarnating himself in humanity but also of him as incarnating himself *in humanity*. He must not be beside or instead of it or act upon it from without; he must be in it and must be it and his acting in it must be its own acting. When God shall have incarnated himself in a redeemed and completed humanity it must equally be a humanity that has incarnated in itself the living God. It will be God who has so fulfilled himself in man; but he will not have done so unless it is also man who has so realized himself in God. It will be both and yet both will be not two but one.

The case becomes more difficult but it also becomes more practically important, because on account of its difficulty it is more liable to misconception and misrepresentation, when we come to study the personal incarnation of God in the man Christ Jesus. The point is that while we see in him a divine person we must see him only in and as a human person. The whole incarnation of the divine Son of God is a divine act, an act of God. But if it is an incarnation and if it is to redeem and exalt humanity it must be an act *in* and *as* man and not beside, through or instead of or in a mere form or semblance of manhood. It is an act of God but it must be equally an act of man or else man is in no way redeemed and completed in it. The difference and difficulty in this case is that whereas in nature we see the Logos of the universe operating in and only in laws or a law which is the law of nature, and in what we might call the generic incarnation or the incarnation in humanity we see the

Logos of humanity manifesting himself in and only in the actual redemption and completion of humanity, when we come to the particular incarnation in Jesus Christ the one person of our Lord is both the Logos who incarnates himself in a human person and the human person in whom he is incarnate. It is perfectly true to say that our Lord assumed an impersonal human nature but it is not true to say that he was impersonal in that nature or that as man he was not a human person and had not all the characteristics and limitations of a human personality. If he had not he was not a man and lived no true human life and is for us no real human righteousness and life. We hope to realize more and more as we proceed that it was the eternal divine nature and predestination of the Logos through nature and through grace to become man—to become as we have said before not only alike in nature but one in person with every man. St. Paul was not content to say, "Christ was a man like me;" he says, "Not I but Christ: *I* live no longer; Christ lives in me." It is the personal human Christ who, because he is the eternal divine selfhood of us, comes to himself in us and brings us to ourselves in him. But if the human Christ is divine, the divine Christ in himself, in his incarnate person or personality and not merely in his nature or purely natural attributes, is human. He is man, the man, the infinitely human, infinitely divine personal manhood of every man; the man in whom every man finds and becomes himself. And in order to be this we must believe that he became man in accordance with all the laws and attributes of a real manhood, through a real human birth, infancy and ignorance, growth in knowledge, will and character, faith and obedience, holiness, righteousness and life. It was the becoming human of the Logos in the flesh of sin and death and the human conquest and condemnation in it of sin and death; in other words it was the triumphant holiness and life of the man Christ Jesus—a holiness that abolished sin and a life that destroyed death—which constitutes him the new man in whom objectively all men have been made new and who in all men subjectively makes them new.

Thus in Jesus Christ the church from the very first recognized the divine personal principle both of nature and of grace, the meaning, end and purpose of the whole creation. He is the eternal mind, will and activity of God revealed in all things, everywhere one and the same. He is the truth of the atom, of motion, law, life, of the soul, of human and divine reason, the world, man, God. If he is God he is also man and nature; he is the unity of God with nature and man.

Therefore while the church identified the Logos, incarnate and preincarnate, with God, for reasons already given it also distinguished him from the Godhead as a whole. The Logos is Θεός but not ὁ Θεός; he is the personal intelligence, will and energy of God and is really or essentially God; but he is not so God as that the whole Godhead is expressed in nature or incarnate in Christ and humanity. So again when the church was conscious within itself of the Holy Ghost as the Spirit and presence of Christ and of God, it was compelled to distinguish him from them even while it identified him with them. There was practically, with inconsiderable exceptions that will be mentioned, no denial of his divinity; there was, with perhaps greater exceptions, no considerable denial of his personality. The true Christian consciousness knows no operation, influence or presence of God that is not God himself; whatever is divine is personal, is God. To it nature is God, events are God, everything is God save those finite spirits to whom in the free will God has given the power to be other than himself and even contrary to himself. So grace is God, not an impersonal, dead influence separate and apart from him, but he himself become human and so capable of becoming as man to every man. The personal Word by the personal Holy Ghost is in every one who is living in him and is in them redemption from sin and life from death. So in himself, in Jesus Christ, and in itself the church knew God as Father, as Son and as Holy Ghost, and was Trinitarian in fact before it became so in thought and doctrine.

CHAPTER V.

THE ORIGIN AND RISE OF ARIANISM.

HERE is probably no heresy that had not something of serious motive in its origin and that did not aim to defend or preserve some element of truth and value. We might be more disposed to question this of Arianism than of any other form of early Christian error. It seems to us now at least to have so little basis of philosophical probability or possibility, its spirit at the time was so merely logical and controversial and so little religious, it was so ready and quick to avail itself of political and secular methods and instrumentalities and its general temper and character as shown in its most conspicuous leaders and representatives were so unchristian that we are tempted to see in it neither seriousness of motive nor interest for truth. So far as it had a religious interest it must be found in its theology, not in its Christology. An incarnation of what is not God in what is not man has nothing in it of the reality and truth of the Christian faith or fact of the divine incarnation and can carry in it nothing of the Christian experience of atonement with God, redemption from sin and resurrection from death. On the one hand Arianism

pushes the distinction between the incarnate Son and the eternal Father to the point of denying the essential divinity of the former, and on the other hand the lower, created and not truly divine person who according to it became incarnate assumed only a human form, body and animal soul, but none at all of the higher functions and parts of a real humanity.

Its religious interest therefore must be found in its theology and most probably in that truth of the divine being and nature that we have alluded to as the monarchia, the unity of God as the principle (ἀρχή) of the universe. Sabellianism and Arianism illustrate the opposite directions in which one and the same theological interest may seek to maintain itself. The motive of both is Monarchian, but while Sabellianism defends the unity of the divine principle by denying any real distinction in it and makes Father, Son and Holy Ghost one in person as well as nature, Arianism attains the same end by widening the distinction of persons into one of nature and so attributing real divinity and original causation only to the Father. The genealogy therefore of Arianism is to be sought in the history of that Ebionite Monarchianism which we saw to be Jewish in its origin. We have seen also how after the teaching of Theodotus and Artemon it appeared in its most conspicuous form in that of Paul of Samosata, metropolitan of Antioch, to whom, through Lucian and the Lucianists, Bishop Alexander attributed the origin of the heresy that broke out under him in Alexandria about the year 318 in the person and teaching of the presbyter Arius.

Such was the direct descent and origin of Arianism; yet there is no doubt that from without it was developed mainly through antagonism to its opposite, Sabellianism. As against this latter many of the church fathers were driven to insist in very strong terms upon the distinction of the persons in the divine Trinity,—so much so that the distinction was sometimes expressed in language which if taken literally would seriously compromise if not destroy the identity of nature. If words used by them be interpreted in the sense and with the technical exactness which they acquired through the long discussions that followed, Origen himself, the ablest of catholic antagonists of the principle of Sabellianism, and several of his greatest followers—as Gregory of Neo-Cæsarea and Dionysius of Alexandria—might be justly charged with this. Athanasius and the later church fathers recognized the fact that such errors of expression arose from personal inaccuracy and natural ambiguity of language and not from unsoundness of faith, but nevertheless the expressions were seized upon and pressed into the service of errors that in part had grown out of them and one or more of the writers themselves were thus made actually responsible for the heresy of Arianism—with which they would have had in fact not the least sympathy. Thus Origen, one of the earliest as well as ablest contributors to the development of the doctrine that was formulated afterward in the term "homoöusion," identity in nature or essential divinity of the Father and Son, used language in emphasizing the distinction between Father and Son against the then emerging principle of Sabellianism which as terms were afterward defined would imply not the difference of personality that he meant but difference of essence or substance—which was just what he did not mean. And in teaching what was on the whole a catholic sense of the natural subordination of the Son to the Father, beside other ambiguous expressions he termed the eternal Son δευτερὸς θεὸς, a term that the Arians adopted and interpreted to mean that the Son, while he may be called God, is so only in a secondary and lower sense than the Father and so really and essentially is not God at all. Similarly Dionysius of Alexandria, intent only upon a refutation of Sabellianism and careless of error in the opposite direction —for Arianism was as yet unborn, though of it his own inaccurate expression was after said to be the seed,— used language that implied that the Son was not "born," as he meant, but "made" of the Father, which he did not mean, and which was developed into the Arian teaching that the Son of God is a created being. Other church fathers are quoted not sparingly as using in one generation and from one point of view terms and expressions which in a succeeding generation and from other points of view are discarded or condemned as heretical. We must remember the natural ambiguity of human language and how unexpressed and inexpressible the church had held those spiritual things to be that were the matter of its faith rather than its knowledge. As it became necessary more and more to define the faith so as to purge it of its perversions, it had only a language which, although the most perfect in the world, was undeveloped in the direction of the new world of ideas and truths that Christianity had opened. A phraseology had to be adapted if not created and then, what was more difficult, adopted by common consent in an agreed sense. In order to do this the church had to select the best or most available words, to separate them from all vague and shifting popular senses and uses and stamp upon them a technical and perhaps arbitrary limitation and exactness which they were very far from possessing of themselves; and then it had to bring itself to a universal consent and agreement to use them only in that sense or at least to understand them in that sense when used in definition of the faith. Thus the two crucial and vital terms finally adopted in definition of the Trinity—the term "ousia" meaning the essence or "substance" of the divine nature in which lies the unity, and the term "hypostasis" expressing the personal distinction that constitutes the Trinity in the Godhead—might have been used and were actually sometimes used before the Nicene Council succeeded in fixing their meaning in senses just the reverse of those adopted; that is "ousia" was used for personality and not essence or substance, and "hypostasis" was used for essence or substance and not personality. And it is easily enough explained how this ambiguity belonged to them in themselves. The church indeed was intent on things, not words; it reluctantly reduced the things of the Spirit to words at all and if it was compelled to devote an infinitely minute and subtle attention to the adaptation and definition of words it was because it had new and high and infinitely important things to express and had to create, although out of existing materials, a language in which truly and adequately to express them.

We can readily understand thus how while Athanasius and the Nicene church fathers saw the truth in what was meant by the church teaching before them, the Arians could also see in much that had been said in that same teaching the suggestion and substance of their own heresy.

In this way catholic antagonism and Sabellianism with its opposite tendencies to Patripassianism and Docetism had unwittingly habituated many minds within the church to such wide distinctions between the Father and the Son as gradually to prepare not only the thought but also the very language that at last found heretical expression in Arius. The circumstances of the outbreak of the heresy are too familiar to require narration in detail. The issue arose between Arius, a leading and influential presbyter, and his bishop Alexander. It secured through the popular qualities and methods of its founder a following among the common people of Alexandria. But its intellectual and theological extension was not there but in the patriarchate of Antioch whence its seeds had been brought and where it found a more natural and congenial home.

A proof that the real interest and motive of Arianism is not Christological but theological, that it was a question not of the value and significance of the person and work of Jesus Christ but of the nature of God, and that its essence is to be found in a deistic conception of God which separates him most widely from both nature and human nature, from the world and humanity, is to be found in Arius's own earliest representation of his contention with his bishop. He addressed to Eusebius of Nicomedia, who was soon to become the real intellectual head and controlling spirit of the movement, the following complaint: "The bishop fiercely assaults and drives us, leaving no means untried in his opposition. At length he has driven us out of the city as ungodly for dissenting from his public declarations that 'as God is eternal, so is his Son; where the Father is, there is the Son; the Son coexists in God without a beginning; ever generate or born, or born without beginning; that neither in idea nor by an instant of time does God precede the Son; an eternal God, an eternal Son; the Son is from God himself.' . . . These blasphemies we cannot bear even to hear; no, not though the heretics should threaten us with ten thousand deaths."

We must remember that with Arius as with the church Jesus Christ was the Logos of natural as well as spiritual creation through the incarnation. He was as far from believing that God immediately created or is connected with the natural world as that he is incarnate in Jesus Christ. The point of his whole position was that God is too exalted and transcendent to be related to the universe except through an intermediary. He who came so near as to mingle himself with the world or who so humbled himself as to become incarnate in man could not be the most high God himself. The very thought is such blasphemy that to bear even to hear it is worse than ten thousand deaths. Consequently the Creator of the worlds, he who became incarnate in the life of humanity, was not Θεὸς, as St. John says, or only so in a secondary and applied sense, δευτερὸς Θεός. He was a being between God and the world of nature and grace, immeasurably higher than it but infinitely lower than he. He was born of God, indeed the only-born or begotten and so alone in the highest sense Son of God, and through him God created the world and redeemed and completed humanity by making him man. But he was only-begotten in the sense that he alone came immediately from God's own hand whereas all things else came from God through him. He was not begotten or born or Son of God in the real sense that makes him in the mind of the church God of or out of God and so of the very essence or "substance" of the Father, but only in the figurative sense in which everything that comes from him may be said to be born of him although infinitely and essentially different in nature. In other words he was not born or Son of God at all but produced by a creative act "out of nothing," not as the church believed by necessary and eternal generation from himself. The Logos was thus a creature, created indeed before all others and even before time itself, for time is one of the creatures, but only differing from them in that, as has been said, he came alone from the hand of God himself and was the instrument of their creation. The Arians indeed turned the very fact of his Sonship or birth of the Father, which to the church meant that he was God of God, into an argument against his deity. It contradicted they said the two very first predicates of the divine, which are that it is underived and eternal. "That which was born, was not before it was born;" we must therefore be able to say even of the only-begotten of God that ἦν πότε ὅτε οὐκ ἦν; "there was"—not a time, for even time was not then—but "there once was when he was not." And as the Arian Logos possessed not the two first so he possessed not any of the real attributes of Godhead. He was not omnipotent, omniscient, or anything else that God alone infinitely is.

The Nicene Council charged against Arius beside the above another heretical tenet from which in the controversy he thought it at least wise to recede. This was the position that the Logos in himself and not merely as man, beside being not eternal and not of the divine essence or nature but created "out of nothing," was not ἄτρεπτος or ἀναλλόιωτος; that is, was not incapable of change or of falling, as Satan one of the highest of created beings had done. He himself was under probation and by his triumphant virtue and righteousness on earth restored and established the world of men. His Sonship was not one of nature or essence but of freedom and choice, a personal and moral, not proper or essential one. It was quite a secondary and subsidiary part but it was a real part of Arianism that this secondary God who was not God, this divine Son of God who was neither Son of God nor divine, became incarnate in a humanity which was not humanity. The bodily or material part was alone human; the rational and spiritual, which is alone essential and real manhood, was in this man not that of the humanity but of the higher incarnate person. So that the earthly life and experiences, sufferings and death of Jesus were no more those of man than they were of God. They were those of a demi-god, demi-man, who was neither God nor man and who from the Christian point of view was neither able to save nor needing to be saved. It is clear that apart from a merely theoretical or theological zeal for the transcendence of a God who can neither touch nor be touched by anything outside of himself Arianism itself could have had no real interest at all in such an incarnation. In fact all in it beyond the barest monotheistic deism on the one hand and the barest Ebionitic humanitarianism on the other,—that is, all that the grand and complicated system of Arianism proper had to add to a simple humanitarian Ebionism,—was nothing but a compulsory concession to the irresistible Christian demand for a human incarnation of God and a divine redemption and completion of man in the person of Jesus Christ. In response to this Arianism pretended to give both and gave neither. In all the tremendous discussion there was nothing on the Arian side either said or thought of the spiritual or religious needs of man or of the self-imparting love and grace of God, nothing realized of that profound necessity which is the meaning and truth of all religion, that infinite love must fill and fulfil all things with and in itself; but everything of a God whose very nature it is to hold himself eternally aloof from all things else, a God whom in his isolation and selfish transcendence it is as absurd for one like Arius to so concern himself about as to prefer ten thousand deaths rather than hear of his soiling himself by contact with us, as it is absurd to think of his condescending to concern himself about so doing.

The true value of Arianism was negative; it acted as a foil for the truth in that bringing out in itself all that Christianity is not it forced the church to bring into consciousness and expression all that it is. And this was only to be accomplished by realizing as fully the real and perfect deity on the one side as on the other side the real and complete humanity of the incarnate Son of God—both of which Arianism denied. With the first of these denials the church for a long time was exclusively concerned; the second remained in the background, and was scarcely recognized as a part of Arianism. But we shall see that just as soon as the first was thoroughly disposed of and settled in the first two general councils, the second came forward to be met and dealt with at even greater length and with more trouble in all the subsequent general councils.

If we turn for a moment from the negative to the positive, from the Arian to the catholic side of the speculations, so far as they have gone, upon the relation of Jesus Christ to God, it is well known that that relation was expressed in two designations, the Word or Logos and the Son of God. Each of these titles had in controversy an advantage and a disadvantage that rendered them according to the point at issue more or less available and so made sometimes the one, sometimes the other the more prominent. On the whole however it will be seen that they were complementary and came to be used to emphasize the opposite aspects of the one truth. The relation of the divine Son to the divine Father was in the church as in the Scriptures expressed by the term "begotten" or "born" and more precisely "only-begotten." In fact this relation if it were not expressed would be necessarily implied by the titles Father and Son, if used in earnest. What possible real relation can Father and Son bear to each other but that of begetter and begotten? Now just this most primary and essential of catholic terms, which was supposed to express the real divinity of the Son, God of God, was as we have seen selected as the basis of the Arian attack upon the catholic truth expressed by it. If the Son was born or begotten, before he was begotten he was not and so was not eternal. The answer had been given long before the objection was made, first and chiefly by Origen, and was already in the possession of the church. It was in the form of the church doctrine of the "eternal generation" of the Son, which meant not only that the divine Son was once for all begotten in or from eternity, so that there was never a time when he had not been begotten, but also that he is of or from the Father by a continuous and necessary process of generation coeternal with himself, because of his nature and not merely of his will or act. The best of several illustrations in common and familiar use was that of the sun which by the very fact of being the sun did not once for all at the beginning generate but forever of necessity generates its radiance. The sun, although it generates or begets, could never have been before or without its radiance. We might say, "Where the sun, there its radiance; the radiance coexists in the sun without any beginning from it; neither in idea nor by a moment of time does the sun precede its radiance; the radiance is of the nature or essence or substance of the sun; and so on indefinitely." In identical language the church expressed the eternal generation of the Son and so his coeternity with the Father; an answer certainly to the Arian contention that if he was born there must have been a time before he was born.

Not only the coeternity of the Son is thus vindicated but also the essential identity of his nature with that of the Father. For in generation the Father reproduces himself and not anything else in the Son; not indeed his personality but at least his own nature and not another. So that we must say of God, not only where the Father there the Son, but what the Father that the Son. The Arians, driven from other points, took refuge in the one attribute of *aseity*, in which they concentrated the whole nature of God. It is the distinctive nature of God to be underived or to come from himself alone (*a se*). A God derived from another than himself by generation or otherwise is not God. They were only determined to maintain that he who is identified with the world by creation or with the lowliness and weakness of humanity by incarnation could not be the most high and only God.

With the church however there was the very different and even more imperative necessity to identify while distinguishing the incarnate Son and the unincarnate Father. And in this the fathers learned by gradual experience the opposite values of the terms "Logos" and "Son" as emphasizing if not exclusively expressing, one of them the identity, the other the distinction. The Logos on the one hand, the divine reason and Word, the wisdom, will and energy of God, might if taken alone be thought of as an impersonal attribute, faculty or function of the Godhead, but it cannot be thought as ever having been wanting to it: God could never have been without self-expression or active will, and so his Logos is coeternal and necessary part of himself, of his very nature and being; while on the other hand the term "Son" must of necessity mean the reproduction and repetition of one self in another self between whom and the first there must be some distinction. If on the one hand the term "Logos" alone were used it might be said that the divine Word, energizing in the natural creation and incarnating itself in the spiritual, need not be personally distinguished from the single personal Godhead; if on the other hand the term "Son" only were used the distinction might be pushed, as by the Arians, to the disruption of the essential identity of the persons distinguished. But if the incarnate one is both Logos and Son he must be both essentially identical with the Father and personally distinct from him. This was afterward in Nicene language expressed by the phrase "God of God"; as God he was one with the Father, as of or from God he was distinct from the Father.

Returning to the term "begotten," the church always recognized different senses and acts in which it might be applied to the Son of God. As Logos of the natural creation he might be said to have come forth from God in the birth or coming into being of the natural creation. He was begotten or born into humanity in his birth of the Virgin. And in his humanity he was begotten anew when humanity in his person was born through his death and resurrection into the Sonship to which it had been eternally predestinated. But the church would never admit that he who came forth from the Father in the birth of the natural creation had not previously existed from eternity in the bosom of the Father, both as Logos and Son, both one with and distinct from him; and this is what was intended to be expressed by the doctrine of the eternal generation.

When driven to make some distinction between the Father and the Son the Sabellians had admitted a temporal but not an eternal distinction. They said that the Logos was eternally contained in the one personality of the Godhead, but in time, in the temporal acts of creation and incarnation, he became distinguished and was then called Son as begotten of the Father in those acts. But in reality he was still the Father, only to be distinguished from him as a different manifestation of himself from that in which he is Father and not Son. On this line some Sabellians avoided Patripassianism by falling on the other side into a sort of higher Ebionism, teaching that it was not the Father himself but only a virtue or energy of the Father that was incarnate in Jesus Christ. Thus the Sabellians held an economic but not an essential Trinity, a Trinity of temporal manifestations but not of eternal persons. Against all which tendencies the church erected the doctrine of the eternal generation as its bulwark and defence.

What gave Arianism a vitality as well as a prominence and importance that it would never have acquired by itself was the accident of its civil and political power and influence. Just when the controversy was well under way in Alexandria the first Christian emperor Constantine the Great was by his victories over his colleague Licinius making himself sole master of the Roman empire and so of the world. It was not Arius and his associates but Constantine and his successors that lifted the Arian discussion into a world-wide and historical significance such as attaches to no other heresy.

There can be no question of Constantine's title to the cognomen of " Great." The victorious career that made him sole emperor and gave him a secure and powerful empire and reign, proved him a great general. The civil administration that reorganized the empire under a new constitution and marked a new epoch if not revolution in its internal history was evidence of his greatness as a statesman. But it was Constantine's policy in reference to Christianity, even though we regard it as nothing more than policy, that constituted his chief claim to greatness. It is useless however to deny his sincere and profound interest in Christianity. It may not have been in the truest and deepest sense a personally religious interest, and it certainly was not such as morally to transform his character and impart to him the spirit and life of the founder of the religion he professed. And yet even here judgment belongeth not unto us; he became a Christian late, in the midst of evil and violent times, and in possession of almost absolute and irresponsible power. We do not know the full secret of his worst crimes such as the execution of Crispus and others of his own household or how much domestic strife, unhappiness, misrepresentation and intrigue deceived and darkened his judgment and apparently, as it seemed to him, necessitated his actions. Again, it may not have been a very profound or correct theological interest which Constantine felt in Christianity, though that may exist in the absence of one truly spiritual and religious. He certainly established no claim to being a theologian and yet it was no mere vulgar or political pretence that he made of being such; he was sincerely interested, and no doubt at times thought himself one. What he said most impressively in public that was theologically true and sound was said perhaps at second hand, and he said much also that betrayed his ignorance. But he had honestly made Christianity his cause and himself its most illustrious and exalted patron and champion and he was deeply and earnestly concerned about it and anxious to represent and further it intelligently and wisely.

Herein was Constantine's true greatness in the matter. He had by his military genius unified the empire and was by his political genius reorganizing its internal administration. But he was great enough to perceive that what he could do in this way from without was not what the world he was dealing with most needed; that it was all nothing and would come to nothing without a moral and thereto a religious reconstitution of individual and personal life and character and of general society. He was the first of the emperors to perceive that old things were passing away and that there was but one thing in the world that was new and capable of renewing it. The old religions had had their day and lost their power and he had not the folly of his nephew Julian to suppose that new life could be breathed into old bodies. Philosophy had outgrown its faith and become critical and sceptical and no longer exercised any positive and constructive influence, and scepticism in thought, as soon as it becomes general or universal, is corruption in morals and disintegration in personal and social life and order. As in material things integration into masses is dependent upon the forces resident in the elementary atoms that compose them, molecular attractions, repulsions, affinities and such like, so does society depend upon the vitality of the spiritual and moral forces resident in individuals, and what social life is public life and politics and the state itself will be. No matter how political his motive there is no possibility of doubting, at first at least and for a long time, the Emperor Constantine's concern for the moral and even spiritual reform of private character and social life in his empire. It has been remarked, in speaking of the failures as well as successes of his personal policy: "Nevertheless we must give him credit for a sincere desire for moral reform and confess that henceforward there was a marked increase if not in nobility of character at least in outward respectability of conduct." He may have succeeded only so far as the outward respectability of conduct, but if he failed to base this upon the deeper nobility of character it was not because he had not aimed to build on this,—as to lay this too in the one foundation of a true faith as well as a pure morality.

Constantine was then the first mind at the head of the world's affairs to realize what Christianity might be to the social and political life of an empire whose vital forces were spent, whose internal bonds dissolved, and which was rapidly undergoing corruption and hastening to destruction. As an actual matter of fact Christianity with all its human intermixture of weakness and failure was the salt that saved the world, that in the disintegration of the old supplied the principle and power of a new integration of personal, social and political life and rendered possible if it did not itself create the new civilization which calls itself by its name and is dated from its birth. And Constantine was the first of the rulers of the world to recognize this and summon it to its high mission and destiny. He did not expect too much but he expected it too impatiently and was disappointed at not finding it immediately all that he had hoped. Perhaps it was his disappointment in Christianity that is responsible for much of what so disappoints us at last in him as a Christian. Alas! Christianity lives and acts, is known and judged only through us and has to carry the weight and bear the blame of all we are, and so always to human vision fails or falls short of what is expected of it. Nevertheless in God's time and way it accomplishes that whereunto it is sent. We shall see that Constantine looked for a united church and a united empire and world as the immediate result of the Council of Nicæa. The immediate result was exactly the reverse; the church and the world were plunged into a state of confusion and strife out of which he saw no hope in his lifetime of the peace and tranquillity of which he had dreamed and for which he sighed. Just this period of his life, succeeding the council, was marked by the greatest vacillation in his own attitude, religiously and theologically, and by his worst excesses and crimes. If he sinned more than others against the religion he had so conspicuously professed, it may be in part at least because he expected more from it and was more than any other deceived and disappointed by it.

More or less predisposed in its favor by inheritance from his father Constantius, who had steadily maintained an attitude of tolerance and kindness toward it, Constantine's actual approaches to Christianity were very gradual. Whether drawn to it in greater proportion by policy, by superstition or by an enlightened intelligence and faith, the process in itself by which he was brought was both a rational and religious one. When in the year 312 he had the vision of the *labarum* and inscribed upon his banner the monogram of Christ, however we may explain the facts or however little he may be proved to have known of Christ at the time, we cannot resist the conclusion that it was, in accordance with the inscription upon the triumphal arch erected in Rome to commemorate his victory, "*instinctu divinitatis*," by an instinct of divinity that he was moved to place himself and his cause under the auspices and blessing of the hitherto despised and persecuted religion which was predestined to the conquest of the world. Christianity had as much to do with his success as he with its future triumphs. On the lowest ground of superstition, the heathen gods were no longer a name to conjure with; their power was gone, and the very soldiers of Licinius felt their inferiority and disadvantage in still offering to them sacrifice and worship in the face of the opposing labarum which was everywhere become a talisman of victory.

By a succession of edicts the Christians were in the year 313 for the first time in the enjoyment of a complete toleration throughout the empire. Constantine was beginning to interest himself in the internal affairs and disputes of the church and very soon had forced upon him that policy of interference in them which was to grow up into the alliance of church and state that has ever since played such a part in the history of both. However impracticable it might be in itself and however unequal he proved to the task of carrying it out, there is no denying him from the beginning, in connection with their relation to each other, an idea and policy that had in it elements of both goodness and greatness.

In his civil administration Constantine strove unsuccessfully to combine two principles which were both strong in him but which it was difficult to harmonize. The first was a real regard in theory at least for the rights of individuals, of private life and natural society; we have spoken of his zeal to animate and reform these as the only basis of public or national strength and prosperity. The other was a passion for organization and order, not only for unity but also uniformity. He wanted the empire and for this end he wanted the church to be one and identical throughout. The chief thing that had attracted him to Christianity was its claim and essential nature to be a bond of perfectness capable of making and destined to make all things one. He saw in its unity and universality an instrument for welding together the discordant elements and parts of the empire and the world. The idea and policy of his life are well expressed in a letter to Alexander and Arius on the subject of their dispute, and nothing can better show the mind and attitude of Constantine at just the point of time at which we have arrived. "Two principles," he said, "had guided his actions: the first, to unify the belief of all nations with regard to the divinity into one consistent form; the second, to set in order the body of the world which was laboring as it were under a grievous sickness."

In his zeal to promote unity in the church, Constantine vacillated between the two impulses or dispositions of which we have spoken, at one time inclined to leave matters to their own natural working and to respect the rights of individual opinions and choice, at another undertaking to enforce agreement and consent by the pressure of legal disabilities and penalties. Neither seemed to succeed and it was without doubt the disappointment of his life that he could not make Christianity and through it the body of the world one and sound and so save it from its grievous sickness.

As far back as the edicts of toleration, the stipulated condition of its toleration was that Christianity should be one thing, undivided by heresies and schisms. But Constantine's personal interference with the faith as well as internal order of the church began against his will and protest when he was forced by pressure from both sides to arbitrate in the quarrel between the Donatists and Catholics of Carthage and North Africa. To decide it he assembled the almost ecumenical Council of Arles in the year 314. And so was established the precedent that was followed by the much more serious personal interference of the emperor in the more difficult heresy of Arianism, and at the greater Council of Nicæa.

When the Nicene Council had completed its labors with apparent unanimity and success Constantine assumed that the matter was settled and the world would be at peace. When a few resisted the pressure brought to bear on them and were still recalcitrant, in his impatience he attempted to force them into agreement, was willing to proceed to the extremest penalty, and did inflict that of banishment. Then, seeming to realize that spiritual unity and harmony could not be effected by material compulsion, he reverted to the opposite policy of conciliation, made friends himself with Arius, was persuaded by his adherents that he was really not as unsound as he had been represented, and insisted upon Athanasius taking the same view and restoring him to communion and to his former position in Alexandria. Athanasius refused and while still maintaining the decrees of Nicæa Constantine began to find himself more and more acting with the Arians against the church. By degrees he succumbed to the wiles and fell under the influence of Eusebius of Nicomedia, the ablest and most unscrupulous of the Arian party, by whom the last offices of religion were rendered him at his death.

So Constantine's policy of unity and uniformity in church and state came to an unsuccessful issue and we shall see that under his successors the failure grew to tragical, almost fatal dimensions and, humanly speaking, all but made shipwreck of Christianity by making the church and the world wholly and hopelessly Arian.

CHAPTER VI.

THE COUNCIL OF NICÆA.

HE conception as well as the realization of the idea of an ecumenical council must no doubt be conceded to Constantine. He was on the way to it when he summoned the synod at Arles, to which St. Augustine afterward appealed as a universal one, and he accomplished it at Nicæa. He himself said publicly, "God it was on whose suggestion I acted in summoning the bishops to meet in such numbers;" and the council at its close declared that "it was by the grace of God and the piety of the emperor in assembling us that the great and holy synod came together." It was not of course that there had not been local councils to meet local exigencies, but there was a long step between these and the conception of the church as the church, the body of Christ, coming together as an organic whole, to bear testimony to its common faith and to give expression to its corporate life. This does not mean of course that either Constantine or the council fully realized at first the significance and importance of the gathering. There was always in the church an instinct and sense of its unity as a single body under a single Head, as the

one bride of the heavenly Bridegroom, as the unity of Christians not only with Christ but also with one another in Christ. There was always the claim of an organic, common, corporate faith and life, in distinction from the more or less incomplete faith and life of individuals even doctors and saints. But the idea of a corporate or catholic utterance or expression of itself through a gathering so truly representative of its whole or corporate self as to make it the voice of the church had not yet fully entered into its mind. There is every evidence of tentativeness and of only a growing certainty and confidence in itself pervading the council; and of course the final verdict of ecumenicity or of its having actually given expression to the general mind came only with the subsequent experience and consent of the church that it had done so.

The records are exceedingly few; they are limited to what was at last agreed upon and subscribed, and this includes only the creed, twenty canons and a synodical letter. Most of our information of the proceedings comes from the later correspondence of Athanasius and of Eusebius, and as these two were not altogether of one mind, as we shall see, their impressions and accounts do not always agree. As most convenient for illustrating the main business of the council, with which we are chiefly concerned, we will consider successively in all their relations to it, (1) the Emperor Constantine, (2) the Arian leaders, (3) the representatives, like the historian Eusebius of Cæsarea, of the conservatives or party of compromise, and (4) the positive and thoroughgoing catholics, like Athanasius, bent on bringing the discussion to some decisive conclusion and action.

1. Constantine had entered with deep concern into the troubles of Alexandria which threatened to endanger the unity and peace of Christendom and of the empire. His first feeling was one simply of amazement and indignation that the representatives of Christianity should excite such discord and risk such consequences upon such slight differences. He was unable to see any cause for so bitter a controversy and writes to Alexander and Arius, urging upon them the insignificance of the issue between them, and entreating them to withdraw their mutual charges and restore quiet and tranquillity to the church and to himself. The letter and the mission of restoring harmony were intrusted to Hosius, bishop of Cordova in Spain, who had for some time been the emperor's closest friend and adviser in matters religious and ecclesiastical. When Hosius returned unsuccessful and no doubt better informed himself upon the true nature and importance of the issue dividing the parties, the emperor began to take a deeper and more serious view of the situation. There were at the time three issues disturbing the church, the old paschal controversy which had come down almost from the beginning as to the day on which Easter should be celebrated, the Meletian schism, a local and purely practical quarrel which had been going on for some time in Egypt, and now this Arian heresy which, arising it may be said somewhat accidentally in Alexandria, was soon shown to have had its real roots farther east in that Antiochian school

of Lucian of which Arius was a disciple. Combining these three questions in the common motive of an ecumenical or world-wide unity and order which always actuated him, the emperor began his preparations for assembling the great council. He wrote letters to all the bishops inviting and urging them to meet with all speed at Nicæa; he himself provided conveyances and other facilities for their journey; and he made every preparation for their welcome and entertainment. The sessions were held in a large church in the centre of the imperial palace. After a number of preliminary and informal discussions, in which much of the ground was laid for the subsequent formal action, the council being duly convened the emperor appeared and took his seat. The address of welcome and of thanks to him from the council has been variously ascribed to Hosius, to Eustathius of Antioch, to Eusebius of Cæsarea, and to Alexander of Alexandria, who either personally or from the importance of their sees were the leading bishops. The bishop of Rome, prevented by age and infirmity from attending, was represented by two presbyters. The emperor as always made a great impression by "his stately presence, lofty stature and gentle and even modest demeanor." He claimed for himself in his reply the position of a fellow-servant among those whom he was addressing; and in urging upon them unity and unanimity, he enforced his exhortation to peace and harmony by producing a sealed packet of charges and complaints which had been preferred to him against many of themselves, and publicly throwing them into the fire. "You cannot," he said, "be judged by a man like myself; such things as these must wait till the great day of God's judgment. Christ has advised us to pardon our brother if we wish to obtain pardon ourselves."

In the regular discussions at several critical points he took a personal part. We might judge from Eusebius that when the latter had proposed his form of a creed it was the emperor who after approving and praising it moved to amend by the introduction of the crucial word "homoöusion." At this time, perhaps as a result of his deeper study of the question with Hosius, he acted with the catholic party; and Eusebius declares that his explanations and arguments had convinced himself and removed his scruples and objections to the term. On the whole however, it is plain that the emperor exerted no undue pressure upon one side or the other of the question. His interest and influence did unquestionably it might be said even force the council to express itself, to formulate the faith of the church; but with the form which that expression took he did not interfere. He seems to have adhered to the principle expressed by him years before when he had angrily repulsed the appeal of the Donatists to him from the decision of the Council of Arles. "They demand," he had said, " my judgment, who myself expect the judgment of Christ. The judgment of bishops ought to be accounted as if God himself was sitting on the tribunal." But when the bishops had spoken, and spoken with a practical unanimity, he assumed that the whole matter was forever closed and did not hesitate to exercise all of his personal influence and his imperial authority to enforce the decision. It is not improbable indeed that his explanations and advocacy of the homoöusion were based not on his own very intelligent comprehension of that term or deep religious interest in it but upon the fact that the preliminary discussions had revealed the mind and intention of the council to impose it.

The council was drawing to a close when, on July 25, A.D. 325, the emperor invited all the bishops to a great banquet in commemoration of the twentieth anniversary of his accession to the empire. The inward unity, harmony and joy that pervaded all minds at the happy consummation of their labors, as well as the outward glory and splendor of the entertainment suggested to the minds of the plain bishops the thought of a foretaste of heaven.

2. The Arian leaders had come to Nicæa full of confidence and hope. When expelled from Alexandria Arius had found among his fellow-disciples of Lucian in the East very able and powerful supporters; he boasted that all were with him except a few heretical and unlearned men. Eusebius of Nicomedia, an imperial city, led the extremer party; but the more moderate and orthodox Eusebius of Cæsarea, the most learned man of the age, represented a large section which, while not agreeing with Arius, had not discovered anything dangerously heretical in his teaching, and so expostulated against the harshness of his treatment. Arius therefore came to the council counting on a support powerful in ability and not insignificant in numbers. In the preliminary discussions he was fully drawn out and did not hesitate to present his whole case. After the formal opening his

opinions were examined in the presence of the emperor, and the Eusebians undertook his defence and justification. It was immediately made apparent that the overwhelming weight of sentiment was against him, and as the discussion proceeded the number of his avowed sympathizers dwindled down to a very few. A letter of Eusebius of Nicomedia, which had perhaps been used as a campaign document, was laid before the council, as also a formal confession of their faith. These on being read were rent in pieces and the party was accused of having betrayed the truth. After this the only question for the Arians was to what extent they could escape utter condemnation and other penalties secular as well as religious, or on the other hand how far they could bring their consciences to accept the action of the council and remain in the communion of the church.

3. When Arianism had been so summarily disposed of, Eusebius of Cæsarea and the conservatives or party of compromise came to the front. They had previously thought Arius hardly treated, but fell in now with the condemnation of his opinions as heretical and blasphemous. They had a creed to propose which would unite all parties, even the Arians, who could all have signed it. It was scriptural, and it accorded with all the traditions and confessions of faith of all the churches. It was in fact the creed in use in Eusebius's own native and see city of Cæsarea, and as it is a good sample of the creeds in use in all churches prior to the Nicene Council, as it was also the basis of the creed for the first time imposed on the whole church by that council, it may be well

to give it as it originally stood. And it may be safely affirmed that, although up to this time each church had its own confession of faith, all based upon the baptismal formula, there was no church in Christendom whose creed did not substantially accord with this of Cæsarea. Eusebius, in his report to his church of the action of Nicæa, writes as follows:

"Our own form then, which was read in the presence of the emperor, and appeared to be right and proper, is expressed in these terms: As we have received from the bishops who preceded us, as we have been taught in the rudimental instructions of our childhood and when we were subjects of the baptismal rite, and as we have learned from the divine Scriptures; as we have believed and taught, both in the order of presbyter and in the episcopal dignity itself, and as we now believe, we present to you our profession of faith. And it is this: We believe in one God, the Father Almighty, maker of all things visible and invisible; and in one Lord Jesus Christ, the Word of God, God of God, light of light, life of life, the only-begotten Son, the first-born of every creature, begotten of the Father before all ages, by whom all things were made; who for our salvation was made flesh, and lived among men, and suffered, and rose again the third day, and ascended to the Father, and shall come again in glory to judge quick and dead. We believe also in one Holy Spirit; believing every one of these to be and subsist, the Father truly the Father, the Son truly the Son, and the Holy Spirit truly the Holy Spirit; as our Lord when he sent his disciples to preach said, 'Go teach all nations, baptizing them in the name of the Father and of the Son and of the Holy Ghost.'"

After Eusebius had read his proposed creed, which was received with entire and universal assent and approbation, there was a pause and then began the real issue between the only two actual parties in the council.

It was perfectly well understood that the motive and intention of the conservatives was not merely to present an unexceptionable confession of faith in which the whole church might come to a uniform use, but to stave off the discussion and decision of a controversy which they were afraid to face. Beyond the mere immaterial advantage of a literal uniformity in their public confessions, what would be gained by the adoption of Eusebius's creed? Everybody would have accepted it and continued just as he was; the Arians would have signed it and been Arians still; nothing whatever would be decided by it. The claim for it was that it was the language of Scripture, and of the traditional faith; the issue made was that it was wrong and unwise to use a language outside of these to express or explain divine truth. But the question was not what Scripture and tradition said— they were all agreed on that; but what Scripture and tradition meant, upon which they disagreed. You cannot interpret and explain Scripture by simple quotation or repetition of scriptural language or expressions, but only by the use of other terms by means of which they might be defined and illustrated. Eusebius's creed was therefore all right as far as it went; but it did not go far enough even to touch, much less solve, the real difficulties of the meaning of Scripture and tradition which were dividing them and which were the reason of their coming together.

4. The thoroughgoing catholic party was thus brought forward and took up the true business of the council. If ever in human history there was a man divinely raised up and endowed to meet and deal with a special emergency it was Athanasius. He had spent some years in the household of Alexander, and there before Arius had given utterance to his heresy and when he was scarcely more than of age, had produced his great work upon the nature of the Incarnation, "the first attempt that had been made to present Christianity and the chief events of the life of Jesus Christ under a scientific aspect." The peculiar qualifications and special preparation of Athanasius have been generally recognized and represented somewhat under the following heads:

A Greek, born and reared in Alexandria, the "emporium for the exchange of the ideas and speculations as well as the products of all climes," he was not only himself endowed with speculative capacity of the highest order but also grew up in daily contact with every existing form of religion or philosophy, and was an observer, student and thinker from his earliest youth.

At the same time he was before all and most of all a student of the Scriptures, and none of his adversaries or antagonists could surpass him in love for these or reverence for their authority. Having to stand for freedom from their mere letter, he was a true interpreter of their mind and spirit.

In addition, he was certainly behind none of his contemporaries in acquaintance, sympathy and accord with the thought and life of the church before him. Called, as he was to be, to stand for the church not only against the world but apparently against itself, he was able to stand alone, until he could recall and restore it to itself, and reëstablish the divine tradition of truth.

Finally it was not the least providential circumstance of the career of Athanasius that his very youth when called into the arena left him a long lifetime in which to labor and to suffer for the principles which none of his contemporaries but himself could have brought to their final and permanent triumph; and that for this he was endowed with not only the intellectual and the spiritual but also with the practical and moral qualifications necessary to carry him through so intense and protracted a strain.

It has been said of Arius that he possessed very highly the logical and dialectical but was devoid of the intuitional faculties. It was just in these latter that Athanasius was strongest. "It was," says Dorner, "his intuitional perception of the Redeemer in his totality that marked out for Athanasius the direction which he ought to pursue." But this intuitional perception of the Redeemer in his totality requires exactly a combination of all the above qualifications, a mind at once spiritual, scriptural, catholic, and in the highest sense rational and practical.

Athanasius was a year or two under thirty, and only a deacon, when he accompanied Alexander to Nicæa. There is no telling to what extent he had already been the inspirer of his bishop in the controversy with Arius, and he went thoroughly armed and furnished for the fray. It is very certain that in the preliminary discussions he quickly took the leading part, and there must have been moments when the issue narrowed down to a duel between the arch-representatives of the opposing causes, Arius and Athanasius. Pen-and-ink pictures of the great protagonists have not been wanting. There was a difference of forty years between their ages. Arius was tall, serious, impressive, insinuating in his bearing and manners; a dialectician and politician, but, in appearance at least, of no mean or vulgar type. He had certainly the arts of mental reservation and dissimulation, and employed them later; but on this occasion undue confidence perhaps led him to be outspoken and open enough. Athanasius was small,—a mere "manikin" the Emperor Julian called him later, in derision,—and with the slight stoop of a student but with a beautiful face which was compared to that of an angel. He went to the council nominally as the private secretary of his bishop, in reality as the controlling spirit and genius of all its proceedings. Throughout these "he was by no means," says Neander, "contending for a mere speculative formula; . . . it was an essentially Christian principle which actuated him." His entire feeling and motive is expressed in his own simple words, "Our contest is for our all." The party, of which he was the real if not the nominal leader, seems not only to have carefully arranged beforehand their policy which was carried through with great moderation, wisdom and skill; but also to have adopted and made up their minds to abide by the crucial term which was destined to become the very effectual test of Christian orthodoxy. They began by giving the Arians full time and scope and even encouragement to expose and so refute and ruin themselves. Then they listened with deference and approval to the conservatives and let it be clearly seen that they had no desire or reason to antagonize them, as indeed there was no issue with them except upon the policy of so defining and interpreting the common truth as to make it clear that they were agreed as to its meaning and not merely as to its expression.

When Eusebius had read and proposed his creed, it was no one of them, who might have created antagonism on the other side, it was the fair-minded and impartial emperor himself whom no one could accuse of partisanship, who commended the formula—but proposed the sole and simple amendment of the insertion of the term "homoöusion." At any rate it was the emperor who in a speech so defined the term and explained away its real or apparent difficulties as to convince the learned Eusebius of its innocence and gain his consent, and perhaps that of many others, to its adoption. No doubt it was Hosius who had prepared the emperor for this important part, but the pardonable design was to accomplish in peace and harmony what the discerning emperor saw by this time that the real minds and wills of the council had come with the determination to accomplish. It might be said that without the aid of the emperor the homoöusion could never have been passed through the council. That may be, but it is very certain that, with the aid of the emperor, no other real definition could have been passed. The providential use throughout of the imperial power in all the councils seems to have been that it acted as an external compulsion upon the council to say something, to come to some real decision. And when it had to do that, as a rule it could only agree upon that which was true; truth alone unites, error only hopelessly confuses and divides. And there was the additional safeguard that no council stood alone and only stood at all if it was in harmony with other councils and with the world-wide and age-long mind of the whole church.

When the ice had been broken by the aid of the emperor other amendments followed, under the cumulative effects of which Eusebius saw his creed quickly transformed from what had been only an instrument of truth into so effective an offensive and defensive weapon against error that it has never since been possible to improve it. The creed as it came from the Council of Nicæa and before it received its final form at Constantinople was as follows:

"We believe in one God, the Father Almighty, maker of all things both visible and invisible; and in one Lord Jesus Christ, the Son of God, begotten of the Father, an only-begotten—that is from the essence (or substance, "ousia") of the Father—God from God, light from light, true God from true God, begotten, not made, being of one essence (homoöusion) with the Father; by whom all things were made, both things in heaven and things on earth; who for us men and for our salvation came down and was made flesh, was made man, suffered and rose again the third day, ascended into heaven, cometh to judge quick and dead; and in the Holy Spirit.

"But those who say that 'there was once when he was not,' and 'before he was begotten he was not,' and 'he was made of things that were not,' or maintain that the Son of God is of a different essence, or created, or subject to moral change or alteration—these doth the catholic and apostolic church anathematize."

In the body of the creed proper the vital additions were the following: Whereas the Arians had used the term "begotten" in the secondary or improper sense of created or made, making no distinction between the generation of the divine Son and the sense in which even the natural creation is called the offspring of God; and teaching that he was only the first begotten or made, and made of the mere will of the Father out of nothing; the creed affirms that he was begotten, not made; not out of nothing, or of things that were not, but of the ousia, essence or substance, of the Father, and so was personally homoöusios, or of identical essence or subtance with the Father. Moreover as against the false anthropology, as well as theology, of the Arian conception of the incarnation, to the article "was made flesh" it adds "was made man," meaning that our Lord took flesh not merely in the sense of a human body but in all that constitutes a true and complete manhood.

The difficulties, inadequacies, and positive disadvantages of such definitions will be done full justice to in the sequel; at present we shall dwell a little upon the necessity of them. Athanasius was as free as any one to regret the necessity of employing terms neither scriptural nor theological but physical and metaphysical in the definition of spiritual and divine mysteries; and he fully admitted not only their insufficiency but their danger. Others before him had regretted and yet had not been able to avoid the same necessity; neither human thought nor human language can represent to perfection the truth of things divine; we can only approximate it by expressing as well as we may the truth of things invisible in terms, which are all that we have, of things visible. When therefore we say that the Son of God is homoöusios, of one essence or substance with the Father, we are fully aware that our own natural and even material associations with the word " ousia " are very apt to mislead in the application of it to the purely spiritual and incomprehensible being of God. But what are we to do? We have no divine language and can only think and speak with the symbols and in the terms at our command. The one thing Athanasius knew and wanted to state in language exact enough, technical enough, definite enough to guard against any evasion or diminution or perversion of it, was the simple primal Christian fact of not only the very humanity but the very personal divinity or deity of Jesus Christ. He summed up and embodied in himself the whole Christian consciousness that all of God and all of man were met, united and consummated in the all-reconciling and all-completing personal work and exaltation of Jesus Christ. As a matter of fact that great essential Christian truth had from the beginning been repeatedly subject to misinterpretation on both sides. Within the church itself the use of scriptural and of ecclesiastical and catholic language and the repetition of true confessions of faith had not saved doctors and even bishops from attaching imperfect and false meanings to the very central article of Christian belief and life. This had culminated in the unscriptural, unchristian, irrational, and irreligious teaching of Arius, held and defended under the very forms and as the true meaning of Scripture and catholic tradition. The time was surely come when it was necessary for the church to define beyond the possibility of misunderstanding at least the vital and distinctive and essential principle of Christianity.

We have repeatedly said that at this juncture the doctrine of the person of Christ was under consideration on its divine and not as before and after on its human side; and the whole dogmatic affirmation of the Nicene Council was contained in its insistence upon the one word "homoöusion." And all that was meant by that was that Jesus Christ was God, in no lower or secondary or different sense from that in which the Father is God; that the incarnation was an act of the divine personal presence and operation in human nature and human life. Not indeed in the sense that the whole Godhead or divine selfhood was contained in Christ, and yet that God was himself and not by any mere impersonal virtue or influence in him.

It has been remarked that while we have no record of the arguments actually employed by Athanasius at the council in defence of the real divinity of our Lord, we can easily gather what they must have been from his letters and other writings; and that they may be reduced to four heads, which we will briefly develop.

In the first place the Scriptures: by which we do not mean the explicit statement of particular passages merely, but that whole mind and meaning of the Scriptures which exhibits Jesus Christ to us as a personal revelation of God himself and not only an impersonal something from him.

In the second place it is involved in the very notion of that unique and real Sonship which the church ascribes to him alone, and which cannot mean anything less than that he receives from the Father the essential nature of the Father, which must therefore be in him as in the Father eternal, and of equal majesty, glory and power; with the sole difference that the Father as father is underived and the Son as son is derived, but eternally so—after the analogy of the sun and its effluence.

In the third place it is required by the very meaning of an absolute religion, of the divine grace and self-impartation and of human redemption and salvation. If Athanasius possessed, as we have attributed to him, that intuitional spiritual faculty which makes the spiritual man a judge of spiritual things, as spiritual things are the test of the spiritual man, we shall expect to find in him not a mere dependence upon the external authority of Scriptures or tradition, which need themselves to be interpreted and therefore understood, but the possession of that spiritual criterion by which the church as a whole through the true representatives and leaders of its thought and mind is the judge and interpreter of revelation and tradition. He appeals accordingly, as we find, to the universal intuitive perception of the truth of God and man, and what must be the meaning of their absolute and ultimate relation to each other in Jesus Christ, if there is to be in him a real divine-human reconciliation and atonement.

Finally, in the fourth place, the doctrine of the real divinity is actually that which has been the teaching of the church from the beginning, whatever may have been the private opinion of individuals. So that revelation, the intuitions of the spiritual reason and catholic agreement and consent are all at one on the essential truth of Jesus Christ.

Under the pressure of the emperor to come to some definite conclusion and decision, under the skilful guidance of Athanasius, under the power of the truth alone to unite and harmonize diverse minds and tendencies, above all under the controlling providence and by the indwelling and helping Spirit and grace of God, the council was brought to a practical unanimity of action. Of the three hundred and eighteen bishops who according to the traditional computation composed the council, there were only two or three at the last who refused to sign the creed. The emperor accepted the result as inspired and banished the recalcitrants along with Arius, and so matters for the moment were settled.

We do not dwell here upon the settlement of the long-standing paschal or Easter controversy, which practically closed the diversity of use that had divided East and West on that point.

The Meletian quarrel was decided against the schismatics, but it was no more dead than Arianism and soon revived along with the latter to give more trouble than ever to the church.

The emperor wrote happy and confident letters to Alexandria and to all the churches, in which he declared that the power of Satan had been thwarted, and that the splendor of truth, at the command of God, had vanquished the dissensions, schisms and tumults which invaded the repose of the church and the empire. "We all therefore believe that there is one God and worship in his name."

CHAPTER VII.

ARIANISM AFTER THE COUNCIL OF NICÆA.

HE events succeeding the Council of Nicæa are so complicated and confused that it is difficult to combine anything like a philosophical interpretation of them with a detailed narration of even the principal incidents. We shall limit ourselves therefore to such details as are actually necessary to indicate or illustrate the onward progress of the matter which we have in hand, the evolution of the doctrine, as distinguished from the truth or fact, of the person of Jesus Christ.

If there had been only the religious question religiously discussed and determined, the task of tracing its solutions and definitions would be comparatively simple and easy; but unfortunately at this point Christianity itself, through its sudden elevation to the position of the state religion, becomes hopelessly mixed up and almost lost in such a seething mass of political intrigue and personal and partisan animosity that it is scarcely possible to trace the real issue through all to its safe emergence at last. And yet, perhaps, except through this admixture and interaction with earthly elements and forces the heavenly truth would not have emerged at all. God in many ways makes the wrath and the folly of men to praise him.

If we should abstract our attention from the selfish and worldly motives and ends that identified and mixed themselves up with the very genuine and profound Christian thought and life of the times, and direct it only to the religious forces at work, we might describe the crisis as follows. A momentous question—the momentous question of Christianity—had been submitted by the church to a general council and the council had decided it. But the question was not therefore decided; the council had judged the question, it remained for the church to judge the council. In a certain sense it might be said that so far as the council itself was concerned, taken as a whole, and still more so far as the church as a whole was concerned, the action of the Council of Nicæa was not yet its deliberate judgment and decision. The fact is, leaving out a very few commanding individuals, for the church the council was the beginning rather than the end of reflection; and we might almost say of it that it spoke first and reflected afterward. So far as the voice of the council was the voice of the church—and we shall see that it was—it was the first thought of the church that was expressed and not, as it is sometimes called, its sober second thought. Not on that account was the verdict the less valuable, but on the contrary that fact constituted its peculiar value. We have seen to what an extent the faith of the first Christian ages was intuitive and implicit, and how slow the great body of Christians was to go beyond the confession of Christianity as an objective fact of divine incarnation and human redemption, and to trust itself to that process of human and rational reflection which would undertake to make the divine mystery humanly intelligible and expressible. It was humanly speaking impossible that the church could have been brought to utter itself as it did at Nicæa without the imperial pressure, amounting almost to compulsion. Speaking then and thus, its utterance was more a testimony or witness to the objective fact in which it believed than an exposition of its own reflections upon that fact. Its great reluctance was not to make a catholic or universal confession of the person of Christ, but to confess him in terms not revealed and not scriptural, and applicable rather to human than divine things. Compelled however thus to define the object of its faith, it did so immediately and on first thought, with a clearness, certainty and decision, of which it would have been more and more incapable the longer it was allowed to reason and reflect. Not that there was no place for reflection and reason; as a matter of fact these, coming after, came eventually to yield a subjective assent and confirmation to the objective testimony borne at once and at first by the instinctive or intuitive faith of the universal Christian consciousness. But it was the peculiar value of the Council of Nicæa that, in the sense and to the extent we have endeavored to describe, its decision was given at the beginning and not at the end of the age of speculative reflection, which it introduced; and, in the words of Dr. Dorner,

"We shall esteem it a special favor of providence that the conscience of the church was appealed to for its testimony and confession while it still retained its [primitive] certitude and authority; and that thus at the very commencement of its voyage, a beacon was enkindled to mark the church's pathway across the stormy seas which lay before it."

Thus it happened that, as our Lord himself coming to bring the peace of God into the world brought at first not peace but a sword, so the great Nicene Council, convened to give unity, introduced a strife and discord such as had never been known in the church before. Hitherto the great silent solid body of Christian people was united without question by faith in facts which they were as satisfied should remain without and above them as children are satisfied not to understand the mysteries of birth and life and growth. The church had instinctively detected and rejected whatever was inconsistent with its faith and life, but doctrinal investigation and speculation, all that we would now call theology, was, as we have said, confined to very few and was viewed with distrust as tending to disturb and darken the simplicity of a faith the truth of which lay in the fact of things without us and not in any reasonings and deductions of our own. Now of a sudden, and unexpectedly to the great mass of them, the simple pastors of simple flocks were brought together from the ends of the earth and made to give in language above their comprehension a scientific or philosophical reason for the faith that was in them. Made to give their verdict as judges, they instinctively raised their voices and closed their ears against every form of open or covert attack upon the true divinity of their Lord, and so bore their testimony to the common faith. Their spiritual sense had not lost its delicacy through too much thought and too little life; they felt intuitively that the Athanasian position was true to their religious wants and their Christian experience, as well as to the Scriptures and the catholic tradition as they knew it; and so they gave their adhesion to it and in the certainty of their first and fresh convictions rejoiced to feel that the Holy Ghost had spoken through them. Even in the council, however, they had not been brought up to this point without doubts and qualms, without hesitation and reluctance. Their faith without knowledge had led them, and they had followed it like Abraham not knowing whither they went. And when the jubilation and enthusiasm over what they had done was over and their elation had grown cold, and their subtle and fine formulæ and definitions came to be discussed and criticised over again apart from the explanations which had made them sound so true, they were by no means as sure as they had been of the truth and value of their action.

It is certainly only in this way that we can explain the almost universal and for a long time apparently hopeless reaction that set against the council soon after its triumphant adjournment. It affected the mind of the emperor himself and wrecked all the shallow hopes he had built upon the sand of his superficial acquaintance with the divine workings of Christianity. And alone, or almost alone, and against odds that it would be difficult to measure, the great Athanasius set himself resolutely and patiently to the task that was to take as many years as the other had taken days, of bringing the church as he had brought the council up to a comprehension and knowledge of itself. In the church as in every individual the passage from intuitive faith to rational knowledge is a difficult, painful and dangerous one. Its path is through thought and doubt back to truth and certainty, and it is not all who return again in safety to the haven of faith from which they started. We shall see how the church passed through it, and we shall not pause to count the sad failures, the faithless and shameful disloyalties and defections by the way.

But, as we have said, the question of the religious progress of the church's thought was complicated with many others of which it is necessary to take account. We must remember that during the time when the imperial policy toward Christianity was turning from persecution to patronage and men had everything to gain instead of everything to lose by becoming Christians, the immediate effect had been to convert the church from a purely religious to a very largely secular and political body. We shall expect therefore to find in even its highest places self-seekers, schemers and politicians as well as theologians, scholars and saints. Of the latter, in all three characters, unquestionably the highest type was Athanasius; and perhaps the various complications that distracted and impeded the church may best be studied by considering them successively in their relation to him as its representative. We shall therefore, referring to him as a standard, pass consecutively in review the subsequent conduct of the several parties which had taken part in the proceedings and almost all united in the conclusions of the Nicene Council; and we shall begin with the inner circle of the Homoöusians themselves, those who had acted most closely with Athanasius, and proceed from within outward.

The council over, and the larger task begun of passing its decisions through the test of the universal judgment, many of those most closely identified with Athanasius, who had most distinguished themselves in the battle for the homoöusion, failed him in just the way to be the source of the greatest weakness instead of strength in the further trials of the truth. A single instance will illustrate how this not unnaturally came about. It had been felt and conceded by some of their strongest advocates that there was danger lurking in the terms and phrases employed to define and defend the truth. Many sound but conservative and timid members had been reluctant to sign the definitions on account of perilous ambiguities to which attention had been called in the debates. That the danger was a real one was soon to be demonstrated by perhaps many more instances than the conspicuous one we are about to give. None of the bishops in the council had been more forward or useful in defence of our Lord's person against the Arians than Marcellus of Ancyra in Asia Minor. Yet it was not long after before he was convicted of holding the homoöusion itself in just that Sabellian sense of which the council had been afraid, and which it had charged as an objection against the term. Worse than that, tried and clearly convicted by one side in the subsequent controversy, he was defended and protected by the other side, including the see of Rome, because of his services in the council; and it was years before his friends were forced by his conduct to give up his cause as a bad one. The effect of such cases could not but revive and deepen the distrust of the decisions which the Athanasians had found so much difficulty in overcoming in the council.

When we pass from the inner circle of the Athanasians to the very large next outer one of the great body of conservatives, who were at bottom opposed to the idea of a universal test at all, who thoroughly distrusted and feared the application of scientific methods and language to the definition of divine mysteries, and who in particular objected to the special terms insisted on by the Athanasians, but who having to define could find no better or other terms in which to do so and so had conformed,— we shall of course not be surprised to find these reviving their scruples and fears, and becoming more confirmed in them and doubtful of their previous compliance, especially as these fears were most artfully and skilfully played upon by the real anti-Nicene party. The leaders of the orthodox conservatives were in addition unfortunately all more or less prejudiced against Alexander and Athanasius. They did not appreciate the depth and danger of the Arian heresy and had never sympathized with what they regarded, in the length to which it was carried, as persecution of Arius. With Eusebius of Cæsarea at their head, as before the council so after it when the personal contentions were revived they found themselves, without being Arians, on the side of Arius and the Arians and arrayed against Athanasius.

Eusebius of Cæsarea, the historian of the church, was without question the most learned man of the age. In all his voluminous literary and religious productions nothing has been discovered to convict him of unsoundness or lukewarmness in the faith. The worst that could be charged against him was that he was liberal or latitudinarian in his judgment of the doctrinal differences of others; he was not warm or strong enough on the side of the truth as it was then assailed and at stake, and was opposed to ecclesiastical prosecutions for heresy. Even this charge has been met by extracts from his works denouncing in turn every heresy of his day in terms to which there is nothing lacking of emphasis or point. That however was his general character, and it is charitable to suppose that it was a constitutional opposition to what to one of his temperament seemed the uncompromising and persecuting orthodoxy of Athanasius that ranged him among the persistent enemies of the latter. Certain it is that in the long series of prosecutions aimed by Arians and Arian sympathizers against their one unanswerable and invincible foe Eusebius was always in the ranks of the prosecutors; and at the very inception of the long and fierce attempt of his enemies to crush him, Athanasius disobeyed the summons of the emperor to defend himself before a council to be held at Cæsarea, on the ground that the prejudice of its bishop precluded the hope of a just trial at that place. With such leaders, there is no question that there was after the council a large party of practically orthodox bishops who were more or less dissatisfied with its results and opposed to their further carrying out under the indomitable and determined lead of Athanasius.

Apart from these personal feelings and motives, we have at this point to take up the real objections of the conservative party, waived at Nicæa but now revived and emphasized, not merely to the general principle of the scientific definition of spiritual mysteries, but to the principal terms, or we may say to the particular term, employed in the Nicene definition.

The first objection to the homoöusion, that the term was not to be found in the Scriptures and that revealed mysteries should be expressed only in the language of revelation, had been met by the rejoinder that neither were other explanatory phrases, the Arian ones e.g., "out of nothing," "there was once when he was not," etc., in the Scriptures. This had weighed with Eusebius, and in his report to his church of his part in the council he says that it had influenced him to join in the condemnation of Arianism. But if Arianism had been condemned on that ground, as by many it was and not for deeper reasons, then the rejoinder of the church was met and the objection remained to the language of the creed. And there is no question that with the great mass of conservatives this objection weighed and continued long to weigh very heavily.

The second objection was perhaps even greater. The term was not only unscriptural, it was uncatholic and indeed anticatholic; that is, it had been distinctly repudiated by the church as unsound. It seems that there was evidence that the great Origen had described the Son as homoöusion with the Father, and Tertullian, in Latin, had used an equivalent expression; and it might have grown naturally and of itself into orthodox and catholic use. But subsequently Paul of Samosata had brought the term into discredit by using it in a sense which led the Council of Antioch to repudiate it in condemning him. Then even the theologians of Alexandria who succeeded Origen had, in their long fight with Sabellianism, come to distrust the word because, in the vagueness of its meaning, it had been used in the Sabellian sense to imply the identity of the Son with the Father in person as well as in essence or nature. There was room therefore for the charge that it was opposed to the catholic mind of the church; and this to very many was confirmed by the exposure in the person of Marcellus of the fact that some at least—and they could not know how many—of the very theologians who had imposed the homoöusion upon the council were not free from the Sabellian taint which the church had feared. Indeed Marcellus, and more openly his greater disciple Photius, were guilty of a Sabellianism which logically resulted in the apparently opposite heresy of Paul of Samosata. Denying any real personal distinctions in the Trinity, they ended not in the one logical consequence of Patripassianism, but in the other which remained open to them—the notion that Jesus Christ was the incarnation not of the Godhead, or the Father, but only of a "manifestation" of the Father. This amounted to nothing more than the incarnation of a divine "virtue" of Paul of Samosata, and both alike ended in a sort of higher Ebionism.

It has been seen that Athanasius himself had felt all these objections to the homoöusion and realized that the word had to be purged from its impure associations, and conventionally separated to its catholic meaning and use, before it could become the true watchword of the church. It was simply not so much the best as the least objectionable and the most effective word that could be found; and he foresaw that it would work its way into definiteness and purity of use and meaning, and so into universal favor and acceptance.

It is interesting to trace Athanasius's own estimate of the meaning and value of the homoöusion. Always understanding it in the sense which was to become that of the church, he was not unnaturally disposed to find in it both expression of truth and exclusion of error more than properly belonged to it. Thus, at one time at least, he interpreted it as including in its predication of the Son not only sameness of essence with the Father but also inseparateness of essence from that of the Father. This would remove a real difficulty in the way of the whole attempt at definition. It was said that the Son was of the same substance with the Father; so it might be said that one man was of the same substance with another man, or one coin with another coin; was that all that was meant? No; something more is meant in the divine relationship than in the other two. While a human son is of the same substance with his father, there is a separation or division of their substances; they are different and distinct not only persons but portions of the common nature or substance of humanity. Two coins of a common substance are distinct not only as individual pieces but as separated portions of the same material. It is not intended to be so represented in the Godhead, as though the different persons of the Trinity were separate portions of the common divine essence or substance, outside of and apart from or side by side with one another. The substance of the Godhead is not divided into a number of individuals but is one and indivisible; and in the one personally differentiated but essentially undivided Godhead we recognize and distinguish Father, Son and Holy Ghost. So to Athanasius the homoöusion expressed not merely sameness or likeness, but undivided and unbroken unity of "ousia" or essence; the Son, distinguished as Logos or Son, is undistinguished as God, from the Father. He has no being apart from the common one of Father, Son and Holy Ghost, but only that distinct and individual mode of being which the church discriminates as hypostasis or personality, and which enables us to distinguish his proper function and operations in the Godhead. In a sense which is true of no other distinct persons—because all others are not only distinct but separate—the Father is always in the Son and the Son in the Father, and neither can be nor be thought apart or separate from the other; what the Son does the Father does, and each is what in distinction he is only in and through the other. When, later, the Semi-Arian party thought to find in the other term "homoiousion"—of like, instead of same, nature—an escape from the possible Sabellian sense of the homoöusion, the argument which prevailed against the substitution was this difference between the two terms, that the former meant just that which it was the merit and value of the latter that it excluded. It was proper to say of two coins or of two men that they were of like or similar substance, but not of the persons of the Godhead; for the term implies that while in one sense they are the same, in another sense they are not the same substance, but different and separated parts of the same. This, it was contended, is provided against in the homoöusion, which means not only that the substance is one in Father and Son but that they are not different parts or portions of the one divine substance.

This little discussion will introduce and illustrate yet another objection on the part of the conservatives to the Nicene terms, which was that they were too physical or material to be applicable to spiritual and divine things. The application of such a term as "substance" to God seems to imply a sort of stuff or material of which he is formed. This of course is not as true of the Greek *ousia* as it is of the Latin *substantia*, but it is still liable to the charge and it was no insignificant additional difficulty with which the Athanasians had to contend. By essence or substance in this connection is meant simply that which a thing is, that which constitutes and defines it; in which sense it may just as well be applied to the most spiritual as to the most material of subjects. That the Son is of the essence or substance of the Father means that he is really God; that he possesses all the attributes and properties that belong to the concept and to the reality of Godhead.

We come however to the real springs and causes of the indescribable troubles of the period when we pass from the great mass of mere obstructive conservatism in the church to the outer circle of real Arianism, which having survived its defeat and condemnation in the council began at once and with the most far-reaching policy to organize victory for itself in a much wider arena and upon a far larger scale. The Arians had measured their strength and discovered their weakness; they were in a hopeless minority, in an opposition which could not secure even a hearing in any representative assembly of the whole church. Moreover the emperor was committed against them; he had so associated the great council with himself and invested himself in the glory of it, that they had no hope of reversing its decisions in his lifetime. Adapting their policy to their circumstances, they withdrew from the frankness and boldness upon which they had too confidently relied; and having given in their adhesion to the letter of the Nicene Confession, they proceeded to evade and pervert its spirit and undermine and destroy its credit. Forming no party of their own, they merged and concealed themselves in the great body of the doubtful and dissatisfied conservatives, and set themselves to the task of fostering their doubts and fanning the flame of their dissatisfaction. So that, as we have seen, a large part of the reaction which set in against the council and of the opposition to Athanasius himself came from, or at least through, those who were if they only knew it at one with it and him and in no real unity with those at whose instigation they were acting. In the next place the Arians set themselves not indeed to convert the emperor but to win him over to at least a policy of personal tolerance and doctrinal indifference. The moderate Eusebius of Cæsarea, who had no sympathy with the positiveness and decision with which Athanasius had carried things, was always of influence with the emperor, whom he extravagantly admired and flattered and whom he no doubt affected with his own latitudinarianism. But more than this Eusebius of Nicomedia, which was before Constantinople the chief seat of the imperial court, had been the spiritual adviser of Constantia, widow of Licinius and sister of Constantine; and through her the Arians reached the ears of Constantine and won him over so far as to convince him that by far too much had been made of the errors of Arius and Eusebius, and that he himself had through misrepresentations been carried too far in his severity against them. By degrees he not only mitigated his own harshness but even brought official pressure to bear upon Athanasius himself to restore Arius and to receive back into communion all who were willing to come. Athanasius could not be coerced, and the Arians were not long in discovering that nothing was to be accomplished by them without his destruction. A series of councils having this end in view sat successively in Cæsarea, Tyre, Jerusalem and Constantinople. Consisting mainly of conservatives, they were inspired and controlled by the Arian leaders, who succeeded finally in restoring Arius and procuring the banishment of Athanasius. From this time on Constantine, while still maintaining the Nicene decisions, was practically associated with the Arian party and, as we have seen, received the last offices of religion from Eusebius of Nicomedia.

To their duplicity and gradual ascendency over the mind of the emperor the Arians added a third line of policy which was carried out with an unscrupulous and unrelenting persistency that seems now inconceivable and incredible. This was to destroy Nicenism gradually by the personal overthrow and ruin of its chief representatives and advocates; a scheme in which they all but succeeded and humanly speaking brought the truth to the very point of utter extinction. Nothing indeed seemed to save it but the superhuman vitality, indomitableness and faithfulness of one man.

They began with Eustathius, patriarch of Antioch, one of the presidents and a distinguished leader in the council. They found no great difficulty in deposing him, and set up a successor; but their action created a schism in the capital of the East which lasted through the century and was the source of endless confusion and trouble.

Unfortunately, as we have seen, Marcellus of Ancyra was fair game and not only furnished a text for the crusade against the alleged Sabellianism and even Samosatenism of the council, but rallied a large following of orthodox conservatives under the banner of the Eusebians and gave a plausible excuse for further prosecutions. And it did not help matters that the Athanasians unwisely defended Marcellus, and that in Rome itself he was never formally excluded from communion.

But Athanasius was their rock of offence, upon which they beat in vain for nearly fifty years until they broke themselves to pieces. Within a year after the council Alexander died and Athanasius succeeded him in the patriarchate of Alexandria, against the fierce opposition of a still powerful Arian and Meletian influence, which was thenceforth at the service of the Eusebian machinations and ready at any time to manufacture whatever testimony was needed against either his public administration or his private character. There was never any attempt as in the case of the others to bring doctrinal charges against Athanasius; they knew him of old, and besides this would have been to impeach the Nicene Council itself, which no one was prepared publicly to do. The ground for beginning proceedings against him was his contumacy in disobeying the imperial command, "On pain of removal from his see, to receive to communion any who desired it," and general alleged acts of ecclesiastical and official tyranny and severity. But these grew rapidly into personal charges against him, so monstrous and ridiculous, so abundantly disproved and persistently revived and reiterated, so absurdly unworthy of the least historical consideration, that nothing can explain them but the supposition that, once involved in their crusade against him, it was a matter of life and death with his enemies to carry it through successfully.

From Cæsarea, whose learned bishop we have seen in the thick of the fight against him, to Tyre, whence not awaiting the foregone conclusion of his condemnation he suddenly took ship and left the council, to face the emperor himself and demand justice of him; from Tyre to Jerusalem, where Arius on new and amended representations of his views was pronounced orthodox; from Jerusalem to Constantinople, where all parties were summoned by the emperor to appear before himself, the case dragged on from year to year. Finally when all the charges were about to be dismissed by the emperor as frivolous and malicious, the new one was suddenly brought forward of his having threatened to distress Constantinople by delaying the sailing of the corn ships from Alexandria. Either because this was too serious and dangerous a power for any individual to be even charged with possessing, or else because the emperor was hopeless of putting any other termination to the endless proceedings, Athanasius was banished to Treves in Germany. It was soon after this that Arius presented himself again before the emperor in person and succeeded in convincing him of his orthodoxy. Constantine commanded that he should be publicly admitted to communion on a set occasion, but on his progress to the cathedral for that purpose Arius was seized with a shocking disease which in a few hours terminated his life.

Soon after this first banishment of Athanasius the

Emperor Constantine died, A.D. 337. The empire fell to his three sons, Constantine II. taking the West, Constantius the East, and Constans the centre. The elder and younger emperors were favorable to the catholic faith, and both at long intervals had the opportunity of serving it effectually in the person of Athanasius. But Constantius, who ruled all the area covered by the Arian troubles, was himself wholly under Arian influence, and from his accession we may date a bolder and more open aggressiveness against the principles and the representatives of the Nicene faith. Athanasius indeed through the influence of Constantine II., whose admiration and friendship he had won in his banishment to the West, was restored to his see at the close of A.D. 338. But in the meantime his arch-enemy Eusebius had been translated from Nicomedia to Constantinople in place of the orthodox Paul, and more vigorous measures were in preparation against him. By Easter of 340 he was in his second exile, this time in Rome where he was kindly received by the bishop, Julius; and in his see the Arian George of Cappadocia had been intruded with bitter persecution of the catholics.

After the failure of repeated attempts by Julius to assemble a council at Rome where Athanasius might have an impartial hearing, the Eusebians, who in spite of many promises could never be enticed thither, took occasion upon the consecration of " the Golden Church," a new cathedral at Antioch, to assemble the ninety-seven bishops present and constitute a council. This was in August, 341, and the council made up largely of conservatives adopted a creed orthodox in substance but omitting the homoöusion, and reaffirmed the action of Tyre in condemnation of Athanasius.

Somewhat later Julius of Rome, despairing of the appearance of the Eusebians but ignorant of their action at Antioch, assembled a council which declared Athanasius innocent, but unfortunately also pronounced Marcellus on his own representation of his views orthodox. Before this, in 340, Constantine II. had been killed in an unwarrantable invasion of his brother Constans's dominions. Nevertheless, Constans sharing his brother's favorable disposition toward Athanasius used his influence as the other had in his favor; and by the end of 343 bishops from East and West were assembled at Sardica, the capital of Mœsia, to review and pass judgment upon the whole situation. But the council came to no practical result in uniting the two sections of the church. The Eusebians were bent on treating Athanasius as already judged and condemned and refused to sit in the council with him. The Western bishops were unwilling to recognize the proceedings by which this result had been reached, but were willing to listen de novo to all the evidence against him and decide the case impartially on its merits. The Eusebians finding themselves slightly in the minority withdrew to Philippopolis where they organized a council and confirmed the condemnation of Athanasius. The reduced council at Sardica pronounced him innocent, recognized the Nicene Symbol as the faith of the church, excommunicated a number of Eusebian bishops, and wrote letters of sympathy to the catholics of Alexandria and Egypt.

Matters were thus further apart than ever. In the East, Constantius and his Arian advisers were provoked to harsher methods and orders were issued that Athanasius and his adherents should be put to death if they returned to Alexandria. But messengers were sent from Constans and from the council in Sardica to Constantius in Antioch; and fortunately a fit of honest and just disgust on the occasion of their reception with the methods of his Arian friends in the city, the convenient and timely death of the intruder Gregory at Alexandria, the pressure of his Persian war, and the influence and threats of Constans combined to move Constantius to a brief interval of tolerance and even kindness toward the catholics of Egypt. The return and welcome of Athanasius in the fall of 346 from his second exile was the occasion of a spontaneous and popular demonstration which was long the great historical type and standard of such events. The next few years were a period of great peace, but in 350 the Emperor Constans lost his life in the revolt of Magnentius. Constantius was for several years engaged in putting down a succession of rebellions in the West, at the end of which he found himself sole master of the Roman world. Then his entire character came out and he set himself to the task of forcing Arianism upon the empire. " His will," he declared, " should serve the Westerns for a canon as it had served the Syrians." In the Council of Arles, 353, and Milan, 355, he personally forced the condemnation of Athanasius upon the assembled bishops by the imprisonment or banishment of all who resisted. In 356 officers of the empire formally handed over all the churches in Alexandria to the Arians. The aged Hosius now nearly one hundred years old, after so long a life of faithfulness to the truth, was forced by imprisonment and torture into signing an Arian creed. And Liberius, bishop of Rome, was released from the irksomeness and hopelessness of exile by submission to the same shameful condition. At Ariminum or Rimini in the year 359, the political bishops succeeded, by guile as well as force, in imposing upon the West a creed omitting the homoöusion (the third of Sirmium), which Constantius then undertook to make the creed of the whole church. It was of this council that St. Jerome gave his famous summary: "Ingemuit totus orbis, et Arianum se esse miratus est."

During this time Athanasius, his seat in Alexandria occupied by George the Cappadocian, his flock persecuted and scattered, his life sought and only preserved from his enemies by a series of hairbreadth and sometimes romantic escapes, was now in flight in the desert, now in hiding among his faithful friends the hermits of the Thebaid, now in disguise among his people, sometimes in Alexandria itself; but never despondent about himself or in despair of the ultimate success of the truth he was in the midst of such a life incessantly busy in defence of the faith, and produced one after another those treatises which contributed mainly to its final triumph and have been ever since an armory of weapons in its defence.

At last in the winter of 361 Constantius died and was succeeded by his cousin Julian. Julian had been educated under the tutelage of Eusebius of Nicomedia, but not without reason had revolted from the religion of his predecessor, whose character he justly despised, and had apostatized to paganism, to the revival of which he devoted much of the interest and energy of his brief reign. The policy of Julian toward Christianity was one of complete toleration, looking more for its extinction by internal dissensions than by outward persecution. From this a sole exception seems to have been made of Athanasius, who after a brief return to his see was again banished, with a threat of something worse if he should attempt to return. Julian however was killed in a campaign against the Persians in the summer of 363, and was succeeded by the Christian and orthodox Emperor Jovian, who not only immediately restored Athanasius but personally applied to him for the correct statement of the catholic faith. This, after convening a council in Alexandria, Athanasius conveyed to him in person in the form of a synodal letter, in which " the Nicene Creed was embodied, its scripturalness asserted and the great majority of churches (including the British) referred to as professing it; Arianism was condemned, Semi-Arianism (Homoiousianism) pronounced inadequate; the homoöusion explained as expressive of Christ's real Sonship; the coequality of the Holy Spirit maintained, in terms which partly anticipate the language of the creed of Constantinople."

This promised to be the end of the long series of troubles, but in 364 Jovian died and under his successors, Valentinian and Valens, the East fell to the latter, who soon gave evidence of a repetition of the policy of Constantius. Athanasius in the spring of 365 made another of those sudden and narrow escapes from violence to his person which were so frequent in his career, and was for some time in concealment. He was however soon restored and spent the remainder of his life, until 373, in the administration of his diocese, in advising in matters of general ecclesiastical policy, and in writing his masterly defences of the Nicene faith.

This rapid and brief sketch of the efforts of Arianism to overthrow the work of the Council of Nicæa by the destruction of its leaders and especially of the great Athanasius gives but a faint conception either of the desperate persistence of Arianism in its determination to possess the world, or of the superhuman endurance and matchless ability of Athanasius in withstanding and defeating it. To him it was given to render the most splendid and successful service in the noblest and holiest cause the world has ever known.

While its alliance with the empire was enabling Arianism to pursue its policy of outward violence, there were changes going on within it that were preparing the way for its own speedy disintegration and destruction. It may be readily supposed that after the death of Constantine the Great and under Constantius it did not continue long to veil itself under the orthodox conservatism in the name of which many of its earlier crimes were committed; or even under the Semi-Arianism, which though apparently nearer to it was really much more akin to Nicenism, from which as Athanasius himself said it

Disintegration of Arianism. 159

dissented more on verbal than on real grounds. Arianism proper soon separated itself and came out in its true colors under such men as Aëtius and Eunomius, who scouting alike the homoöusion and the homoiousion boldly set up against them the symbol of the heteroöusion. They frankly admitted that there was no middle ground between an absolute sameness of essence and nature in the Father and the Son and an absolute difference. Between the divine and any, no matter how exalted, created nature there was an infinite distance quite as far from "likeness" as from "sameness." In a series of councils Arianism proper gradually diverged from all half-way positions, and under the titles Eunomians (from their leader), Anomœans (ἀνόμοιον), Heteroöusiasts (ἑτεροόυσιον), etc., openly avowed the non-divinity of the Son of God.

Under this process it became progressively apparent to the great mass of conservatives, Semi-Arians and other more or less orthodox dissenters from the Nicene definitions that there was indeed no middle ground for them; that like the dove without the ark they had been hovering over the face of the deep looking in vain for some other rest to the sole of their feet, and none other existed. The moderation of Athanasius in dealing with the Semi-Arians combined with his sublime and unshaken confidence in the truth and final triumph of the Nicene faith must have had no little to do with the final absorption of the great mass of them into the body of the church. When they began at last to appreciate the true nature and outcome of Arianism and to be perplexed by their own position, Athanasius wrote of them as "brothers who mean essentially what churchmen mean. He will not for the present urge the homoöusion upon them. He is sure that in time they will accept it as securing that doctrine of Christ's essential Sonship which their own symbol, homoiousion, could not adequately guard. But while exhibiting this large-minded patience and forbearance he is careful to contrast the long series of Arian, Semi-Arian and conservative creeds with the one invariable standard of the orthodox; the only refuge from restless variations will be found in the frank adoption of the creed of Nicæa." His confidence was justified and his hope realized in the now rapidly approaching collapse of Arianism, and the general gathering in of the long-distracted flock into the Nicene fold.

The explanation then of the protracted Arian agitation of the fourth century, divested of its purely human selfish and political elements and considered only in so far as it was religious, may be stated as follows. It included within itself every possible shade of dissatisfaction with the positive and scientific definitions of the Council of Nicæa, from the mere conservative reluctance to exclude by such definition at all to the most real and radical Arian opposition to the truth defined, viz., that of the divinity of the Son of God.

In the course of the agitation the mind of the church was effectually aroused and quickened and every resource of thought and language was tested in every direction to discover some more perfect or less imperfect mode of expressing and explaining the truth of the Scriptures and of the church with regard to the person of Jesus Christ. The result of over fifty years of criticism and experiment, of hesitation, doubt and distraction, brought the church around before the Second General Council to the acceptance after the fullest reflection of just what, before reflection at the suggestion and by the guidance of a few great souls, it had instinctively and intuitively seen to be the truth at the first.

CHAPTER VIII.

THE FIRST GENERAL COUNCIL OF CONSTANTINOPLE.

THE reign of Theodosius the Great was scarcely less opportune and decisive for Christianity than that of Constantine the Great. It gave in the Second Ecumenical Council the opportunity just when it was needed for gathering in the results of the long discussion that succeeded the First. Constantinople closes the Arian controversy only in the sense of reaping the conclusions and giving final shape to the decisions which the logic of fifty years of experiment had practically already brought to a determination. The later council appears peaceful and tame in comparison with the earlier, because the hostile forces just gathered in all their freshness and might at the one were spent and dead at the other. Its conclusions were all foregone; the easy displacement everywhere of Arianism by Nicene orthodoxy was accomplished without serious disturbance, because Arianism was exhausted and ready to pass away, while Athanasianism had but attained its strength by wrestling and was prepared to enter upon and run its course.

We have seen how long Athanasius stood almost

alone in the theological defence of the great doctrine of the Trinity, whose scientific statement was to be the outcome of his labors and sufferings and which was forever after to be associated most closely with his name. But through him and the exigencies of the times there was arising a great school of theologians hardly inferior to himself, in whose hands his work was to attain almost complete and final perfection. Not to mention Hilary of Poictiers in the West, in the East the three great Cappadocian bishops, Gregory of Nazianzus, Basil, and Gregory of Nyssa, were all born about or not long after the date of the Council of Nicæa, and had added their labors to those of Athanasius before that of Constantinople.

In an important point the scientific statement of the doctrine of the Trinity was left incomplete in the mind of Athanasius and in the definition of Nicæa. It will be remembered that in the discussions of that definition the brunt of controversy had fallen upon the word "ousia"; was the Son of God in the relation of his nature to that of the Father homoöusios or homoiousios, or heteroöusios, of the same or similar or other and dissimilar essence or substance? The point so far not only attained in thought but also reduced to successful expression in the homoöusion was the essential and real divinity of the Son of God. In all the discussions the fact also of a personal distinction, and an eternal distinction, between Father and Son had been equally insisted upon and was no doubt involved or implied in the language of the Nicene Creed. But it had not been expressed in any definite single term which had commended itself to all or most of the Nicene theologians, or to the mind of Athanasius himself, as exactly designating the place of the distinction, as "ousia" did that of the identity. It was finally agreed that in the Godhead there was one ousia, but there were three hypostases; the first of these terms was already fixed but the second was not, nor any equivalent for it. It was the Gregories and Basil who mainly effected the determination and separation of the term "hypostasis" to this specific sense and fixed it in the use of the church. The thing expressed by it is vastly more delicate and difficult to be understood or expressed than the meaning of the other term, "ousia." The theologians of the fourth century, while feeling the necessity of a word designating the distinctions in the Godhead and exhausting the resources of the Greek language to find one, would never have consented to the use of a term so strong as our English one "person," which requires the most careful guarding and explanation not to express too much. The distinctions in the Trinity are indeed essentially personal and in one sense no other term will properly express them; for in Father, Son and Holy Ghost just what we recognize in each is a subject of living activities who must of necessity be discriminated from the others and who bears relations to the others, and this is just what we mean by a person. But the different personal subjects within the Godhead ought not even remotely to be compared, which our use of the term "persons" almost compels, with such differences and distinctions as exist between men who are not only wholly distinct but wholly separate and apart from one another. From this false impression by association the Greek hypostasis was free, and yet even with that advantage the tripersonality was in danger of running into a tritheism, to which we are vastly more liable.

Thus in the East " hypostasis " was gradually becoming the term expressive of personal distinction, in competition however with the other term *prosopon*, the equivalent of the Latin *persona*. In the West *persona* was preferred, while *substantia*, the exact etymological equivalent of " hypostasis," was used in the other sense, of " ousia," essence or substance. In this confusion and conflict of expressions there was of course much friction and misunderstanding among those who were at bottom agreed. But as time went on and it was made more and more apparent that among the orthodox it was simply a question of the meaning of words and not any difference in the understanding of things, it was peacefully and tacitly agreed that in Greek and in Latin the one truth should be expressed as best it might, in the terms that were least insufficient and misleading. It is however unfortunate that the Westerns should be limited, if they were so, first to the term " substance " for " ousia," which goes the furthest toward imparting material conceptions into the notion of the divine nature, and afterward to the term " persons " for " hypostases," which implies popularly at least the widest not merely distinction but separation between the three persons in the one divine substance.

Although we have already, perhaps at too great length, anticipated it, it will be necessary in order to indicate the additional length or depth to which Trinitarian speculation was carried by the great theological school of this period, to review the course of Trinitarian thought up to this point. This course has been on the whole an a posteriori one, a reasoning back from the facts of the incarnation, through those of nature and creation, to the essential and internal nature of God himself. The original impulse began with the religious and practical necessity of recognizing the real divinity of the Son of God, incarnate in Jesus Christ, as afterward of the Holy Ghost, incorporate in the church; and yet at the same time of personally distinguishing these from each other and from the Father,—that is to say, distinguishing them as different divine subjects with whom we deal personally, and who deal personally with one another, in their several offices and functions. This was at once the scriptural representation, and a representation necessitated by the practical and devotional life and worship of the church. "Baptism doth represent unto us our profession," and baptism brings us into a spiritual and personal relation of unity and fellowship with "the Father and the Son and the Holy Ghost." From this baptismal formula grew up all the church confessions and the general creeds, every one of which involved the threefold personal relation; and so the threefold personal distinction was wrought from the first into the mind of every individual believer, as it was the confession of every congregation and the common faith of the whole church. The church was never for one instant in danger of losing the sense of the absolute unity of God; yet to it the Son and the Holy Ghost were as truly God as the

Father, while it could never be said of either of them that he was the Father.

In the second place we saw how immediately the church passed back from the Christological to the cosmological significance of our Lord. He was the head not only of humanity but of creation, the end and final cause of nature as well as of grace. Now as in the incarnation so in the creation the rational, ideating, creative principle and cause of the world, that which is manifest in phenomena, cannot be anything else than God ($\theta\epsilon\grave{o}\varsigma$) and yet it is not God ($\acute{o}\ \theta\epsilon\acute{o}\varsigma$). That is to say, it is not the divine ousia but the divine Logos which is revealed in creation. Just as it is not a man's being but his thought or mind or will which is expressed in those productions of his which are from him but are distinguished from himself; only with this difference, that while in man's productions the objectified thought or will becomes separated and ceases to be living and personal, that of God can never be so but is always personal and himself, though it may need equally to be distinguished from himself.

That the Trinitarian movement was a more or less conscious or unconscious solution of the truth which lay just half-way between deism and pantheism may be illustrated historically as well as speculatively. The principle underlying pantheism may be described as "substantiality," that of deism as "creationism." According to the former all being or existence is of the substance of God, an evolution or extension of himself; according to the latter it is not of the being but of the bare will or word of God. The one sees the world only in God and God only in the world.

To the other, the world and God are wholly not only distinct but separate one from the other. Now the bare statement of the facts makes it apparent that as the earlier development of Christianity was between the deism of Ebionism and the Gnostic pantheism of Docetism, so its progress in the period we are considering lies between Arianism and Sabellianism, which are to a certain extent their successors on opposite sides of the truth. On the one hand Arianism represents the barest and baldest creationism; it not only puts the world outside of God, but separates it the furthest possible from him by making it the creation of a creature. On the other side Sabellianism, in its original form and in its revival by Marcellus, through the denial of essential and eternal distinctions in God, is constantly running into the pantheistic extreme of confounding God himself with the world. God who is eternally and essentially one and without distinctions *becomes* three in the economy of creation and incarnation. But the Son, for example, who is manifested in these divine acts is only a different manifestation of the one divine person and is really identical with the Father. So that it is the Godhead, and not the Logos or Son of God only, who is revealed in creation and incarnate in Christ. Now Trinitarian theism, as developed in the theology of the period, not only avoided the error of either extreme but was able to hold and to do full justice to the truth of each. It fully holds the truth of creationism as against the pantheistic error of substantiality. All works of God, like creation and redemption, are in a true sense outside of him and must be distinguished from him; they are revelations or manifestations not of his ousia or being but of his Logos or objective self-expression; not of himself but of his personal wisdom and power and love. On the other hand, the world is not in the Arian sense outside of God and God outside of it, but each is, in a truer sense than the Sabellian or pantheistic one, in the other. For though the Logos who is the inner and ideal truth and reality of both creation and redemption is not ὁ θεός, he is θεός. By which is meant that while he is not also Father and Holy Ghost, he is nevertheless not apart from them, but in indissoluble union with them is the one only and living God; he is not, after human analogies, the separated and impersonal, but the living, personal and inseparable wisdom, will and Word of God.

If however Trinitarian theology had not gone back further even than these Christological and cosmological evidences and illustrations of its truth, it would have left the inner personal distinctions in the Godhead a matter not of necessity to the being of God himself, but only necessary to the existence of such objective activities as those which we designate creation and redemption. In other words the distinctions of the Trinity would be relative not to God in himself, but only to the outward activities of God in those things which are not himself. Athanasius and the theologians after him fully realized this, and already opened up that rich and endless field of philosophical as well as theological speculation which since then has so abundantly demonstrated the fact that the personal distinctions within the Godhead, which the church as best it may has formulated in the doctrine of the Trinity, are necessary not only as a basis of true relations of God to his works of creation and redemption, but as a condition of his own being. God as bare simplicity and homogeneity, as unity without differentiation or distinction, cannot be thought as being or doing anything at all. If God is in himself a living God, and does not merely come to life and activity in the external world; if within himself, and not for the first time in it or in relation to it, he possesses reason, intelligence, affection, will and energy,—then we must say that those distinctions which through the world and ourselves we recognize and call the Trinity must have existed before ourselves and the world; for without them God could not have been himself, and could not have created the world and us. All the fathers whom we are now considering express, with the illustrations which are still in use, the fact that if God is bare unity and absoluteness we cannot predicate of him wisdom or knowledge, love, will or action. If we cannot think of him otherwise than as eternally all these, then there is in him from eternity that ground of personal distinctions which is the condition of his being what he is in himself, as well as of his doing what he does in the world.

The connection of these reflections with the Council of Constantinople is this: as we have said, the interest and value of that council lies not so much in what it accomplished itself—though that was something—as in what it indicated and represented. We may say that the Council of Constantinople swept up together and removed the debris of the controversy inaugurated by that of Nicæa. When we speak of Arianism being swept away by it, we do not of course mean that this was literally and universally so. There was no little life and survival still to be found in it in spots, and it long continued to exhibit vigor and vitality among the Gothic nations Christianized and civilized by the great Arian missionary and bishop Ulfilas. But if we look not at the actual, in themselves less interesting and valuable, details of the council but at the changes intellectual and spiritual which had taken place since the Council of Nicæa and which it was to sum up and measure, we shall find that what had taken place was the thinking out and formulating of a great religious and theological philosophy, before which Arianism was destined to evaporate like the dew before the sun. The fact is, its political and other external alliances had given to Arianism a strength and importance of which it was wholly devoid in itself. Its religious deficiencies and weakness were not more fatal than its utter lack of any rational or philosophical truth or probability. Its use was only to provoke and arouse the genuine Christian thought and investigation and expression which has become the permanent possession of the church and which with all its inevitable, and from the first acknowledged, deficiencies and imperfections is the most valuable contribution that any age has made, or probably will ever make, to either practical religion or religious science and philosophy.

We saw how the period of the Nicene Council had so flooded the church with politics, worldliness and selfish and partisan ambition that one who goes into the details of the subsequent controversies finds it hard to discover in them or under them any real movement and progress of genuine religious and Christian thought and life. And yet out of that confusion and strife emerged the scientific and final formulation of the essential principle of true Christianity, the real deity of the incarnate Son of God. An Athanasius cannot be an isolated and disconnected phenomenon. Behind him and a few others like him, and visible only through them, was a great underlying mass of living, loving and suffering Christian faith and life. They were but the organs or instruments by which it wrought out its faith and life into knowledge and expression.

So again, when, upon the accession of Theodosius, Arianism had run its course and worked out its own condemnation; and Semi-Arianism found itself suspended over a void with no place of compromise between Arian denial and Athanasian confession of the Son of God; and conservatives were beginning to flock back like doves to the ark which, as they had discovered, offered the only resting-place for the sole of their feet; and finally when the emperor himself began his long and strong reign by summoning the church and the world back to Nicenism and orthodoxy, it is not strange that, with instinctive presentiment of the inevitable, a current should set in toward the church which should bring in with it many whose return was actuated by no deep Christian principle. There is certainly more than enough to disgust and repel one who looks only upon the surface of the events as they were now to follow. The greatest soul connected with the Council of Constantinople, with a courage and manhood that suffers by comparison with Athanasius the Great, withdrew from it and from the patriarchate of Constantinople, with a noble lament for the degeneracy of the times and the hopeless selfishness and disorder of the church, to seek refuge and salvation for himself in the privacy of his ancestral village and home. But that there was a Gregory of Nazianzus there and a Gregory of Nyssa by his side—Basil, the strongest spirit of the three, was dead—gives assurance that there was much more. And even under the strife and confusion of the human passion and littleness that disgusted them they might have read more clearly than they did the triumph and acceptance of the principles of Christian theology and philosophy for which they, like Athanasius before them, had so patiently labored and studied and suffered.

We might indeed be disheartened and perplexed by any narration of the public fortunes of Christianity at this period, as indeed at almost any period; but let one go deeper and familiarize himself with the thoughts and lives, the self-denials and sacrifices, the studies, the intellectual and spiritual attainments and achievements of the Basils and Gregories of this time; let him reflect that Gregory Nazianzen spent ten years, from twenty to thirty, studying philosophy in Athens in preparation for his lifelong devotion to theology, and that Basil his fellow-student was not his inferior; let him remember that there must have been a soil out of which such men grew, and but learn the names of the mothers and sisters and friends at home who nurtured and influenced and stimulated and encouraged them,—and however one may blush or smile at the abundant folly and weakness that appears upon the surface it will be impossible to doubt or ignore the continuous presence and grace of God and the living power of Christianity in the church. There is abundant proof in contemporary literature that while the bishops were being swayed here and there by political and worldly considerations; or what was much more common by their own indecision, and vacillation with regard to issues and questions upon which they were compelled and yet were not prepared to take sides; the great body of the faithful permitted to live in peace and leave thought and speculation alone were actually living lives of as deep and sincere Christian faith, devotion and charity as have characterized any age of the church. Of the heads of the church, scarce given between councils and conferences time to say their prayers or leisure to learn their own minds, Hilary might write as he did: "Since the Nicene Council we have done nothing but write the creed. While we fight about words, inquire about novelties, take advantage of ambiguities, criticise authors, fight on party questions, have difficulties in agreeing, and prepare to anathematize one another, there is scarcely a man who belongs to Christ. First we have the creed which bids us not use the Nicene consubstantial (homoöusion); then comes another which decrees and preaches it; next, the third excuses the word 'substance' as adopted by the fathers in their simplicity; lastly the fourth which, instead of excusing, condemns. We determine creeds by the year or by the month, we change our determinations, we prohibit our changes, we anathematize our prohibitions. Thus we either condemn others in our own persons, or ourselves in the instance of others, and while we bite and devour one another, are like to be consumed one of another." And yet even among these warring bishops there was a St. Hilary who took his part, and where there was one there were more; and let any one read the life and writings of St. Hilary and ask himself whether he belonged to Christ. It is only God who knows how many even among the bishops had not bowed the knee to the Baal of imperial patronage or pressure but remained true in their hearts to the faith and life of the gospel of Christ. On the other hand, with regard to the simple faithful lay people, Basil could write as follows of the attempt to impose Arianism upon them in Asia Minor—and yet stronger pictures are drawn of the condition of things in Egypt and elsewhere: "Matters are come to this pass: the people have left their houses of prayer and assemble in deserts,—a pitiable sight; women and children and old men, and men otherwise infirm, wretchedly faring in the open air, amid the most profuse rains and snow-storms and winds and frosts of winter; and again in summer under a scorching sun. To this they submit because they will have no part in the wicked Arian leaven." Again: "Only one offence is now vigorously punished,—an accurate observance of our fathers' traditions. For this cause the pious are driven from their countries and transported into deserts. The people are in lamentation, in continual tears at home and abroad. There is a cry in the city, a cry in the country, in the roads, in the deserts. Joy and spiritual cheerfulness are no more; our feasts are turned into mourning, our houses of prayer are shut up, our altars deprived of the spiritual worship." All this is not the description of a worldly and irreligious population.

To illustrate by particular instances, Gregory Nazianzen had a Nonna for his mother, as Augustine a Monica. Let us select almost at random among the holy women, the mothers and sisters and wives of that age, the example of the wise counsellor and guide in his youth of the great Basil. Gregory Nazianzen and Basil had spent many years together in the universities of Athens, and on their return rose at once to great repute in their respective homes. Gregory indeed repudiates the idea of either his friend or himself having been seriously influenced by ambition or love of praise; "but Basil's excellent sister, Macrina" —we are told on good authority—"judged him less indulgently and more truly. She found him on his return from Athens inordinately elated, puffed up with the pride of philosophy and science, and looking down with contempt on his superiors in dignity and rank. He had put on the airs and habits of a fine gentleman, and without being stained with the vices of the city was not altogether insensible to its pleasures. It was a period of some peril to the young and ardent rhetorician, the object of universal admiration. Macrina proved his good genius. Her warnings and counsels saved him from the seductions of the world. Basil describes himself at this period as one awaked out of a deep sleep, and in the marvellous light of gospel truth discovering the folly of that wisdom of this world in the study of which nearly all his youth had vanished." Such glimpses behind the scenes, from what was going on upon the public stage to what was hidden from sight in the secrecy of private Christian homes, are necessary at once to console us for the intrigues and violence of Christian partisans and politicians and to account for the presence and rise in their midst of Christian scholars, theologians and saints than whom no other age has known more or greater.

We have seen that the purpose and result of the Council of Constantinople was simply to disestablish Arianism and restore Nicenism. Its first canon ratifies the Nicene Creed in its original form, and anathematizes the several different degrees, on either side, of Arianism and Sabellianism; and besides these another heresy, which as pertaining to our Lord's humanity and not his divinity forms not like them the subject-matter of previous ones, but the transition to a new controversy, viz., Apollinarianism, which will next demand our attention.

It has usually been accepted without question that what we possess as the Nicene Creed, or what is often called for greater exactness the Niceno-Constantinopolitan Creed, is the creed of Nicæa with the addition at Constantinople of the fuller sections upon the person and office of the Holy Ghost. But even leaving out these (and of course the later Filioque clause), our so-called Nicene Creed has so many, inconsiderable as well as considerable, divergencies from the real Nicene confession of faith that it may well merit more consideration than we can give it here. For one thing, no little importance had been attached not only to the ὁμοούσιον but to the ἐκ τῆς οὐσίας of the original form. If the first expressed the oneness of essence or substance against Arianism, the second was thought to declare the distinction of persons against Sabellianism. But the second has been left out, and it is somewhat unaccountable not only why this but why certain other and more indifferent changes should have been made. On the other hand the clause "God of God" or "God from God" is inserted, which was not in the original; and it may well be claimed that the gain of this phrase quite counterbalances the loss of the other, for it just as well expresses distinction from, along with oneness with, the Father. But there seems to be not only no reason given why these changes should be made, but no proof that they were made by this council, and the explanation of them has yet to be discovered.

With regard to the additions which the council did make, the question which had arisen under the name of Macedonius was not, as we might now suppose, as to the separate personality but as to the real divinity of the Holy Ghost. The Macedonians were only a sect of Arians applying to the Third Person of the Trinity the same irrational and irreligious speculations which had been applied to the Second. They held the Holy Ghost, as they held the Son, to be a creature, of different and inferior nature from the Father. There is no real issue involved in the discussion which has not been already considered and we need not devote further consideration to the heresy.

As to the practical legislation of the council bearing upon the organization and government of the church, the famous canon providing that " the bishop of Constantinople shall hold the first rank after the bishop of Rome, because Constantinople is New Rome," was probably directed primarily against the repeated and recent interferences and meddlings of the older patriarchates of Alexandria and Antioch with the affairs of Constantinople. The effect was rapidly to make Constantinople in the East almost what Rome had been without competition or question in the West. The bearing of the canon upon the question of the ground and nature of the supremacy of Rome, making it political rather than ecclesiastical, as also that of the equally well-known canon of Sardica, providing for certain appeals to Rome, does not concern our present purpose and has been abundantly dealt with by others.

CHAPTER IX.

APOLLINARIANISM

AMONG Catholics and heretics, among anathematizers and anathematized, prominent in the Council of Constantinople or made prominent by it, we discovered one thinker who had passed through and beyond the Trinitarian controversies of the fourth century, and was already busy with all the Christological problems of the fifth. Apollinaris, or Apollinarius, bishop of Laodicea, was at once among the most literary and scholarly men and among the most acute and profound theologians of that great age. He was thoroughly in accord with all the catholic results of the first two general councils, an Athanasian of the Athanasians; and his mind ran on naturally, though perhaps prematurely and too hastily as we shall see, to the application of Trinitarian principles to the question of the divine-human personality of Jesus Christ. That is to say, he was the first to carry the theological discussions of the fourth century on into the Christological ones of the fifth.

Jesus Christ being divine, in the sense now once for all determined, in what sense and how could he be also and at the same time human? There had been those, though not many even so late as the third century, who had held that our Lord was primarily human and only secondarily divine; that is, he was a man essentially like other men who became or was made divine through the union of God with him. He was ἔνθεος ἄνθρωπος, a man filled with God; which might mean either filled with the impersonal influence or grace, the wisdom, goodness and power of God; or that the personal Logos, or perhaps Spirit, of God was in a peculiar sense united with him and made him the organ of his personal self-revelation and operation in the world. According to the first view, our Lord was one person and that a human person; it was only his life and character and conduct which by the grace of God in him were divine; *he* was a man. According to the second view, he was necessarily two persons in one; he was (1) the particular man or human person with whom the divine Person had entered into union, and (2) he was the divine Person of whom the other was only the human organ or medium of self-revelation and communication.

Now after the Nicene Council and its thorough confirmation in the Constantinopolitan, no one who was in any sort of union or sympathy with the mind of the church could hold any view of the primary humanity of Christ. The person of our Lord, in perfect harmony with his own self-consciousness and with the scriptural conception and representation of him, had in the mind of the church assumed such a universal, theological and cosmological as well as human significance, that it was impossible to regard him otherwise than as primarily a divine Person. He was not a man who had received God into himself but God who had taken man into himself, not a man who had become God but God who had become man.

Of this primary deity and only secondary humanity of the Lord the victorious Nicene theology was full; and no one more so than Apollinaris. Now it will be readily seen that at such a moment it would be impossible at once, at least from the Athanasian side, to render to the humanity all that was due to it, to enter fully into all the significance of the function of the human side in the joint divine and human process of salvation. And yet it was necessary that the human part as well as the divine should be recognized, and recognized in all its totality. Salvation is a divine act; it is primarily a divine act. That God redeems, sanctifies and spiritually completes is as essential a part of his divine ἐνέργεια in the universe as that he creates. Indeed it is the same, it is that higher spiritual creation in which he completes and reveals the natural, and explains, vindicates and justifies all his works. The incarnation of the Logos in the spiritual redemption and glorification of personal humanity is only the continuation and interpretation of his whole cosmical and natural activity in the inanimate, irrational and impersonal creation. Through the evolution of the universe God comes to himself in man; there is no lower selfhood or personality in which he could manifest himself personally. Fulfilling himself through all, he only fulfils himself in that in which it is possible for him to be himself. For God is essentially not substance or force or energy; all these he could be in an impersonal and inanimate world. He is reason, freedom, love and personality, and all these he could become only in a world of reasonable, free and loving persons, who are his children and in whom he reproduces and fulfils himself. All this will one day be a scientific fact as well as a religious truth,—in the day when all the things of the spirit shall become verifiable facts of observation and experience, objects of sight and not only intuitions of faith. Then it shall be seen that the ultimate truth of universal evolution is that the natural is completed in the spiritual; that God through all nature comes to himself in man—not the man who is but a part, though the highest part, of nature, but the man who is also the incarnation of personal Godhead. In Christ the church sees indeed a man, but not only a man; it sees all men and the whole creation taken up into and made one with God, through God's own fulfilling himself in them. When Christ is complete, the teaching of Christianity is that God will be all in all, and all will be in God, and yet not cease to be itself but only truly begin to be itself in him. But God does not fulfil himself in nature through violation of the uniformity or limitation of the universality of nature's own laws. He fulfils himself in it and not in suspensions or contradictions of it. And in humanity as a whole God will incarnate himself in the redemption, sanctification and exaltation of itself, and not merely in activities in or through it which are not itself. So precisely in our Lord, the end of the divinity in the humanity is not to take its place and do something instead of it; it is simply to supply the conditions and impart the means by which it shall completely and perfectly become itself. The divinity of Jesus Christ is seen in the realization and reality of the humanity in which it is incarnate, and not in the displacement of it or the substitution of something else for it.

This side of the truth of Christ is what Apollinaris ignored. In his view the humanity of our Lord wholly disappears in his deity; or rather it never truly appears, nor plays any essential part in the drama of the incarnation. There is an infinite significance in what God is and does in the visibility of his humanity, but none whatever in what humanity does and becomes in the person of Jesus Christ.

Passing by however for the present what was lacking in the system of Apollinaris, let us look at what there was in it of truth and of permanent value for the knowledge of the person of Christ. Apollinaris saw first and saw with no little depth and penetration that the incarnation so far from being an unnatural or irrational thought was the very truth of both nature and reason. He who was from eternity the divine thought and will and purpose of the creation, and of its personal and spiritual culmination in man who was to be the end and fulfilment at once of it and of himself, was from eternity predestined to incarnation. What was the Logos in the universe but the ideation of man, what was man but the actualization of the Logos? The Logos was eternal humanity, the eternal idea of humanity which was to be actualized in time through the creation. The true end and destiny of man is to be that which the Logos will become when he shall through the creation have actualized himself in time. The Logos and man are then the eternal and the temporal of one and the same thing; the Logos is man, the eternal of him; and man is the Logos, the temporal of him. So that each in becoming the other is only becoming himself; the eternal Logos temporally in and through creation realizes or becomes himself in man; and man who temporally realizes the Logos in himself eternally realizes or becomes himself in the Logos. The incarnation is accidentally, because of the fact of sin and the fall, human redemption; it is essentially, and would be if there were no sin or fall, human and cosmical completion; because humanity and the whole creation in it is complete only as it realizes its divine idea and law, which is that through incarnation the eternal personal Logos shall realize or become anew himself in it. What was to be accomplished for and in all men through the generic incarnation of the Logos, through the whole of creation and in the whole of humanity, could only be so by means of his particular incarnation in the individual person of Jesus Christ. For Christ is not only individual but generic man. He is not only a man but all men, who are to be included in him in the church which is the body of the incarnation and in which the Logos is to realize or anew become himself. Apollinaris in this way teaches the eternal humanity of the Son of God, as also therefore, in idea at least, the eternal divinity of man; and so the eternal predestination and preconstitution of the Logos and man to become one in the incarnate Son, both God and man.

The great and comprehensive truth contained in this representation might have been carried out with substantial orthodoxy and with no little gain to the theology that preceded it, if it had been within the grasp of a single mind, and that the first to deal scientifically with the most difficult of problems, to see all the sides and provide for all the interests involved. That God must become man, must personally realize or become anew himself in the highest of his creatures, from the very nature and necessity of the divine Word to become that which it means, to actualize itself in that of which it is the idea, was a great thought. What he needed next to see and to say was that God can be or can fulfil himself in anything or in any person only in the own being and self-fulfilment of the thing or the person. He cannot be in it to efface or destroy it, to make it not itself or save it from the necessity of being or becoming its own self. He cannot be in nature to make it not nature, or in man to make him not man. It is perfectly true that man can only fulfil or become himself as he fulfils the Logos, and that he can only do so as the Logos fulfils him by fulfilling or becoming himself in him. But the self-realization of the divine Logos in man must not be at the cost or at any diminution or detriment of the part which man must take in realizing the Logos, for it is in this that he realizes and becomes himself. In other words the divinity must not be at the expense of the humanity in a process the end of which is that the divine Word is to accomplish itself in the highest being or becoming of man. The incarnation must be the supreme deed and attainment of humanity as well as of deity. Man in it must become his completest, highest and fullest self. If on the contrary God is to take the place of him or of any part of him, if he is to be to him in any way instead of himself, or to spare him any trouble or pain of being himself or himself becoming himself, then the incarnation is no true human redemption and completion, for God is in him to his hurt and not help, to his diminution and not increase. It is as necessary that the man himself and all the man shall be in the incarnation as that God shall be in it. And that is what the church fathers did not yet fully see, though they implicitly held it and in terms asserted it and instinctively as in the case of Apollinaris condemned and rejected any denial of it. It is easy to realize as they did that in Christ we are in God—in the divine atonement, redemption and eternal life—to accept his part in the total and consummated results which he has wrought in our nature, without equally realizing the significance and necessity of the human part, in a realized and actual spiritual freedom and life of ourselves in God. And in Jesus Christ what that age—like our own—needed most to see in him, because it saw it least, was not the divine fact of God incarnate but the human fact of man redeemed, humanity free from sin and alive from death. And if in him we see not only the freedom but the redemption, or becoming free, and not only the life but the resurrection or making alive of humanity—then the humanity he assumed, to redeem and raise from the dead, was that which needed to find in him its freedom and life.

It is beside our purpose as it would be impossible in so brief a space to give an outline of the system of Apollinaris which should at once expose its defects and errors and do justice to its depth and truth. Our aim is not an historical exposition of successive theological or Christological systems, but only the illustration through them of the principles which entered successively into the constitution and evolution of the true doctrine of the person of Christ. Apollinaris was one and perhaps the greatest of those who taught an incomplete humanity of our Lord, and who must be ranked on the Docetic side of the truth of Christology. It would not however be as just as it might seem to dismiss him with the charge of teaching that the Logos assumed in his human birth only a natural body and animal soul, while the place of that higher part in us which we call the spirit was supplied by himself, and that therefore our Lord had no truly human rational and spiritual nature. For we must remember that he held that the Logos was himself human, that he was the eternal higher or spiritual truth or side of humanity, who in order to become like us and as one of us needed only to assume the material or natural of which he was already the supernatural or spiritual. From his point of view he could claim to hold the very completest and fullest humanity of our Lord, because he held him to be the heavenly and divine fulness and completeness of it. He was the eternal humanity who only needed to take to himself the lower accidents of our material and mundane condition in order to become like us, and by redeeming us from these make us like himself. If then he assumed not all but only some and the lower elements of a human nature in his birth into the world, it was because he already possessed or rather was in himself its highest element, and only needed these lower ones in order to enter into our temporal and earthly condition.

We may not perhaps then be able to say that the Christ of Apollinaris was not a true and complete man in all the actual as well as ideal truth of human nature, but the objection which may not lie here lies elsewhere with equal force. To the Docetism which in whole or in part impairs the completeness and reality of our Lord's human nature and life, we say: Of what use or interest is it to us, beyond that of a mere exhibition or external representation, that God and not man, that God under a semblance of humanity should present to us a spectacle of human victory over sin and sorrow and death? What we want is not a divine ideal but a human actuality of these things. We want to see ourselves who groan under the bondage of sin and death free from sin and alive from death. Show us this in Christ and we will see in him a real, because our own, redemption and resurrection. We believe in a divine redemption but only in one that exhibits itself in an actual human freedom. We believe that in Christ God redeems, but only because we see in Christ, in Christ's own sinlessness and holiness, that man is free. And man can be only freely free; it must be the freedom of himself, of his own will and his whole self. It must be himself fulfilling God's will as well as God's will fulfilling itself in him. Jesus Christ is redemption both active and passive. He is divine redemption manifested in human redemption, God's freeing revealed in man's freedom. If Jesus Christ were not as man free from sin and risen from the dead, we should not accept him as God freeing from sin and raising from the dead. The cause is seen only in the effect, and the effect exists only in the cause.

Now Apollinaris, appreciating the Christian demand that the incarnate Son of God must be really and completely human, makes him so indeed in a sense which in terms cannot be denied. The person and personal life of Jesus are certainly in the highest sense human, but it is only because the divine Logos is himself eternally, and independently of his incarnation, human. And what humanity is this of his which is so holy and living and divine? It is only one which was so before, which is inherently and essentially and necessarily so and never had been or could be otherwise. What redemption then has he wrought, what sanctification imparted, what glorification accomplished? The holiness, the life of Jesus, what was it but the mere display of the perfections if not of God only, yet of a divine, ideal, eternal humanity—very different from that which the Son of God came to seek and save, to sanctify from sin and raise up out of death. No, what we want and what we find in the holiness and the life of

Jesus is not that of a divine humanity which knows nothing of sin and death, but that of our own earthly poor and sinful humanity which he stooped to lift out of the mire and the grave and infinitely to quicken and enrich with himself. And as he took nothing other than ourselves, so he has not exalted us at the expense or cost of ourselves. As our whole humanity was present and acted in him, arose and walked, believed and lived, obeyed and was holy, put off itself and put on God, arose from the dead and ascended up into heaven, so in losing we but find ourselves in him; he in no sense or measure takes the place of ourselves, but himself becomes our true selves and fulfils us in fulfilling himself in us.

The difficulty with Apollinaris as with most Christians now is that he was so concerned that our Lord should be God that he was not sufficiently willing he should be man. Under the shadow of a great and valuable truth he contrives that he shall be man without the humiliation of becoming the man which nevertheless divine love came into this world to be and was. He brought his human holiness along with him when he came; as many of us fancy that the Holy Ghost was sent before mechanically and miraculously to prepare it for him in our flesh before he came, lest he should be contaminated by contact with human unholiness—not knowing that he came himself to take our unholiness and make us holy, to take upon him our defilement and make us clean. Not of course to take it in himself, but upon himself; he took our sin and death upon him in assuming our flesh; he redeemed us from sin and death in his crucifixion of the sin and resurrection from the death of our flesh.

A reference to the origin and motive of Apollinarianism will throw additional light upon the matter. Apollinaris developed his system in opposition partly to the Arianism that preceded and partly to the Nestorianism that was to succeed him and that in principle though not yet in historical form was already beginning to appear. In opposing Arianism on one side Apollinaris fell unconsciously into its error on the other. To Arius, in the first place, our Lord was the incarnation of a superhuman but not a divine person, and secondly he was incarnate in not a real humanity; his whole earthly activity was that of the superhuman and not of a human being. Apollinaris antagonizing the first of these positions fell himself into the second. He demonstrates the natural necessity of an incarnation of the divine Logos or Son himself; but he conceives his incarnation in a humanity not a whit more actual or real than that of Arius. The activity of our Lord is solely a divine one, or human only in so far as there is an aspect of humanity in the divine Logos himself.

We shall see how the great school of Antioch had a tendency from the beginning to stand for the human aspect of our Lord, as that of Alexandria did for the divine. About contemporaneously with Apollinaris, Diodorus of Tarsus was originating those views of our Lord's person which in the beginning of the next century were to result in the Nestorian heresy. The Antiochians made so much of the humanity of our Lord, they dwelt so much especially upon the personal elements in his human life, as practically and with some of them actually and avowedly to make him a human person. Now our Lord is without question a divine person, and if he is also a human person then he is a conjunction of two persons and not only one person in two natures. This is the doctrine of the dual personality of our Lord which was beginning to loom up and of which Apollinarianism was the deadly antagonist.

To Apollinaris it seemed inevitable that if we concede to our Lord a complete human nature in the sense of not only body and soul but also spirit, if we make him man in the complete sense in which we are, then we make him a human person as well as a divine one and so two persons. Moreover if he is man like us, then he has a human and a free will and is mutable ($\tau\rho\epsilon\pi\tau\grave{o}\varsigma$) or capable of sin. But we must think not only of the Logos but of his humanity as above this, and of the redeeming work of God as so divine as to be free from any human contingency or possibility of miscarriage. And so, to avoid any such consequence, he lifts up the humanity into the divinity; he makes it in itself so divine that there is nothing of our humanity left in it at all—nothing of the humanity which our Lord actually assumed in order that he might purge and cleanse it by himself and present it to himself all-glorious, without spot or wrinkle.

We do not mean to say that the motive of Apollinaris was not a right one, and that there was not a necessity for something to be done to conserve the unity of our Lord's person; but only that he did too much and went too far on the other side. Though we say that our Lord is very God and also that he is very man, we cannot say that he is two. We might even find it necessary to say that he is a divine person and that he is also a human person (which is identical with saying that he is a man, or to speak of the man Christ Jesus); but we cannot mean by that that he is two persons but only that he is a person who is both divine and human, and personally both; that is that he is one person in two natures or modes of being. To Apollinaris this seemed impossible; two, he said, cannot be one. The difficulty is a very real one and will give us trouble enough, as it gave the church for several centuries without being solved at the end of them. But Apollinaris's mode of getting rid of it will do no better than the old Docetic expedient of denying the human outright. The fact simply is that the actual and historical Jesus Christ, the Christ of the gospels and the church, was a man with a human will and human freedom, who by the grace of God through his human faith overcame sin and destroyed death; and so redeemed and exalted human nature and human life to its true human destiny of oneness with God and eternal life; and in his humanity which is ours, once sinful and now holy, once dead and now alive, we all are now sanctified and risen. The true Christian explanation of this act and fact is, that as it is human so also is it divine, and that there could have been no such human act that was not divine; that Jesus Christ as man so realized or exhibited in himself the divine reality of humanity because as God he so humanly realized himself in humanity. And moreover not only was the complete humanity of our Lord an historical fact, but only as human could he have been really divine. God fulfils himself in and not instead of or as a substitute for his works, whether they are natural or spiritual. We repeat that a redeeming God only reveals himself in redeemed humanity.

Of course according to Apollinaris since our Lord brought his humanity and his human holiness with him into the world, he was complete from the first; he had no real infancy or growth; he learned nothing, acquired nothing, encountered and overcame no real temptation, was in no true sense made perfect by the things he suffered nor really touched with any feeling of our infirmity. He may have been perfect God and in Apollinaris's sense perfect man,—but he was no perfecting God for he perfected nothing, nor perfected man for he was perfected in nothing. But to take away this is to take away the very end of the divine incarnation and all the meaning of human redemption and completion in and through it.

Apollinarianism was the forerunner of all the Monophysitism of the succeeding centuries. In denying the double personality he denied along with it the double nature of our Lord. The eternal divine-human or human-divine of the Logos in his view expresses only two aspects or sides of a single nature, as on the one hand it comes eternally from God as its origin, and on the other looks forward to humanity as its end. Jesus Christ is throughout one person, one nature, one activity, not the atonement and oneness of God and man.

The element of truth in Monophysitism is not that the divine and the human natures even in our Lord are the same; that the divine is human and the human divine, as Apollinaris taught; or that in the union they become the same, as the Monophysites taught; but that there is a natural relation or affinity between them which predestinates and predetermines them to a union and unity of the two. The divine Logos is predestined to take the natural and the human into himself and the human to receive the divine of the Logos into itself. It is the nature of God as love and fulness to communicate and fulfil himself in his creation as it becomes capable of receiving him. It is the nature of man as creation's crown of susceptibility and conscious need of God to be taken into personal and free union and unity with him. This truth had been seen by the church fathers long before Apollinaris; by Irenæus, Tertullian, and Athanasius especially. Athanasius speaks much of an ἕνωσις φυσική, a natural unity, of the divine and the human in Christ. "Bearing the image of the Logos and destined for him, humanity arrives at the actuality of its possibility, at the substance of its form, in a word at its perfection, when the Logos enters into vital unity with it." "As its archetype, one aspect of the Logos' own essence stood in affinity with humanity, and called for manifestation in actuality. This actuality was acquired by the Logos when having connected himself with the man Jesus he set forth in him the perfected humanity. Accordingly the ἕνωσις φυσική is that union which is demanded by the essence or conception of both, and in which the idea of both first attains realization;—humanity, because its nature remained imperfect, its creation as it were incomplete, without the incarnation; deity, because even its nature, to wit, its ethical nature, could not satisfy itself until it became man" (Dorner, on Athanasius). The difference between this truth and Apollinarianism is that while according to the former the divine and human come naturally to union in the earthly incarnation of the Logos; according to the latter the divine merely brought into the world, in a Docetic and unreal incarnation, an ideal humanity which it had always possessed.

But when Apollinaris presented the alternative of his own view, and charged that a whole deity and a whole humanity in Christ were two and could by no possibility be one, and not only two natures but two persons,—the theologians of the fourth century were not prepared at once to refute this by presenting the true solution of this new difficulty. They had reflectively vindicated and stated the divine nature and personality of the Lord. They held, as yet only intuitively though just as firmly, the true humanity and were as ready to affirm it. They knew that he was perfect God and perfect man, but how to combine the two natures in a single person without detriment to either was not the task of that century but of another, and much more than another.

It was natural that the age which had with such ability and with so much difficulty and suffering stood for the side of the real divinity of the Lord should unconsciously and unintentionally feel and appreciate less the importance, in its details as well as in its totality, of a scientific analysis and construction of the real humanity. But besides this, we have seen that the Greek genius, and much more so in Alexandria than in Antioch, predisposed it rather to the ideal than to the actual and practical side of religious truth. Christianity was naturally to the Greek much more an activity, a revelation, of God in man than an activity, a redemption and freedom, of man in God. He was more disposed therefore to dwell upon what God was and did than upon what man was and did in Jesus Christ. The theologians of the fourth century, filled with the Trinitarian questions and decisions and, through the transcendent influence of Athanasius, being of the Alexandrian rather than the Antiochian temperament, did not feel all the difficulties of combining a real humanity with the real divinity of the Lord. Apollinaris indeed in his premature and one-sided thought was only exposing a tendency which existed in themselves, though they did not permit it to run into heretical expression and condemned it when it did so in him. For while they held the real humanity as a whole, they were unconsciously not holding it in all its details or in all the parts that were necessary to the integrity of the whole. Jesus Christ was God and man, but he was with them, too, so overpoweringly and controllingly God that he was very infinitesimally man. The humanity in the Godhead was as a drop of honey in the ocean. In the overwhelming self-fulfilment of God in man there was very little self-realization of man in God. The human consciousness, will and freedom, the human becoming-divine of the man Christ Jesus, all but disappear in the omnipotent and irresistible becoming-man of the divine person. But, as we have so often said, God does not really become man, he only remains himself, in a manhood which does not also itself humanly, freely and personally become divine. It is not in the material body but in the human will and freedom, in the human righteousness and life, of Jesus Christ that the Logos most truly and savingly incarnates himself. No matter what the danger of falling into the error of a dual personality, or the difficulty of ascribing to our one Lord the whole activity of God and the whole activity of man, we must not get over it by making human salvation any less an act of man in God than an act of God in man.

Christianity may be viewed as a revelation of God in man; or it may be viewed as an actualization or realization of God in man. If the first aspect is dwelt upon too exclusively, the part of the man in it will be made too little of. It will be even of secondary or no importance that the man, the humanity, shall be a real one at all, if only the revelation is made, or the idea conveyed. But the end of God in Christ is not to show God but to save man; it is not even the truth of God except as the means to the redemption, freedom and life of man. What God has done in Christ is to be read simply and solely in what man has become in Christ.

In saying that Athanasius and his school, which means the theology of the fourth century, represented this tendency to the ideal rather than to the actual, to the divine rather than the human, side of the incarnation, we are only saying that they did not work out both sides of the truth with equal clearness and thoroughness; that something remained to be done by others.

CHAPTER X.

NESTORIANISM.

HE theology which Apollinaris had apprehended and in part anticipated was not long in making its appearance. Indeed it was already in suspense and was immediately precipitated by his attack. Nestorianism and Apollinarianism are simply the opposite extremes in the Christian thought we have been endeavoring to depict, and are each only the denial of the other. We shall find after this that every attempt to discriminate the human from the divine in the person of the Lord is liable to be branded with Nestorianism; and every effort to emphasize the unity of the human with the divine, with Apollinarianism. And this, because Nestorius did undoubtedly divide the aspects to the destruction of a real unity, as Apollinaris united them to the effacement of any real distinction.

Nestorianism had as to its origin and development comparatively little to do with Nestorius, in whose person it was afterward condemned and by whose name it has become known. It had been slowly growing for a long time in a congenial soil. And we must see in its origination quite as true and necessary a motive as we discovered in Apollinarianism, though it resulted in quite as wide an error and heresy. Indeed we shall find its motive just in an exaggeration of the objections which in behalf of the church itself we have already presented to the system of Apollinarianism.

The two great patriarchates of the East, before they were both overshadowed by Constantinople, seemed to be naturally constituted to represent the opposite interests of Christianity. We have seen how from the first Alexandria made itself the representative and champion of the divinity, while Antioch quite as consistently espoused the cause of the humanity of the Lord. The characteristics of the two schools quite remarkably fitted them for these opposite functions. The temper of Antioch was scientific and rational; it seized upon the human and natural elements of Christianity and saw in it the meaning and truth of man and of the world. That of Alexandria was spiritual, intuitive and theological; to it Christianity was the revelation and manifestation of God. The difference was best shown in their methods of biblical interpretation. The exegesis of Old and New Testaments which was the forte and pride of the great teachers of Antioch was literal, grammatical and historical; the exposition of Clement, Origen and their successors in Alexandria was allegorical and mystical. At Antioch the question was, what did the human authors intend to say; at Alexandria what did the Holy Ghost mean to convey.

It would be unjust to claim that Apollinaris represented the Alexandrian school, but he did represent their side or tendency carried to its extreme. That extreme was to represent Jesus Christ as essentially divine, with certain human predicates which however fell very far short of a complete and real humanity. The opposite or Antiochian extreme was to represent him as essentially human, with certain divine predicates which fell equally short of a real and personal deity.

The school of Antioch culminated at the close of the fourth century, after Diodorus of Tarsus, in his great pupil and disciple Theodore of Mopsuestia, regarded in the East as the greatest of biblical scholars and commentators, and the real founder so far as there was one of the organized tendency which was to become known as Nestorianism. When we say that any sincerely and genuinely Christian theologian—as undoubtedly Apollinaris and Theodore were, on opposite sides,—represented one side of the common truth of Christianity, it is not to be inferred that he consciously denied the other. This is especially true at that time of the very inception of Christological science, when although there was a church truth there was not yet a church doctrine of the person of Christ. But at the end of the fourth century no theology could have originated within the church which did not intend to hold, and believe itself to hold, the reality of both the divinity and the humanity in a real incarnation. We only mean to illustrate the fact that nothing short of a catholic doctrine, a doctrine of the mind of the church as a whole, could be broad enough and comprehensive enough to embrace at once on all its sides the totality of the truth of Jesus Christ, and that prior to such a doctrine no one theologian did or could so hold the whole truth as not unconsciously to deny or mutilate some one part in the supposed interest of some other part. If Athanasius himself, who could so clearly see and so exactly define the divinity of the Lord and who unquestionably equally affirmed his humanity, had undertaken to define the latter also in terms of the then knowledge of it, in all its essential elements and details, he certainly would not have done it to the permanent satisfaction of the Christian consciousness. He and his contemporaries, holding it in its unresolved totality, wisely left its analysis and definition to be worked out as it was in the church's gradual and wise rejection of the opposite errors and reconciliation of the opposite truths of Apollinarianism and Nestorianism; just as their own Trinitarianism had been the outcome of the long struggle between the opposing principles of Sabellianism and Arianism.

Theodore of Mopsuestia then approached the question of our Lord's person from the Antiochian, that is to say from the human side. As Apollinaris had undertaken to show how the incarnate Logos is man, so Theodore undertook to show how the man Christ Jesus is God. And with the widest differences their methods are similar in one respect. Apollinaris proves an inherent and eternal humanity in the deity of the Logos, Theodore establishes an essential and natural divinity in the humanity of the man Jesus Christ. His anthropology is peculiar and must be somewhat understood in explanation of his Christology. In a somewhat modernized form we may give its substance as follows:

The whole creation is naturally to culminate in man, who is not only its head but who recapitulates, reconciles and unifies it all in himself, as its summary or epitome. As in him spirit and matter apparently so opposite and contradictory unite in one human nature, so it was natural that all the contrarieties of the whole universe should eventually meet and be reconciled in him, in an all-comprehending unity. Indeed in him the infinite and the finite, eternity and time, God and the creation, were met and were destined to be harmonized. Man is by nature the cosmic god, the image and likeness of the absolute and hypercosmic God. But he was all this not merely physically and naturally but spiritually and morally; and so he was to become it not by a merely natural and necessary evolution but in the exercise and development of his personal and free spirit. In other words, man's place and part in the world as its natural bond and unity was to be accomplished by a process in which humanity was spiritually as well as physically at once to realize itself and the whole creation in itself. In this humanity had failed, and its failure to accomplish its natural high function and destiny is sin, which breaks up the harmony of the universe and reduces everything to discord and contradiction. As the bondage of creation came through man's sin, so its freedom can be restored only through man's redemption from sin. But man's redemption, while it can come only from God, can come only through and in himself and can consist only in the restoration of the freedom and ability of his own will and personality to discharge his function by realizing himself and completing and perfecting the world. Only man, the cosmic god, himself restored and completed, can restore and complete the cosmos in the image and likeness of the absolute God. Therefore when the heavenly Logos, whose earthly image man is, comes down to redeem and restore him, his presence and operation in him are not at the expense of the freedom or the personality or personal activity of the man; for these are just what he is come to restore.

The Logos, according to Theodore, might be conceived as entering into man in Jesus Christ either κατ' οὐσίαν, or κατ' ἐνέργειαν, or κατ' εὐδοκίαν,—either by natural or essential union, or by union of power and operation, or by personal union or the free union and unity of spirits and wills. The first is impossible; the infinite and omnipresent essence and nature of God cannot be contracted to that of a man. It cannot be the second, for the power and activity of God are in all things and this would not distinguish Christ from all other persons and things. It can only be the third, the union of the divine good will and satisfaction with the perfect faith and holy obedience of the man Christ Jesus. The union therefore of God and man, the divine Logos and his human image, in Jesus Christ is a union of wills, of spirits, of personalities. Human personality must not be obliterated and supplanted in Jesus Christ; it must be redeemed and completed by the restoration to it of its freedom, power and efficiency. The human in Christ is not simply a predicate or quality of the divine, it is something in itself; the divine in it is not instead of it but for the sake of it, not to diminish but to increase it. "I am come that ye may have life, and that ye may have it more abundantly." The human in our Lord is therefore above all things personal and free and complete. Whether or not it might have been possible for Theodore to preserve the essential and vital truth in his system without involving a duality of persons in his conception of our Lord, he certainly did not succeed in doing so. It seemed to him vital that our Lord should be a human person, a man in whom humanity should recover its place and function in the world and so restore or attain the unity, harmony and consummation of the universe. With the man Jesus Christ through whom this was to be accomplished, the Logos, whose image or cosmic self he was to be, united himself, became one; not, as we have said, ὀυσίᾳ,—so as himself to become homoöusion with us, —nor ἐνεργείᾳ, by mere operation in him; but εὐδοκίᾳ, by the spiritual and moral unity of consenting and harmonious wills and spirits. The Logos did not literally become flesh or man, but only figuratively did so in that he entered into a spiritual and moral union and unity with the man Christ Jesus. The man was not the Logos but only one with him, and the Logos was not the man but only one with him. Spiritually and morally they were one person, essentially they were two persons, a divine and a human, become one in will and act. Not otherwise than thus did it seem possible to Theodore to preserve in the unity of the incarnation the necessary freedom, completeness and relative independence of the human factor. In this way the distinction of the two factors is most certainly obtained; whether it was not at the price of the loss of their unity there can be with us no question; but we need not doubt, indeed no one acquainted with Theodore himself can doubt, that he believed himself to have secured that too and to hold the catholic doctrine.

Of course the difficulty begins when we ask ourselves who and what this particular human person is who was to be one with the divine Person, and through whom humanity and the whole creation were to be restored to unity and harmony. It was necessary that it should be a person, and that God should foreknow that it would be, who would as freely and yet as infallibly unite himself or be united with the Logos as the Logos with him; for the union begins in and is perfect from the moment of the conception in the womb, and yet is throughout free on both sides and the act of both persons. If the human person is truly human he must have a human growth and progress under human laws and conditions, and must continuously himself will to be one with the Logos, as the Logos wills to be one with him. In this way human salvation is not only a double act, but the act of two persons willing and acting as one. If we ask how it was that this especial person was thus enabled from the first and all throughout to be one with the Logos and so to effect human redemption, Theodore's answer was that in the fact of his miraculous birth there was imparted to him the advantage of a special fitness or affinity, without impairment of his real humanity and freedom; and that his union with the Logos and fulness of the Holy Ghost insured the rest.

It is clear enough from the foregoing representation that Theodore held not only that our Lord was two distinct natures but was two distinct persons,— the eternal Logos or Son and a man specially constituted not merely to be his visible organ and manifestation but to enter freely and personally into union and conjunction with him. The term συνάφεια, by which he expressed this not one-sided but mutual and free conjunction, was intended to affirm that God did not "become" but entered into union with man, and that personal humanity was as much as personal deity a party in the union. As marriage makes two persons one flesh, so in the incarnation of which marriage is but a faint reflection and symbol the Logos and the man become one person. But it is a union not *substantialiter* but *spiritualiter;* not ουσια or φύσει, but γνώμῃ or σχέσει, by mutual disposition, affinity and consent.

Of course Theodore made every effort to minimize the duality and to emphasize the practical unity of the person of Christ. In fact it is only in such an analysis of the ultimate constituents of his system that the duality appears. In his voluminous works and the general teaching of the school nothing more would appear than a distinct emphasis of the human significance of the life and work of the Lord. The school of Antioch believed itself to be asserting the catholic view of the incarnation against Apollinarianism in which the human element was reduced to nothing. And during the life and very wide activity of Theodore no charge was made by the church against his teaching, although it was so broadly disseminated as to gain him the title of *Magister Orientis.* He was the intimate and dear friend to the last of the great Chrysostom, who was of Antioch and of the same school. Theodore's studies and teaching were primarily exegetical, and the image of the human Jesus of the gospels, in its every trait and detail, in the simplicity and reality of his very and complete manhood, was the starting-point of all his thinking; that Jesus was more and not less man by reason of his union with the Logos was the principle of his Christology. To him practically if not essentially Christ was one person; he thought of him not as mere divine Logos nor as mere human Jesus but as the two become one in the one will and activity of the Christ who is at once Logos and Jesus, God and man. It is unnecessary to enter into further criticism of Theodore's position until we get to the time when the church was forced by the progress of Christological science to take it up and analyze it, and to pass judgment upon it. We can see now at once both the right motive in it and its final and utter unsatisfactoriness and untenableness.

Theodore did not seriously object to the application to the mother of the Lord of the term "Theotocos," the point upon which later the whole issue was made and the principle involved analyzed and exposed. He admitted a limited *communicatio idiomatum* by which, in consequence of the closeness of the union and the practical oneness of the Logos and the man, the predicates of one could be applied to the other and we might say that God was born and suffered and died; but he deprecated the growing custom of employing such language, which he thought strained and savoring more of Apollinarianism than truth. Practically the person born of the Virgin might be called God, but essentially he was not God and the Virgin was not Theotocos, mother of God. More exactly she should be called Christotocos, though literally she was only anthropotocos, mother of the human nature and personality in Christ.

It was wholly through the enormous and widespread influence and popularity of Theodore, whom all the East called master and believed as he believed, that the subsequently condemned and generally abandoned Nestorianism yet maintained such a hold in the farther Orient that it continued for a long time to overshadow the true faith and has perpetuated at least its name to our own times.

It was in the year 381—that of the Second General Council—that John, to be known afterward as Chrysostom, was ordained deacon in Antioch his native city, where during the next fifteen or more years he established that astonishing reputation as a preacher from which he received his name. In 398 Chrysostom was forcibly removed from Antioch where he was idolized and consecrated bishop of Constantinople. Chrysostom and Theodore were fellow-students, first under the great heathen sophist and rhetorician Libanius and afterward under Diodorus bishop of Tarsus, the founder of the later school of Antioch. Under him they both, we are told, "learned the common-sense mode of interpreting Holy Scripture (rejecting the allegorizing principle) of which they became such distinguished representatives." "It is as an expositor of Scripture that Chrysostom is most deservedly celebrated. His method of dealing with the divine Word is characterized by the sound grammatical and historical principle and the healthy common sense introduced by his tutor Diodorus, which mark the exegetical school of Antioch. He seeks not what the passage before him may be made to mean, but what it was intended to mean; not what recondite truths or lessons may be forced from it by mystical or allegorical interpretations, but what it was intended to convey; not what may be introduced into it but what may be elicited from it." Chrysostom was not a theologian in the sense of having constructed any system of his own; he was a preacher and an expositor. And we do not know at all that his Christology was that of Theodore, whose practical spirit prevailed much more, happily, than his speculative errors, as we shall find in his successor Theodoret. Perhaps he did not go so deeply into the analysis of the grounds upon which he held the real humanity as also the real divinity of the Lord. But in his temper and teaching he was, behind the ardor of the orator and the outward occupations of a practical administrator, most certainly an Antiochian. Chrysostom's difficult, active and painful administration of the see of Constantinople was terminated by his overthrow and exile. And after an interval under other successors of some twenty years, during which the memory and influence of his greatness and holiness had deeply impressed itself, his seat there was, less fortunately or happily, filled by another representative of the school of Antioch, Nestorius a pupil and disciple of Theodore of Mopsuestia.

Nestorius was of the personal disposition and was now in a position to bring forward and obtrude upon the general view, in the most aggressive way, the principles which had peacefully pervaded the patriarchate of Antioch. He was zealous for orthodoxy, as he believed, and uniformity; and he lost no time in setting about enforcing them. In his very first sermon he boldly addressed the emperor in an appeal to coöperate with him to that end: " Give me, O prince, the earth purged of heretics, and I will give you heaven as a recompense." Whereupon, with or without the emperor, there ensued a general suppression and expulsion of Arians, Novatians, Quartodecimans, Macedonians, and so on. Under the term " orthodoxy," Nestorius was ambitious to extend and make universal the principles of his master Theodore and had brought with him as his chaplain a theologian of Antioch, more zealous and perhaps more learned than himself. To this man, Anastasius, and to Nestorius the prevailing church doctrine outside of the influence of Antioch seemed to be mere Apollinarianism, with which it was necessary to make some decided and positive issue in behalf of the truth of the church.

The issue was joined and the gauntlet publicly thrown down by Anastasius in a discourse in the cathedral in which he exclaimed: " Let no man call Mary Theotocos, for Mary was but a woman and it is impossible that God should be born of a woman."

The new position thus enunciated was publicly indorsed, defended and expanded by the bishop himself in a series of sermons.

The point made was intended for the whole church, and so the whole church came not merely to investigate the propriety or impropriety of the title "Theotocos," but gradually to call into question the fundamental principles of the theology of Antioch. The term "Theotocos" was by no means a new one; it had had the very highest sanction for its use in the church and was familiar everywhere. To the theologians of the Alexandrian school it was very expressive as emphasizing the divine personality of the Lord. It was naturally distasteful to those of Antioch, as at least an exaggeration and as ignoring or denying the human personality. In addition to its important bearing upon the question of the person of Christ it had become more popular through the growing veneration and worship of the Blessed Virgin, whose person and office it magnified. For this reason and in the interest of peace and harmony Theodore had withheld any objection to its use, contenting himself with what he deemed the necessary explanations. Nestorius however evidently thought that the time was past for compromise, and on this word the issue was made and the battle of the Third General Council begun.

The challenge was quickly accepted on the other side, and just where and as might have been expected. The battle-field was Constantinople but the contestants were the two rival patriarchates. Indeed there had been an old contention between them for the control of the potent influence of the Eastern capital. It had been their interference in its affairs, their attempts to influence its episcopal successions and their meddling with its disputes which probably influenced the action of the Second General Council in giving it precedence over them. But that did not at once mend the evil. On the occasion of the appointment of John Chrysostom, Theophilus the overbearing and violent bishop of Alexandria had had his candidate, and was only brought by imperial compulsion to take his part in the consecration of an appointee from Antioch. He soon after placed himself at the head of the opposition which was gathering against the high policy and strict discipline of Chrysostom, and devoted the energies of a most determined character to compassing his downfall. He was indeed personally discomfited and defeated and escaped only by flight the wrath of the people of Constantinople, whither he never ventured again. But his intrigues continued and contributed no little to the overthrow in the end of the great preacher, saint and bishop; of whom Theophilus in his partisan blindness was capable of believing, and saying in a public invective: " He was not what he seemed to be; his guilt transcended all possible penalties; in the world to come he will endure an eternal penalty. . . . Christ himself will condemn him to be cast into outer darkness."

Theophilus had been succeeded in Alexandria by his nephew Cyril, who in his youth had been with him in Constantinople in the prosecution of his proceeding against Chrysostom, and had inherited as he carried with him through life his uncle's hostile judgment of the great preacher. Cyril's own intemperance and intolerance had certainly not in the earlier years of his episcopate fallen short of his predecessors'. His connection with the excesses and outrages mutually inflicted and suffered between the Christians and the heathen and Jewish population of Alexandria, and especially those associated with the name of the philosopher Hypatia, is familiar matter of history. And though the exact degree of his complicity or responsibility will never be known and possibly has been exaggerated, enough is known to indicate his spirit and temper. A change for the worse had assuredly come over the successors of Clement and Origen and of Alexander and Athanasius. The spirit of tolerance and charity, of moderation and sympathy, had been succeeded by one of keen, fierce, vindictive and not over-scrupulous orthodoxy.

The truth of history requires that this should be said, and we cannot shut our eyes to the ample and sad illustrations of it in the events that are to follow. But even in those events, in which the ordinary and earthly eye detects only the play of the bitter and bad passions of men, we can see if we look deeply enough the logical and orderly working out of the most divine and human issues and interests. Nestorius and Cyril, Antioch and Alexandria, now fairly pitted against each other, may represent very much of the merest jealousies and bitternesses of human strife; but it is nevertheless true that underneath all this the two parties to the strife were each, with no little faithfulness, conscientiousness and ability, representing a vital principle at that moment vitally at stake not only for themselves but for the whole world and for all time. The question of the divine in Jesus Christ personally, freely and fully realizing itself in the human, and at the same time of the human freely and fully and personally realizing itself in the divine, is no trifling one; in it is focussed and brought to an issue the whole question of the divine-natural and the divine-human constitution of the world and of man. It is true, as Irenæus said, that Jesus Christ " in se recapitulat longam dispositionem hominis," and not only of man but of the whole creation. To know him is to know them, for it is to see them in God and God in them. Alexandria had developed the truth of God in man. Antioch had undertaken and was ready now to submit and defend its attempt to develop the truth of man in God. Each charged the other with its error and failed to see its truth. It was charged against one side that it taught indeed the self-fulfilment and revelation of God in man, but at the expense of the humanity which was reduced to a mere visibility or at most to a mere instrument or organ of the divine. Everything distinctively human, human knowledge, human will, human freedom and character and activity, human personality, were absorbed and lost in the divine. If there was a fulfilment of God in man in all this, there was certainly no fulfilment of man in God, but only a complete supplanting and obliteration of him.

Against the other on the contrary it was charged that its preservation of the human was through denial of any real being in it of the divine. The so-called incarnation was not God in man at all, but only God with man; it was an external personal relation and not an internal personal identity, a συνάφεια and not an ἕνωσις. In principle the Logos was no more Christ or Christ the Logos than other men; he was only more closely associated with him through the superior faith and piety of that particular man. The incarnation was thus nullified to save the humanity from being absorbed and lost in the divinity. The Logos and Christ were not really one but continued two; and no sanctification of a man however complete can make him an object of our adoration and worship or constitute him all men's redemption and salvation. At most he can be to us an illustration and example of human salvation.

Matters had got to the point where each side could see the deficiency or the error of the other, but not to that at which the truth of both sides could be successfully embraced in a common statement. It is possible to hold as the church did that God is complete in man and man is complete in God in the one person of Jesus Christ, without at all realizing the difficulty of practically carrying out into detail that double truth in its integrity on both sides. It is very certain that there was a real, and a very important and difficult issue raised between Cyril and Nestorius. And it was only an accident that it was raised by them in particular; it would have come inevitably without them at about the same time and in about the same way.

There were, as always, agents from Alexandria in Constantinople, and no sooner had Nestorius thrown down the gauntlet than Cyril was prepared to take it up. In fact even before the dispute arose Cyril had already, like Athanasius, produced his initial treatise upon its subject-matter. He did not assume any new position through antagonism to his opponent. His position was the logical Alexandrian one. He was the honest and veritable successor, and intellectually and theologically no unworthy one, to the great Athanasius. Indeed his uncle Theophilus, although less honest and of worse temper, was no mean theologian and had inherited and transmitted the orthodoxy of the school. And in the discussions to ensue Cyril frequently manifests at least a doctrinal and theological if not personal appreciation of the genuinely religious interests involved, not less true than that of Athanasius himself. He dwells even less upon the mere revealing and teaching and more upon the actually regenerating and redeeming function of the incarnation, and in a way to show that he had fully felt its necessity in thought at least if not in personal experience. But why not in both? Men are generally as much better as they are worse than they appear; the heights and the depths meet in us all. And it would seem that in that age wider extremes of good and bad could coexist in one man; men could be both better and worse, both higher and lower, than it is possible to be at one and the same time now.

Cyril began by making the issue that Nestorius had raised the subject of his annual paschal pastoral in the spring of 329, but without personal allusion to Nestorius himself. Especial excitement had been aroused among the monks by the attack upon the Theotocos, and Cyril in allaying this proceeded further in an elaborate circular letter to give the catholic use of the title as indicating not, as Nestorius had charged, that the Virgin was mother of the Godhead in a heathen sense, but only of the humanity in our Lord. "But," he continued, "since it was not a man who was born of her but God the Word in human form or nature, therefore he whose mother she was was God and she was mother of God." In the more and more heated correspondence that ensued Cyril certainly at first strives to keep the discussion free from personal complications and subordinate to the interests of the truth. His analysis of the position of Nestorius is acute and masterly and evinces nothing more than a religious as well as scientific regard for the theology and the Christianity of the church. If he had had a Theodore instead of only a Nestorius to deal with, and if it had been possible (at any time, but especially in that contentious age) for the two parties to think out sympathetically, from their opposite points of view, the common truth of which they were both in search, much good might have been gained and much evil averted. But Christians are as human as Christianity is divine, and even human passions are among the means to divine ends.

News of the excitement created by Nestorius in due time reached Rome, and he himself in a letter to the Bishop Celestine incidentally alludes to the measures he had felt called upon to take with reference to the heathen representation of the Virgin as mother of God; and asks his judgment of the matter. Celestine kept the subject a long time under advisement upon the excuse of having to get it properly translated and considered; and meantime he was in correspondence with Cyril with whose views he finally and entirely concurred. It was due in great measure to the Roman mind and character and to the peculiar qualities and limitations of the Latin tongue, and not only to any especial wisdom or prudence of the Roman bishops, that their relation to all the questions of speculative doctrine which agitated the church was not a controversial but a judicial one. They never contributed to results but only weighed and passed judgment upon them. It was very naturally their policy to be silent in discussion and to balance conclusions. Lacking the more subtle and philosophical qualities of mind, they left the analysis and definition of principles to the Greek intellect and language which seemed to be specially constituted for it, and played the part of the common sense which tests and passes judgment upon the decisions of the reason. Undisturbed by the sophistries which mingle with and confuse theoretical disputes and by the personalities and partisanship engendered by heated controversy, they were better qualified to represent the universal practical religious instincts and experiences, and in the light of these to be dispassionate and impartial judges of discussions which they could not always follow and of results which they could never have attained.

Celestine when he was ready summoned a synod in Rome, which from the standpoint of Cyril condemned Nestorius. He then wrote to Cyril to add his authority to his own, and that they should conjointly proceed to the excommunication of Nestorius and the provision of a successor for Constantinople, unless he should repent of his heresy within ten days of his receipt of their action. Cyril on his part, on receipt of this communication from Rome, gathered a council of Egyptian bishops and at the beginning of November 430 addressed to Nestorius a fuller letter, the points of which were summed up in twelve anathematisms in which he called upon Nestorius to unite, directed against the specific errors with which he was charged: " That Immanuel is not really God and the Virgin not Theotocos; that the Logos was not personally joined to the flesh; that there was a connection of two persons (συνάφεια); that Christ is a God-bearing man (θεόφορος); that he was a separate individual acted on by the Word and called God along with him; that his flesh was not the Word's own; that the Word did not suffer death in the flesh;" etc.

In reply Nestorius issued twelve counter-anathemas. And Cyril having opened the way with a lack of care and caution that afterward he found very hard to explain, to an attack on his own views, John of Antioch, Theodoret and others of the Eastern bishops now also entered into the controversy with charges against him of Apollinarianism.

But before all this, and in fact before Cyril's messengers had reached Constantinople with the twelve anathemas, the Emperor Theodosius II. had placed a temporary quietus upon the whole controversy by issuing a summons for a general council to be held after Easter of the following year, 431, pending which all proceedings were ordered to be suspended.

CHAPTER XI.

THE COUNCIL OF EPHESUS.

YRIL had of course the immense advantage over Nestorius that the matter of controversy was the heresy of the latter, and not any possible deficiencies in his own faith. But beside this he was very much more than a match for him, not only in his transcendent ability as a controversialist and his irresistible personal energy but in the political arts which the character of the times rendered an essential element of success. The one advantage that Nestorius possessed in the favor of the emperor, who was on his side and was personally prejudiced against Cyril, was only a source of weakness to him; inasmuch as it led him through undue reliance upon it to neglect the necessary exertions and precautions for securing to himself a fair and favorable hearing. Nothing was done on his part, while nothing was neglected on the other.

The council met in Ephesus in June A.D. 431, and was at once taken possession of by Cyril and the local bishop Memnon, who packed it with their suffragans. The sentiment of the city was unanimous against Nestorius who, realizing the hopelessness of impartial treatment and dreading violence to his person, absented himself altogether.

In Constantinople itself Cyril was no less actively at work. The monks of the city were aroused and set to influence and terrify the weak mind of the emperor. Before the council closed Alexandria had almost impoverished itself in costly presents and bribes to influential members of the court and the imperial household. And in course of time no labor or expense was spared to excite or foster dissensions among the favorers of Nestorius. By October the whole thing was over; Nestorius had been deposed and banished; Maximian had been consecrated in his stead, and Cyril was plying the latter with suggestions and advice how best to complete and establish his victory.

We are however mainly concerned not with the politics but with the progress of the doctrinal interests involved, and to this we direct our attention. On one side of the question at issue Cyril, although not alone, was almost as overshadowing and supreme as Athanasius had been in the conflict with Arianism. On the other side matters stood about as follows: Between the emperor's call in November and the convening of the council in June the patriarchate of Antioch had been awaking to the issue unexpectedly raised between it and Alexandria by Nestorius's action in Constantinople.

The temper there at the time was moderate and conservative. The speculative error of Theodore which had not in him led to practical heresy—for there is much room for logical inconsequence between speculative and practical opinion and thought—had been much softened down and was in a fair way to disappear gradually in the minds of his successors at home, not one of whom can now be convicted of heresy. If Antioch and Alexandria could have been kept from the bitterness and blindness of controversy, they might soon have coalesced in the common faith, with no other difference than that of wholesomely and helpfully occupying opposite and complementary points of view, each professing also to hold the truth of the other.

John of Antioch was at the time patriarch; and Theodoret, a native of Antioch but at this time bishop of Cyrrhus near the Euphrates, was the representative, not inferior to any of his predecessors, of the scholarship and learning of the school of Antioch. In personal character and ability, in sanctity and devotion, in eloquence and culture, Theodoret combined without diminution the qualities and gifts of Chrysostom with those of Theodore. And he was quite as free as the former from the doctrinal expressions and positions which laid the latter open to the charge of heresy. Indeed the sequel proved that John and Theodoret and most of the school of Antioch, but for the complications that followed, were already prepared to meet the opposite side more than half-way upon the ground of the common truth. On the other hand it might be repeated, once for all, with reference to all such reflections upon how things might otherwise have happened, that the truth or right never does get settled peaceably or otherwise than by the sword of human strife and passion. And the discussions and disputes of this as of the preceding century were none too much, if they were even yet enough, to develop and reconcile the issues lurking at the root of the church's doctrine.

It happened that Theodoret and a number of other bishops were assembled in Antioch, probably for the consecration of one of their number, when in the fall or winter before the council the summons reached the patriarch from Rome and Alexandria to join in the excommunication and deposition of Nestorius of Constantinople, unless he should at once recant his errors. It produced great excitement and indignation, because it was not believed in the East that Nestorius's objection to the title "Theotocos" proceeded to the extent of unsoundness in the faith. While more intemperate in other respects Nestorius had not gone —and probably never did go—so far as Theodore had in the implication of a double personality in our Lord; and was not Theodore still the venerated master of the East, whose name had not been sullied with any charge of heresy?

But notwithstanding all this, a letter was immediately prepared and sent to Nestorius imploring him to yield, and not involve the whole church in discord upon a point about which there was no substantial disagreement. The title "Theotocos" had been consecrated by orthodox usage. Theodore had wisely and moderately forborne from objection to it, and it was susceptible of a sense which was true and acceptable to all. This letter is so admirable in form as well as spirit that it has been usually ascribed to the pen of Theodoret, although it was sent in the name of John.

But Nestorius was fixed in his determination to abide by the issue. With his reply he sent the Twelve Articles or anathematisms of Cyril, which had been received in the meantime. Now unfortunately, as has been said, these articles were at the least unguarded in expression and conveyed to the mind of the Antiochians, sensitive on the other side, a distinct impression of Apollinarian error. That is to say, Cyril used language which we shall consider later, which meant to them if not in itself a oneness of nature as well as a unity of personality in the incarnate Lord and so a denial of any real manhood in him. Several answers to Cyril were at once prepared and circulated, one of them by Theodoret, and all based upon not only insufficient but false views of his opinions. Thus all Antioch was involved in the quarrel of Nestorius and preparations were made for an irrepressible conflict at the forthcoming council over irreconcilable differences.

As soon as Easter and its octave were over, John assembled at Antioch his suffragans and prepared for his departure to Ephesus. He was delayed by a famine and troubles in the city and by bad weather and accidents on the way. It was a six weeks' journey at the best, and messengers sent ahead found Cyril provoked by the delay and impatient to begin. John regretted and explained his slowness, but hoped to embrace his brother within one week more and be ready for business. Besides this formal message he had privately instructed several of those who had gone ahead to say that if he should be still further delayed they should proceed without him. Cyril impatiently seized upon this as a pretext and forthwith convened the council. And when John and the Syrian bishops arrived on June 27th, within the time specified in their message, they found that the council had been in session for some days and its work practically accomplished; Nestorius was deposed and excommunicated. The forty-odd Antiochians were provoked by the discourtesy shown and the advantage taken of them into a course which for intemperance and violence unfortunately out-Cyrilled Cyril and placed an impassable chasm between the two parties. Refusing on their arrival to accept any attentions or explanations or to see any of the opposite faction, they proceeded before even removing the dust of their journey to hold a conference in their inn, in which they deposed and excommunicated Cyril and Memnon and anathematized their supposed opinions. And so the great gathering of bishops was instantly and hopelessly split into two hostile and irreconcilable councils, each anathematizing the other for opposite heresies of which probably none present were really guilty. The representatives of the bishop of Rome arrived later and at once added the authority of Rome to that of Alexandria in condemnation of Nestorius. For some time longer both sides were eagerly pressing their claims upon Theodosius II. and awaiting his decision. At length after much vacillation the emperor inclined to the side of Cyril but refused to confirm any penalties against the Oriental bishops. So the council broke up and the bishops returned to their homes with no new doctrinal decisions and the net result of the personal condemnation of Nestorius,

No sooner however were the parties to it dispersed than the quarrel began to assume a less serious and violent character. The change was no doubt largely due to the desire and determination of the emperor to effect a reconciliation and to the consciousness on the part of the Eastern bishops that the weight of the church was against them. The emperor was especially anxious to effect a better understanding between John and Cyril, and this was facilitated by the fact that each of these was feeling the need of exculpating himself from what he thought to be false and unjust impressions as to his position. Cyril had been busy even at Ephesus, while the case of the two parties was in suspense before the emperor, writing a defense of his misunderstood Twelve Articles. He subsequently wrote to Maximian a disclaimer of the views imputed to him and was now preparing a vindication of himself to be submitted to the emperor. John of Antioch and his party on their way home, while still under the fresh sense of their wrongs, had halted at Tarsus to hold a new council, in which the deposition of Cyril was confirmed and the members pledged themselves never to consent to that of Nestorius. Soon after another was held at Antioch which was much more largely attended. At this the Twelve Articles of Cyril were condemned, the Nicene Creed was declared to be a sufficient confession of faith, Athanasius's exposition of it in his epistle to Epictetus was adopted as the expression of orthodoxy, and finally—indicating the beginning of the change toward better feelings—Six Articles were drawn up as a basis of possible reunion.

The emperor had been unsuccessful in his first efforts to bring John and Cyril together in a private interview, but on receipt of the Six Articles of Antioch, which had been sent to him by the aged and venerated Acacius of Berœa, Cyril wrote to John a letter that opened the way to further and closer approaches. Cyril implied that his own Twelve Articles, which he had been at so much pains to explain, would not be allowed to stand in the way of a reconciliation, disavowed and condemned the heresies attributed to him, and insisted upon nothing but concurrence in the condemnation of Nestorius. Through the good offices of Acacius, who seemed to have singularly combined the respect and affection of all parties, John admitted that the letter of Cyril certainly cleared him of any charge of heresy, and sent to Alexandria one of his bishops, Paul of Emesa, to confer further upon the differences between the patriarchs and the terms of reconciliation. There were still obstacles in the way, but Paul acted with prudence and tact, explained and smoothed away difficulties, pleased both bishop and people by one or more sermons preached at Christmastide, in which he took occasion to express his views of the incarnation, and returned to Antioch with terms of communion upon John's signature of which Alexandria and Antioch should be one again.

After some delay and a little imperial pressure John accepted the terms, and in the spring of 433 sent to Cyril the formulary of reunion with his signature. He concurred, in spite of the pledge at Tarsus, in the sentence of Nestorius and the condemnation of Nestorianism. Cyril replied in a letter beginning, "Let the heavens rejoice and the earth be glad!"

The Oriental party however did not all follow their head. Most of them could have joined in the condemnation of Nestorianism but not in the sentence of Nestorius, because they did not hold him guilty of it. And besides that they had solemnly agreed at the Council of Tarsus not to abandon a man in whose substantial orthodoxy they believed and at whose unjust treatment they were indignant. Nestorius was now in a monastery near Antioch with which in earlier life he had been connected and where he was kindly received and treated on his return by the bishop and the whole church of Antioch. But at no stage of his career had he shown a very attractive spirit, and perhaps his persistent obstinacy and intractableness at this juncture, as well as the satisfactory explanations and the conciliatory temper of Cyril after the council, had wrought the change in John's mind. To these causes however must be added the good management and judicious pressure of the imperial officers, the wisdom and tact of such episcopal advisers and helpers as Acacius and Paul of Emesa, the moderation of Celestine of Rome and his successor, and John's own prudent consciousness that he was on the losing side.

Besides those who acted thus with John, there were two other sections of the Antiochian party who took a different stand. First there was a very large one represented by Theodoret and those like him who repudiating Nestorianism refused to condemn Nestorius. Theodoret had thrown himself prematurely and bitterly into the doctrinal controversy with Cyril and had not personally shown himself in it at his best. Upon Cyril's subsequent explanations, and in the subject-matter of his negotiations with John, he had frankly admitted that Cyril had cleared himself of heresy. But Cyril's one condition of intercommunion was the condemnation of Nestorius, and in the way of this was not only the pledge to stand by him but the continued faith in his innocence. There being no doctrinal ground of separation it was of course only a question of time how soon this section would be reconciled with the church. They seemed by degrees to admit that there was something that the church had need to condemn under the name of Nestorius, whether he himself was formally and technically guilty of it or not. Theodoret himself joined in the condemnation late in the sessions of the next general council at Chalcedon. But the spirit of irreconcilable and undying hostility to "Egypt" was concentrated in the person of the good and holy bishop of Hierapolis, Alexander, and a small section of men of the same temper, who persisted, against the disinclination of the authorities to resort to severity, in suffering the loss of all things and preferring death in exile and poverty to intercommunion with the heretics of Alexandria.

So far for the external history of the downfall of Nestorius. It is quite a different matter when we come to ask ourselves what progress had been made toward the solution of the doctrinal problem that constituted the sole interest and value of the whole dispute. The one point gained might be said to be the final settlement of the question of the double personality; the language of Theodore and Nestorius would never afterward have been possible within the church. But that was in process of settling itself and would not have survived long to trouble the peace of the church. The idea of a Christ who is two persons, the Son of God who becomes man only in the sense of being morally reproduced in a human person as his free image or likeness; and a man who is the Son of God only in the sense that he morally images and reproduces him in himself, is too untenable and impossible in itself, and falls too far short of the church's faith in a real incarnation, to have perpetuated itself. Cyril had truly stated the question at issue to be, "Whether Jesus was a human individual (no matter how closely related to God), or whether he was the divine Son himself appearing in human form. In the former case the Son of Mary must be regarded simply as a very highly favored saint; in the latter, as a divine Redeemer." But there were practically none now of the opposite party who would not freely concede as much. While then under the term "Nestorianism" the error to which the Antiochian doctrine inclined was condemned, and effectually condemned, on the other hand was the truth from Antioch which the church needed, and which was sought to be added as the complement and completion of that from Alexandria, in any fair way of securing recognition and appreciation? At that moment most assuredly not. Cyril is singularly clear and sound in detecting the logical tendencies and dangers of the opposite side, but of the possibility of a contribution of truth from that direction such as was to be recognized and accepted in the Council of Chalcedon, he and his party seem as yet to have caught no inkling. It is true he makes now a nominal concession to John in which he seems to be giving up something and accepting something, but he was not long in making it apparent that he had no such meaning.

In accepting the Six Articles of Antioch as the basis of the reunion Cyril gave his approval to a confession of faith which, though submitted to him now simply as that of John, was in reality that drawn up by Theodoret for presentation in the name of all the bishops of the East to the Council of Ephesus. In this formulary our Lord is defined as being " of one essence (homoöusion) with the Father as to Godhead, of one essence with us as to manhood. For there took place a union of two natures; wherefore we confess one Christ, one Son, one Lord. According to this idea of a union without confusion, we confess the holy Virgin to be Theotocos, because God the Son was incarnate and made man, and from his very conception united to himself the temple assumed from her." In this formula, it will be observed, there is an explicit recognition of the two natures united without confusion in the one person of the incarnate Lord. It was just this distinct acknowledgment of the two aspects, divine and human, in the incarnation that the Orientals had insisted upon, and when Cyril thus admitted it their objection was removed and John and Theodoret both accepted it at the time as satisfactory assurance of Cyril's orthodoxy from their point of view. But it is very evident that

Cyril did not mean it as they received it. Either the concession was not made in good faith or else Cyril was very far from conceiving or appreciating the truth, and the importance of the truth, for which the Orientals were contending. This will appear from all his subsequent conduct.

As many of the Easterns thought that John had yielded too easily and too much, so the followers of Cyril felt that he had gone too far in the compromise effected between them in his acceptance of the phrase "two natures." In justifying himself he explains what he means by it and proves very conclusively that it is very far short of what the Orientals understood or would have been satisfied with or what the Council of Chalcedon afterward taught. He points out the natural distinction and necessary difference between the nature of God and the nature of man, which before the incarnation are manifestly two natures and are combined in the person of Jesus Christ. But they are two only before the incarnation; in their union in the incarnate One they cease to be two and become one. After that, the mind may still conceive them as two but in fact and in operation they have become one and are not to be distinguished in their activity.

If this is so is there any room or possibility for a real human life of our Lord or is it possible to say that he was a man? The contention of the Orientals was not theoretical but practical; they demanded that, after and in the union, the human nature, the human life and activity of the Lord should have its proper significance and value in the act and fact of the divine-human atonement. If there was but one nature in the incarnate One, then either he was no longer God but only man or no longer man but only God or no longer either but only something half-way between both. The catholic truth is that our Lord is, after and in the incarnation, both God and man in the complete nature and activity or operation of both, so that in his every act and quality and character we can say, and mean it, that he is very man and also very God.

So, after and in spite of the contrary assurance in terms and his acceptance of the two natures united without confusion in the person of our Lord, Cyril continued to hold as before what the Antiochians really objected to in the doctrine of the " one nature." It is not that he was guilty of bad faith so much as that he never did see the other side sufficiently to understand or appreciate the truth of its claim. It is true that it is common still to maintain that what he means by the μιὰ φύσις, the one nature of the Incarnate, is the single personality in the two natures; and every now and then Cyril succeeded in convincing his opponents that that was his meaning, just as every now and then detached sentences may persuade us of the same thing; but a careful weighing of his own explanations, as of those of his modern apologists, convinces us of the contrary. It would be unjust to charge him with heresy, and in doing so we should implicate even greater and much holier doctors than he before him. But it is very certain that at Alexandria one side, one half, the truth was not only undeveloped, but in the mind of Cyril and still more in the mind of his successor seemed incapable of taking root. They were so satisfied with what they had done that it seemed impossible for them to conceive that there might be something more to be done. To them the two natures, distinct before, became practically one after the union in Jesus Christ. The one divine Person acted indeed in both, or under the form of both, but it was a single and thus a divine activity. It was God and not man who lived and spoke and acted in Jesus. The human nature is indeed acknowledged as acting according to its own laws in certain lower functions, as in the bodily wants, sufferings, etc. But these are not distinctly human, they are animal; the human begins properly in the consciousness and the will. And the humanity of our Lord's consciousness and will is to be found in a freedom, a choice, a limitation and growth, a reality of weakness and temptation, of faith and obedience, which are not possible in a system that denies the continuance in the incarnation of a true human nature and human conditions.

Cyril simply does not advance a step beyond the stage of Athanasius in this direction. As a whole and implicitly there is the opposite of any denial of the very humanity of the Lord; but in detail there is no full understanding and valuing of the part of the human activity in the true end and result of the incarnation. The atonement is solely something which God did, not also something which man did.

Of course so hollow a compromise and reconciliation could not be a very lasting one and this was not long in becoming apparent. We saw how anxious the emperor was for the reunion and how large a part he had in effecting it. When it was accomplished, he undertook to enforce conformity to its terms, and the pressure gently applied at first to John of Antioch himself was by degrees and in the end much more decidedly brought to bear upon those who, like Alexander of Hierapolis, utterly refused to be reconciled. The agitation and resistance only served to give a new impulse to the circulation and study of the works of Theodore, and produced the impression of a revival of the principles that had been only superficially touched and were very far from being permanently extinguished in the person of Nestorius. It so happened that the good and charitable Proclus, the successor of Maximian at Constantinople, who had done much to bring the opposite parties together by impartially recognizing them all as in full communion with himself, wrote to the Syrian church urging them, on their part in the interest of the reconciliation, to disavow and condemn certain extracts which he had collected as liable to prejudice their claim to orthodoxy. These extracts were in fact drawn from the works of Theodore but it was not so stated and no mention was made of his name. Unfortunately the messengers thought good to insert officiously the name that the tact of the bishop had wisely omitted. The condemnation of the extracts would consequently as it now stood carry with it that of Theodore himself. No doubt John and Theodoret and the great body of the Oriental bishops were quite ready at the time to disavow the objectionable language, but none were willing to begin at this late date to affix to the great and venerated name of Theodore the stigma of a heresy with which the church had not charged him and of which however in terms he might have been guilty they at least did not believe him in spirit or life to have been so. And if he had been, no doubt they would still have felt that in themselves, his disciples and successors, it was suffering a gradual and natural correction and oblivion, and that just the one way to revive and renew it was to disturb the peaceful and revered memory of Theodore.

Cyril himself was forced to recognize the weight of the above reasoning and when it came to the point counselled against any formal condemnation of the person of Theodore. But he could not be blind to the fact of the revival throughout the East of the great reputation and influence of Theodore, whose works the Nestorians were industriously circulating. It looked as though the heresy, slain in the person of Nestorius, were undergoing resurrection in the far greater and more influential person of its real author. Gladly would Cyril have extirpated in the root in Theodore that which it now appeared had only been lopped off in the branches in Nestorius. Unable to reach his person or to stigmatize his memory, he devoted his last years to the refutation of his works and to this task all his thoughts were directed when in A.D. 444 he was cut off in the midst of his zeal and labors for the truth.

The estimate both of the personal character and of the doctrinal service to the church of Cyril of Alexandria will always be one of the problems of history. With regard to the former, after all has been said of his faults and limitations, and they were great, his sincerity, his courage, his devotion to the truth as he saw it will never suffer from that closer acquaintance which is necessary to enable one to judge him fairly. The subordination of the claims of concrete charity to those of abstract orthodoxy seems singularly to characterize the Greek Christianity of that age and Cyril was a conspicuous instance of the type, but the intolerance and violence of his youth seem to have been at least modified by age and experience, and we may hope that he ended with somewhat less of the knowledge that puffeth up and somewhat more of the love that buildeth up than he began with.

With regard to the latter point, the contribution of Cyril to the doctrinal progress of the church, it was great but also critical and negative. The net result of the Council of Ephesus was the condemnation of Nestorius and Nestorianism. He was successor to Athanasius in that like him he was the master spirit and pilot of one of the ecumenical councils of the church, and he stood for the same truth; but his greatness and his service, in so far as they were an actual factor in the history of dogma, were exhibited in defence not in construction. Cyril added no new element in the development of the doctrine of Christ; it is a question rather how much he obstructed its true progress.

While the Alexandrians were thus with difficulty restraining their hands from the attack upon Theodore and the principles of the school of Antioch, the

Antiochians on their part had ceased to attach any value to the disclaimers and explanations of Cyril with reference to his principle of the μία φύσις, and under the leadership of Theodoret were beginning to organize the attack which, with many alternations of fortune, was finally to result in victory for them in turn, at the Council of Chalcedon.

CHAPTER XII.

EUTYCHIANISM AND THE COUNCIL OF CHALCEDON.

HE preparations on both sides for the renewal of hostilities resulted in overt action first on the part of the Orientals. In 448 a local council was in session in Constantinople under the presidency of Flavian, who had succeeded Proclus as patriarch. In the midst of this council, which had been called for quite other purposes, Eusebius bishop of Dorylæum, without previous notice, preferred before Flavian charges against a monk of his city of disseminating false doctrine. This was the archimandrite Eutyches who for many years had presided over a monastery of three hundred monks, and during that time had never once emerged from his cloisters. When he was summoned to appear and answer the charges, it was for a long time impossible to prevail upon him either to present himself in person or to submit a statement of his views. The determination and persistence however of his prosecutor Eusebius finally compelled his presence and examination, and he was pronounced guilty of heresy.

Eutyches was a fair representative of the extremest and narrowest section of the following of Cyril upon the subject of the single nature. He taught that the person of the Lord was of or out of two natures, but not in two natures; that is, that the natures were two and distinct prior to their union in the act of incarnation, but that after that act they were one. So that in the incarnate Son the human nature was no longer the same as ours; even the body of Christ was by union with deity made different from that of other men. Of course there was in such a view no longer any even pretence of room for the slightest really human volition or action in our Lord. He was simply God willing and acting through a human visible form and outward appearance. Such extreme instances naturally only threw Theodoret and his party back into distrust of Cyril's own disavowal of denying the real humanity. Nevertheless the council acted with extreme moderation and caution; the condemnation of Eutyches was expressed in the very words of Cyril in his letters to Nestorius and John of Antioch.

The condemnation of Eutyches was quickly followed by a much more decisive and fatal movement from the other side. In Constantinople Flavian had had from the moment of his consecration a bitter personal enemy in Chrysaphius, the infamous minister of Theodosius II.; and in him Eutyches now found a friend who was ready for any measures by which the tables might be turned against Flavian and in favor of himself. Through him the imperial influence could be relied upon to undo the action of the council.

On the death of Cyril of Alexandria in 444, he was in turn succeeded by his nephew Dioscorus, who seems to have combined in his person all the bad qualities of his great-uncle Theophilus and his uncle Cyril, without the redeeming ones of the latter. At once violent and dishonest, and possessed only of the energy and persistence without any other qualification necessary for the part, his ambition in life seems to have been to play the rôle of the great bishops of Alexandria who before him had guided and controlled general councils and been the representatives of the orthodoxy of the world. He at once took up the task that Cyril had dropped, of extirpating Nestorianism in its root by anathematizing the memory of Theodore and destroying the credit and influence of Theodoret. He proceeded at once to the most violent and unscrupulous attacks upon the latter, disregarding and ignoring the most temperate and convincing demonstrations of his innocence of all the charges brought against him. But it was Dioscorus's opportunity; he had the emperor at his back, and Nestorianism was to be crushed finally and forever in the persons of its real representatives, dead and alive. Theodoret could get no hearing even from Theodosius more than from Dioscorus, although his letters of vindication and explanation have been accepted from all sides in the church as models of piety and orthodoxy. He was deposed and confined in a monastery, where he was dependent upon friends for the bare sustenance which he would consent to accept at their hands. But from this retreat his correspondence with the outside leaders of the church, Leo, Flavian and others, no doubt accomplished all that his personal activity could have.

The other line of Dioscorus's policy was to procure

the reversal of the condemnation of Eutyches and therein the defeat and discomfiture of the opposite party. With a view to this the emperor was easily induced through Chrysaphius to call a general council to be organized and controlled to that specific end. The council met in the summer of 449 at Ephesus, and has become famous or infamous under the designation fixed upon it by Leo the Great of Rome, of Latrocinium or the Robber Council. Dioscorus was made president by the emperor and from his throne with the coöperation of the imperial officers directed and controlled the proceedings with an absoluteness and irresponsibility that was unknown in any previous council. The Council of Constantinople that had tried Eutyches was brought into question and upon the pretence that its proceedings were to be reviewed and judged by the decisions of the general councils of Nicæa and the first Ephesus the bishops who had taken part in his condemnation, with Flavian at their head, were put upon their trial. Theodoret was specially excluded from the right to sit in the council. The records of the action at Constantinople were publicly read, the charges against Eutyches reviewed and all his answers accepted as the sound doctrine of the church. Then Flavian and Eusebius, who had been the prosecutor of Eutyches, were condemned and deposed and the other bishops who had united with them were by the violence of Dioscorus and the support of the imperial officers terrorized into signing their condemnation and the acquittal of Eutyches; and even this did not secure some of them from subsequent deposition. Flavian, who had almost alone had the strength and courage to oppose the violence of Dioscorus, received at the hands of the more brutal monks physical injuries that soon after resulted in his death.

Thus was the temporary advantage of the Antiochians overwhelmingly reversed by the most crushing defeat. And yet perhaps nothing could have happened better calculated to secure to them at last the consideration of their side of the truth which had hitherto been withheld by the church and in all probability could never have been secured from Alexandria, the traditional leader and representative of catholic thought. Dioscorus had not only done everything in his power to bring odium upon his own cause but he had left nothing undone to alienate the powerful allies who had hitherto made common cause with Alexandria. The see of Athanasius and Cyril had especially always carried with it the great weight and authority of the sympathy and support of Rome. The seat of St. Peter was now occupied by the greatest of its bishops up to that time, and its first great theologian, Leo I. Leo had been carefully studying the course of events that followed the condemnation of Nestorius. Upon his condemnation at Constantinople Eutyches had confidently appealed to Leo and the bishops of the West, upon whose side as associated with the cause of Cyril he naturally supposed himself to be. Leo also corresponded at the time with Flavian and letters passed between him and Theodoret. His impression of Eutyches was that of a weak and narrow man who had fallen into error through ignorance rather than wickedness.

Dioscorus also no doubt counted at first upon the support of Leo and the West—he seems to have had no misgivings about being the true successor of Cyril and representative of Alexandria. But his ambition and violence blinded and drove him on to neglect and disregard and at last even to defy and excommunicate his great traditional ally.

Some time before the meeting of the Latrocinium Leo embodied his judgment of the whole doctrinal question at issue, with regard to the two aspects of the person of Christ, in a letter to Flavian, " Epistola dogmatica ad Flavianum." This treatise, commonly known as the " Tome of St. Leo," became one of the most influential as it is still one of the most celebrated of the patristic writings. In it he undertakes, without condescending to controversy or discussion, to lay down the faith of the church with regard to the two natures in the one divine personality of our Lord. The letter was hailed with great favor and applause throughout the East, and Theodoret wrote to Leo expressing his entire sympathy and accord with it.

Armed with this letter and with another addressed immediately to the council, the legates of Leo presented themselves before it and took their seats. But the letters were never received or read and no notice was taken of them in the proceedings. Dioscorus was able to say afterward that he had more than once proposed that the communications from Rome should be laid before the council; but they were not, and no one doubted that if Dioscorus had been in earnest the council would have heard them. In the violence that disgraced beyond all parallel the closing scenes, only one of the Roman legates could withstand the intimidation that carried everything before it sufficiently to utter his "Contradicitur" to the proceedings. He was more fortunate than Flavian in escaping with his life to carry the disgraceful story to his master, whom he was to succeed in the see of Rome as Pope Hilary.

The so-called general council broke up with Dioscorus in possession of the field and all the East at his feet. No doubt he saw himself a third to Athanasius and Cyril in the history of catholic dogma, and for a brief while his ambition felt itself satisfied.

But Leo was now in the field, stirring every energy to wipe out the shame of the Latrocinium by substituting for it the action of a real general council of the church. His grief and indignation knew no bounds but did not paralyze his efforts and determination to repair the damage done to the faith and honor of Christendom.

The position and character of Leo the Great during the more than twenty years of his reign—from 440 to 461—were singularly impressive and commanding. It was given to him more than to any other man to organize and consolidate that spiritual empire in the West which was to hold society together in the disintegration and decay of the secular power, and to transfer to the Christian church the authority and ability that were lost to the Roman state to mould and assimilate the barbarian hordes that were overrunning the Western world. The credit was given to him of personally overawing and turning back Attila the Hun from the gates of Rome and of softening if not wholly averting the excesses of Genseric the

The Synod Sustained by the Emperor. 249

Vandal. It was necessary for the function that the church was to discharge in acting as a bond to society and especially in receiving, subduing and civilizing the inflowing tides of barbarism that it should present everywhere a united and compact front, and Leo devoted much of his earlier energies to extending and establishing the authority and control of the apostolical see over Gaul, Spain and the whole of the West.

In this he had the advantage of an absolute influence not only over the Western Emperor Valentinian III., but over his mother and wife, so that the imperial heart and arm were with him in all his schemes for the unification and organization of the spiritual power of the church.

Yet while all-powerful and practically without resistance in the West, Leo was at this juncture powerless in the East. He had indeed a noble and powerful ally at court in the person of Pulcheria, the remarkable sister of Theodosius II., who had been the friend of orthodoxy in the person of Cyril in the General Council of Ephesus as she was to be so to Leo in connection with the Council of Chalcedon. But through the machinations of Chrysaphius Pulcheria was powerless at this time and the weak emperor was in the hands of Eutyches and Dioscorus. Leo implored him to at least let matters stand as they had been prior to the proceedings against Eutyches, to give no authority to the disorderly Council at Ephesus and to authorize the assembling of a really ecumenical council in Italy. But to his appeals and those of the whole imperial family of the West he had no reply from the emperor but a defence of the freedom, regularity and authority of the Latrocinium. Meantime Dioscorus, who continued to have things his own way, had excommunicated Leo. Anatolius, supposed at first to be his adherent and instrument, had succeeded Flavian at Constantinople. The rest of the East was still intimidated by the action of the Council of Ephesus and the determination of the emperor to enforce its decisions.

Suddenly in the summer of 450 the whole aspect of matters was changed by the sudden death of Theodosius II. and the accession to the throne of the pious and orthodox Pulcheria. To strengthen herself Pulcheria married and associated with her in the empire the able General Marcian, and in both these Leo and the catholic faith found old and tried friends. Instantly the ecclesiastical atmosphere began to clear. Anatolius of Constantinople signed the famous Epistle to Flavian which was the condition of communion with Rome, and was ranged on the side of Leo. The Eastern bishops who had been intimidated into compliance with the decisions of Ephesus breathed again and one by one explained and recanted, and everything bade fair to fall back of its own accord into the orthodox channel.

Marcian had been prompt to take up Leo's desire for a really ecumenical council, but Leo himself now under the changed aspect of matters began to hesitate, especially since Marcian while anxious to concede everything else to him seemed firmly and quietly to disregard his request that the council should depart from precedent and go to the West. But matters had gone too far; the council was called, first for

Nicæa but subsequently for Chalcedon; and Leo, only stipulating that dogmatic questions should not be stirred anew and treated as doubtful or unsettled, prepared to take the leading part in it.

The time and conditions all happily conspired to favor the views and designs of Leo, which were not wholly restricted, as we shall see in the end, to a dogmatic interest in the church's faith. The imperial courts East and West were wholly with him. Dioscorus was involved in the ruin that the cause of Eutyches had brought upon itself by the proceedings of Ephesus. In all the church there was not a single commanding personality to stand by his side and share with him the influence and honors that were to be all his own. The council though summoned by the emperor was assembled by his authority—" te auctore, " Marcian had written to him—and was to be presided over by his legates.

The Council of Chalcedon met early in October and was composed from first to last of over six hundred bishops. Dioscorus having entered and taken his seat was made to leave it and take his place among those under accusation. When Theodoret and those deposed at Ephesus entered as members, there was a loud outcry from the opposite side against their reception, but they were admitted as accusers.

The council began its proceedings by ratifying the decisions of the preceding ecumenical ones, Nicæa, Constantinople, and Ephesus, with apparently for the first time some discussion of the verbal differences introduced into the Nicene Symbol upon no recorded authority, to which allusion has already been made.

Charges were brought by Eusebius of Dorylæum, the original accuser of Eutyches, against Dioscorus for his treatment of Flavian and himself at the Latrocinium. Both Dioscorus and Eutyches were condemned and excommunicated.

Leo had stipulated that the council should make no new definition of the faith, assuming that it was already determined and sufficiently stated in his Tome, which was now generally accepted. But Marcian was resolved that the two parties should not separate without putting their own hands to a formula of concord which should compose their differences and insure peace. Without dwelling upon the successive steps by which this end was secured, we may now pass to a consideration of the general dogmatic results of the great Council of Chalcedon, which have controlled the faith of the catholic church from that time to this, with only a few supplementary and explanatory additions by the later general councils of Constantinople.

In the first place the catholic creed, as has been said, was recited and accepted separately in both its forms, that of Nicæa and that of Constantinople, and the Council of Ephesus was recognized as ecumenical. "On the doctrine of the Trinity," it was declared, "those creeds required no further explanation nor was any other faith to be taught or creed proposed for acceptance to converts from what heresy soever, under pain of deposition in the case of the clergy and excommunication in that of the laity." On the mystery of the incarnation the synodical letters of Cyril to Nestorius and the Easterns and the Epistle of Leo to Flavian were received as correct expositions of the truth, the former as against the heresy of Nestorius, the latter against the opposite one of Eutyches. So far only the council was disposed to go, but Marcian required that it should make a definition of its own upon the point immediately at issue. After much vacillation from side to side and much firm insistence and even suggestion on the part of the emperor, the famous symbol of Chalcedon was passed and all the above-stated action appended to it as constituting together the Chalcedonian Decrees. On October 25, 451, the action was subscribed by the whole council, the Roman legates alone attesting that they subscribed but did not define. Marcian and Pulcheria attended in state the closing scene and the emperor modestly and appropriately addressed the parting bishops in much the same spirit and with quite the impressiveness of Constantine at Nicæa.

With regard to the doctrinal formularies included in the decrees, it is of course unnecessary to say anything further of the creed or creeds. We may pass by also, as already considered, the letters of Cyril exposing the fallacies and errors of Nestorianism. It is only as against a specific heresy that the mind of Cyril stands forever as the exponent of that of the church. Against the limitations and deficiencies of his own views on the opposite side all the remaining action of Chalcedon stands equally as a corrective if not a protest.

With regard to the Epistle to Flavian it is necessary to say something more in connection with the subject of Eutychianism which is still before us. The Tome of Leo in connection with the symbol of the council effectually accomplished its immediate end, and the council in taking a positive step parallel and supplementary if not quite equal in magnitude and importance to that of Nicæa fully entitled itself to be received as ecumenical. It fixed once for all the second of the two constituent elements that were to enter into the church's doctrine of the person of Christ. For the first time, alongside of the Athanasian statement of the real divinity of the incarnate Lord was posited something like a corresponding and adequate statement of the reality and actuality of his humanity. The two natures were affirmed to be not only in themselves and before the union but in their union in the one Christ each complete in all the faculties and functions proper to it, so that our Lord is in his human life and activity as complete and perfect man as he is also true and perfect God. "Leo says clearly and this constitutes his merit that the fundamental truth of Christianity is sacrificed quite as much by a curtailment of the humanity as by a curtailment of the divinity of Christ" (Dorner). " God so became man that each nature and substance preserved its distinctive characteristics while both were conjoined in one person." The true God was born in the entire nature of a true man; he was *totus in suis, totus in nostris*. As the divinity was in no wise diminished or changed by incarnation in humanity, so the humanity in no sense ceased to be itself or to act according to its own constitution and laws by assumption into the deity.

Substantially identical in position with Leo's treatise is the symbol of the council itself which we will now give in full:

"Following the example of the holy fathers, we teach and confess one and the same Son, our Lord Jesus Christ, the same perfect in deity and the same perfect in humanity, very God and very man, consisting of reasonable soul and flesh, of the same substance with the Father as touching his Godhead, of the same substance with us as touching his humanity; in all things like to us, without sin; begotten of the Father as touching his Godhead before the æons; begotten in the latter day for our redemption of the Virgin Mary, the mother of God, as touching his humanity; one and the same Christ, Son, Lord, only-begotten, in two natures acknowledged unmixed, unchanged, undivided; so that the distinction of nature was never abolished by the union but rather the peculiarity of each preserved and combined into one person and one hypostasis; not one, severed and divided into two persons, but one and the same Son and only-begotten, him who is God, Logos and the Lord Jesus Christ. And inasmuch as the holy synod has formularized these things in all aspects with all accuracy and care, it decrees that it be not allowed to propound any other faith either in writings or in thought or to teach it to others. Whosoever dareth to act in opposition to this decree shall be deposed if of the clergy, shall be excommunicated if of the laity."

The general result of the Council of Chalcedon has been summed up substantially as follows: It is conceded to be not improbable that personally both Nestorius and Eutyches were treated unjustly by the

Councils of Ephesus and Chalcedon. They suffered not so much for principles distinctly held or avowed by them as for consequences deduced by others from their teaching. "But although the synod may have been unjust in condemning the men, it was not wrong in deciding that the two theories of Nestorianism and Eutychianism, to which henceforth a dogmatical instead of a merely historical significance attached, should be anticipatorily laid down as buoys, pointing out to the church the middle course along which its voyage must proceed. The symbol of Chalcedon may be characterized as a declaration on the part of the church that no doctrine of the person of Christ can lay claim to the name of Christian which puts a double Christ in the place of the incarnate Son of God or which teaches either a mere conversion of God into a man or, vice versa, of a man into God" (Dorner).

Thus once more was the church brought to condemn both of the opposite tendencies to which the course of its thought was always subject. In putting its foot at once upon Nestorianism and Eutychianism it was crushing again on the one hand the Ebionitic tendency that under its attack upon the term "Theotocos" only veiled a denial of the real deity of the Son of Mary, and on the other hand the Docetic tendency that in its assertion of the one only incarnate nature of our Lord taught the virtual absorption and loss of his humanity.

Nevertheless the immediate—and perhaps we ought also to say, the permanent—effect of the Council of Chalcedon was and remains a disappointment. The church had accomplished in it more than she either knew or intended, and it remained for far-off future ages that have scarcely yet arrived to take the Council of Chalcedon at its word and honestly construe the person of our Lord in the totality of his manhood as well as his Godhead. It is one of the not infrequent instances in which the collective voice of the church has seemed far in advance of the individual minds that have given it utterance. Of this there is no better illustration than in the case of Leo himself, the master mind and controlling spirit, though not personally present at the Council of Chalcedon.

We have not underrated the greatness of either the mind or the services to Christianity and civilization of Leo, as a far-seeing statesman and an able and powerful organizer and administrator. But if Leo's was a great practical it was not an equally great speculative, philosophical or theological genius. His mind, character and policy were the highest reach and illustration of that type which we have already briefly described as distinctively Western and Roman. Incapable by mental constitution of contributing to the scientific formation and development of doctrine, averse by policy to taking part in it, his genius lay in the line of the practical wisdom and common sense whose function in the church was to pass judgment upon the results of thought and impart to them the authority and weight of catholic authority. The merit and value of his Tome arose from the fact that while the parties engaged in the problem of thinking out and stating the opposite aspects of the person of

Christ were unavoidably liable to the double danger, each, of ignoring both its own error and its antagonist's truth, Leo was in the position of an equally interested and personally unoccupied spectator who could see the drift and danger of both. The brilliancy, power and apparent originality of the Tome are mainly not in the thought but in the statement and in the incomparable tone of authority in which the culture of ages almost attains perfection. He excludes the error on both sides, he affirms the truth on both. But he did neither of these in such a way that both sides could see it, and therefore he did it to the permanent satisfaction of neither side.

Why did not the solution of Chalcedon satisfy? Leo saw that the tendency of Nestorius was to a higher Ebionism and he accepted and reaffirmed the sentence of Ephesus upon him and it; he saw that the end of Eutychianism was a subtle but patent Docetism and he procured a final sentence upon it at Chalcedon. Thus the real deity and the real humanity, the presence together in the one person of the Lord of two natures, the divine and human, distinct, unconverted and unconfused, yet indivisible and inseparable, were affirmed as plainly and positively as words could express them. One might ask, What more was needed or possible? The answer is that the mere affirmation, no matter on what authority, of two opposite and apparently irreconcilable facts is not a real and therefore cannot be a satisfactory solution of the problem of their coexistence. The only solution is so to explain the facts as to show that they are not irreconcilable but rather mutually require or postulate each other. The difficulty with Leo, as with the mind of the church as yet, is that he did not himself so understand either the divine or the human nature in our Lord as to present a satisfactory and convincing picture of their unity. His unity of the two natures in the one person was simply an affirmation. It was not so construed or explained as to render it to the speculative or reflective mind any less inconceivable or impossible than it was before.

Leo however and all the West with him were perfectly satisfied that the Tome and the symbol had done all that was necessary and that the question was settled forever. Jesus Christ in his incarnation is very God and very man, *totus in suis, totus in nostris*, complete in all that constitutes Godhead, complete in all that constitutes manhood. But how can this be so? And how is it so? The answer with them was, practically: By the omnipotence of God, and the authority of Leo's Tome and the symbol of Chalcedon. That part of the mind of the church which had created the symbols could not be satisfied with such a closure of the question. Divine omnipotence and human authority combined cannot of themselves constitute a dogma. That requires in addition a δοκεῖ, a *placet*, from the universal spiritual understanding and experience of spiritual and rational men. The full question actually before the church at the time was not merely: Is Christ both God and man? That, in terms at least, all held. But it was: How is he both God and man; how shall we blend and combine the two into one, and see and construe and accept the unity? It was only in the inability and the effort to do this that one side fell into an unreality of the deity, and the other into an absorption and loss of the humanity. Leo succeeded admirably in affirming but not at all in explaining the duality in the unity and the unity in the duality. And the Greek world at least went on in its task of thinking out the problem as though nothing had been said at Chalcedon.

It is easy to show that in this instance, as in many others, without a proper conception of the διότι it is impossible to hold the ὅτι. Leo himself, through disregard or misconception of how Christ is complete in both natures, unconsciously does not hold the completeness of both natures in him. Indeed it is scarcely an exaggeration to say that Leo could not reconcile the unity with the duality for the reason that he held neither a real duality nor a true unity. Let us test this in detail.

First with regard to the two natures: Our Lord, he says, is in his incarnation *totus in suis, totus in nostris*. That is, he is complete in all the attributes of his deity, which are unchanged by his assumption of humanity, and complete in all the characteristics, the faculties, functions and activities of our humanity, which is not supplanted or swallowed up but only quickened, heightened and realized by its union with deity. This is what his words mean, and they are true.

But when we come to ascertain what are the *nostra* in which Leo sees our Lord's humanity complete, what indeed are they? He says, for example, very truly and admirably—and this is what is catholic in him—that " it is the catholic faith that in Christ Jesus there is neither humanity without true divinity nor divinity without true humanity. Neither of these received without the other would avail for our salvation and it is of equal peril to believe the Lord Jesus Christ either God only without man or man only without God." But he goes on to say that "the denial of a true flesh is fatal." Why? Only " because it is a denial of the capacity for the bodily pains and sufferings which our Lord endures for our salvation." There is no really human significance given by Leo to any activity or experience of our Lord higher than those which are corporeal. The Son of God has merely assumed a nature in which it may be possible for deity to undergo experiences and sufferings of which it is incapable in its own nature. All the action of our Lord in the flesh is only divine, it is only his passion which is human. On the contrary we say that if Christ was *totus in nostris*, then he was human in all the activities as well as the passivities of a rational, free, moral and spiritual, and not only a corporeal, manhood. His highest act of faith in God, his supremest attainment of self-sacrificing love and obedience, his entire conquest of sin and victory over death, were as truly human acts and activities—and needed a thousandfold more for our salvation to be truly human—as his merely bodily passion. It is characteristic of the position still occupied by Leo to see the reality of our Lord's humanity in the facts of his hunger, thirst and weariness, of his physical birth and death,—that is to say in functions (ἐνέργειαι) which are not distinctively human at all but only animal, which so far from being the whole of us as men do not even belong to us distinctively as men.

In the second place, not only does Leo incompletely apprehend the *nostra* or "ours" in which the church through him affirms our Lord's human completeness, but he introduces into our Lord's personal consciousness and will and acts a duality, different indeed from that charged against Nestorianism but hardly less objectionable in itself. The human Jesus thinks, knows, wills and does this as God and that as man. As man he is hungry, as God he feeds the multitude; as God he says, " I and my Father are one;" as man, " My Father is greater than I;" as man, "Where have ye laid him?" as God, "Lazarus, come forth." He thus humanly manifests, exhibits to our very senses, a double consciousness, volition and action, passing at will from one to the other aspect of what cannot but appear to us as a twofold personality.

The above is sufficient to indicate the grounds of the charge that Leo had not yet arrived at a satisfactory conception or appreciation either of our Lord's completeness in each nature or of his unity in both. But neither had he any conception of any lack in his own views or in their expression; and the misfortune is that at this critical moment his supreme personal and official weight of authority closed the great living question pressing upon men's minds and hearts for further solution, and not so much settled it as fixed it as it stood, forever unsettled, in the Western Church. For the contribution from Rome to the supplementary work of the Sixth General Council is only a reiteration of Leo's position, and further than that Rome has not moved since.

The doctrinal results of the Council of Chalcedon were sufficiently satisfactory to Leo, although he would have preferred that it should not define but simply accept his own formula of the faith; but there were other results that were far from satisfactory to him. It was characteristic of Leo that throughout his career he subordinated and consecrated his great personal gifts and powers to the task of consolidating and extending the paramount authority of the Roman see. Beside that his far-seeing statesmanship fully appreciated the practical importance and even necessity of this, the traditional theory of the divinely derived supremacy of the chair of St. Peter had attained in his hands a relative if not yet its most fully developed completeness. And there is no question that apart from his dogmatic interest in the faith of the church he was actuated by the perhaps secondary but certainly powerful motive and hope of turning his doctrinal influence and weight to good account in the extension of his practical scheme. It was the first opportunity the Roman see had had of extending its prestige and authority in the East through any paramount or even prominent part in a general council, and everything conspired as we have seen to make it a very great opportunity.

Leo had been anxious, in the interest both of the doctrinal and the practical ends which he had in view, that the council should meet at Rome or should not meet at all; but this part of his request Marcian silently but firmly ignored. The emperor was throughout resolved to further the doctrinal purposes of Leo but quietly to thwart and defeat his political scheme of aggrandizing Rome, especially at the expense of Constantinople. The council itself too seemed to be conscious of Leo's designs, and while it made many and great admissions and concessions upon the surface, its general disposition and its final action were to set itself against them. It had been a matter of traditional right and propriety that the ecumenical discussions and determinations of the catholic faith should take place in the East, where they could be conducted by Greek thought and in the Greek tongue; and the suggestion of a general council to be held in the West was itself received as an innovation. The threat by which Marcian finally brought the bishops to agreement upon the symbol was that if the council adjourned without agreeing it would be to meet again in Rome. Indeed the council in itself was not only not in sympathy with what might be Leo's practical schemes but if left to itself its doctrinal conclusions would have been both conceived and expressed in far greater independence of him. Nothing but the most pointed intervention of the emperor brought either the meaning or the form of the decrees sufficiently near to his mind to avert on the part of the Roman legates the withholding of their signatures and their withdrawal from the synod.

We see thus three elements finally combined in the decisions of Chalcedon, Leo, Marcian and the body of the council itself, no two of which were wholly at one. The emperor alone perhaps was successful and satisfied in all points with the result. He secured his formula of concord; he kept the council in dogmatic accord with the mind of Leo; and at the same time he had, as we shall see, advanced the ecclesiastical claims of the imperial see of Constantinople and thwarted the aggressive ambition of that of Rome. With regard to the council we shall see immediately and abundantly that the decrees of Chalcedon were rather the beginning than the end of controversy with regard to the main subject-matter of its action.

As for Leo, while the dogmatic result of the council was on the whole a triumph for him, largely through the emperor, his practical plans, at least not without the emperor, sustained a distinct rebuff. It will be remembered that the Second General Council, held in Constantinople, had decreed that the bishop of that city should have the primacy of honor after Rome, on the ground that "it is itself New Rome." This decree had long given great offence and had not been acknowledged at Rome, because it assumes that the primacy accorded to it rested upon purely secular and political grounds and not upon a divine right. At Chalcedon it was thought necessary for practical reasons and was desired that the jurisdiction of Constantinople which had been growing up under that decree should be reaffirmed and confirmed. The emperor, the senators and the people of the imperial capital were interested in pressing the measure, and the council was not averse to reiterating its own version of the primacy which had from the first naturally attached to the political and secular centre and capital of the world. With this view the twenty-eighth canon was adopted, which provides as follows:

"The fathers gave with reason the primacy to old Rome because that was the royal city; and with the same object in view the one hundred and eighty pious bishops gave equal primacy to the chair of New Rome." This canon confirming the action of the one hundred and eighty bishops at Constantinople was enacted against the determined opposition of the Roman legates and with full knowledge of the fact that Leo and his predecessors had steadily refused to acknowledge the action then ratified and confirmed. The ground of offence is thus stated by Leo himself: " Secular importance cannot confer ecclesiastical privilege "; " Alia est ratio rerum sæcularium, alia divinarum." The Roman bishops based their claims upon the divine prerogatives of St. Peter. The council as yet continued to base them upon the " gift of the fathers," and stated the reason of them to be that the natural capital of the world ought to be the spiritual capital of the church.

CHAPTER XIII.

THE MONOPHYSITES AND THE SECOND COUNCIL OF CONSTANTINOPLE.

HE action of the Council of Chalcedon was the first general recognition and triumph of that side of the truth of Christ which had been represented by Antioch. How barren the victory was and was to remain for many ages could scarcely be appreciated at the time. In terms it was all or almost all that could be desired. What more can be said than that our incarnate Lord is *totus in nostris*, if only the words be allowed to mean all they say? And what less or more do they say than that he was in all points like as we are, sin only excepted? But unfortunately, as we have seen, neither Leo nor the church fully meant as yet all the truth that in the providence of God they were made to bear witness to. The gain was there, but it was stored up and laid aside for future use. The two facts, of the very Godhead and the very manhood, of the completeness of the two natures in the unity of a single personality, were destined to lie side by side in the treasury of the church's thought a long time before they should enter into a really organic and vital union. Indeed have they done so

yet? What more can we claim than that we more and more see that in themselves they do exist in such a union and that more and more also we appreciate the fact that the integrity of neither can be truly maintained at the cost of that of the other? Against the council's own symbol there is nothing to be said. Nor anything against that in the Tome of Leo which was accepted by the council as the statement of its own doctrinal position. What we object to in Leo is not his facts but his philosophy. That he marked out the channel for the church's future course and as it were located the Scylla and Charybdis between which it was necessary to steer is a service of which the credit can never be taken away from him. But it remains that the hypostatical union as he understood it was still very far from being the true organic unity of Godhead and manhood in the person of our Lord. And there was this irreparable harm, that the weight of his personal greatness in combination with the now full-grown authority of the chair of St. Peter, at least in the West, was sufficient almost to arrest the further development of the truth of Christ. The East will indeed continue for a few centuries longer to think, but its conclusions will beat themselves in vain against the rock of Roman fixedness and stability. And the East itself, without the balance and correction of the now no longer plastic and responsive practical good sense of the West, will think more wildly and futilely; until, with one final summation of itself in John of Damascus, its thought too will sink exhausted into a stereotyped orthodoxy incapable of further change.

For the present then the advocates of the integrity of the two natures in Christ were satisfied, and there was no further complaint from the Antiochian side. It was only when considerably later the representatives of the actuality of our Lord's humanity undertook to develop and apply the Chalcedonian definition in accordance with the truth of its letter that it was discovered that that was not intended and would not be permitted. The trouble now was on the other or Alexandrian side, with the many who could not see that with the Chalcedonian assertion of the two natures any satisfactory representation was given them of the unity of our Lord's person. The result of the experiment at Chalcedon, and especially of Leo's own presentation, was rather to convince very many that a distinction of the natures after the union was inconsistent with any real preservation of the unity, and there arose a school of scientific Monophysitism which was often more than a match in argument for the truer intuition but inferior science and logic of the church teachers. This new movement we shall first briefly sketch historically and then endeavor to characterize doctrinally.

The publication of the decrees of Chalcedon, as has been said, was only the signal for a new outbreak of Monophysitism throughout the East. To the great body of monks especially it came with the meaning and force of a compulsory universal establishment of Nestorianism. Everywhere the most determined opposition was instantly developed; first of course and chiefly at Alexandria, but also in Jerusalem, Constantinople, and even Antioch the Monophysites exhibited an unparalleled and violent activity. Marcian's decrees enforcing uniformity followed one another in rapid succession. In A.D. 457 he was succeeded by Leo I., who perplexed by the fierceness and apparent hopelessness of the strife conceived the idea of testing the real mind of the church by a very natural though novel method. All the metropolitans were instructed to procure the judgments of the bishops subject to them not only upon certain issues raised by the enforcement but also upon the general question of the validity of the decrees of Chalcedon. Some sixteen hundred bishops responded, from all quarters of the empire, and the verdict was overwhelmingly in favor of the decrees. Nevertheless the Monophysites, making up in activity for their inferiority in numbers, continued more than to hold their own in the great centres of the East.

In the year 470 Peter the Fuller succeeded in displacing the orthodox incumbent from the patriarchal throne of Antioch. This Peter was very active and successful in propagating Monophysite views and sentiments by incorporating them through liturgical changes into the public worship of the church. Many of his interpolations acquired immediate and general popularity and were adopted even in catholic churches. Thus in the Trisagion he introduced a clause in which the triune God is addressed as having suffered for us: "Holy God, Holy Strong One, Holy Immortal One, who for our sakes wast crucified for us, have mercy upon us!" Thus under the form of Theopaschitism was revived the old spirit and principle of Patripassianism, and it became perhaps the most insidious and successful of the aspects in which Monophysitism continued not only to hold its own against the church but also to make its way within it, until in the Fifth General Council it won a decisive success if not a permanent victory. The phrases " mother of God," " God was crucified " and the like, while containing a precious truth which the piety of the opposite side was not disposed to contradict, were nevertheless characteristic of Monophysitism and were part of a systematic reference of the whole incarnate activity of our Lord to his Godhead, and an ignoring of all personally human activities in him. It is to be observed that this aspect of Christianity always appeals most powerfully to the heart of the popular faith. In proportion as it is less moral it has the appearance of being more religious. The more mystically we surrender our minds and wills and selves to the operations of the divine grace, and the less reflectively we strive to realize our own parts in the process of regaining our freedom and life in Christ Jesus, the more honor we feel ourselves to be doing to God who is our sole salvation.

The Emperor Leo I. was succeeded A.D. 474 by Zeno, who favored the catholics, until in the year 482 he was led into a fatal scheme of reconciliation the effect of which was only the more wildly and helplessly to divide the two parties. We have not thought it necessary for our purpose to go into the details of the violent and often bloody strife that immediately followed the Council of Chalcedon in Alexandria, the proper home of Monophysitism. At the juncture we have now reached the rival claimants of the patriarchal throne were appealing to the church at large for recognition. Rome favored the orthodox candidate, but Acacius of Constantinople and the Emperor Zeno were unfortunately persuaded that to recognize the Monophysite contestant, Peter Mongus, would be to begin at the heart of all the trouble over a gradual compromise and reconciliation. Mongus affected a moderation and desire for peace that lasted only until he had attained his object, but under the influence of his representations the emperor with the aid of Acacius drew up and issued an edict of union that was known as the Henoticon (ἑνωτικὸν). It was a confession of faith based upon the first three general councils and ignoring that of Chalcedon. All disputed terms and phrases were avoided and the issues dividing the parties carefully kept out of sight. The effect, as has been said, was only to multiply the number of parties and to increase the irritation between them. Each side was divided into two, of which the most politic and least sincere accepted the compromise, while the zealots withdrew into a wider and more embittered separation. Then outside of these were the very many of all views who resented the presumption of the emperor in promulgating a doctrinal formula in his own name. The right of the emperor even to force the church to define and then to enforce the definition had been long recognized, but Zeno was the first to undertake himself to declare what was the faith of the church. Rome of course resisted the compromise; Pope Felix III. after long remonstrating in vain excommunicated Acacius. The excommunication was disregarded in the East and the result was a schism which lasted for nearly forty years. In 491 Zeno was succeeded by Anastasius, who during a reign of twenty-four years persisted faithfully and conscientiously in carrying out a scheme of conciliation that kept all the capitals of the East in perpetual and fruitless turmoil and strife. Justin, who succeeded to the empire in 518, was orthodox and during his reign of eleven years the centres of controversy for the most part returned to the fold of Chalcedon. Acacius and the Emperors Zeno and Anastasius were stricken from the diptychs; communion was resumed with Rome and the West; Alexandria alone remained true to Monophysitism and thither the leaders of the party betook themselves and bided their time.

The long and illustrious reign of Justinian began A.D. 527. The Empress Theodora was an ardent adherent of Monophysitism and under her patronage the sect revived and reorganized itself everywhere. Even in Constantinople a covert Monophysite was through her influence elevated to the patriarchate. Justinian himself began his reign as a positive and decided Chalcedonian, but was not long in contracting the imperial mania for acting the part of a theological as well as political mediator between the parties. His first movement of concession toward the Monophysites was in connection with the Theopaschite controversy originated by Peter Fuller's liturgical interpolations. The popularity of the added phrase, " God who wast crucified for us!" had grown steadily in the intervening years. There was a devotional and religious element in it that appealed to the mystical spirit in us which welcomes the closest approach and identification of God himself with us in our extremest experiences. It seemed only to involve the same principle which the church had already affirmed in its formal adoption of the Theotocos. If it was God who was born of the Virgin, it was God also who was crucified upon Calvary. There was a revolt against Leo's distribution of the actions and passions of our Lord between the Godhead and the manhood, the miracles to the former, the sufferings to the latter. There was but one subject of all the actions and the passions, the divine Person incarnate, and Leo's position was but a latent Nestorianism. The liturgical formula had found acceptance in Constantinople. In Justin's reign an effort was made, but without success, to gain recognition for the amended form of the Trisagion. The attempt was transferred to Rome, where Pope Hormisdas condemned the formula as heretical. But under his successor it found favor, and the ablest Western theologian maintained that it was orthodox to say that "one of the Trinity was born and was crucified." Justinian's first act of conciliation was to sanction the formula by a special edict issued A.D. 533. Twenty years afterward the Fifth General Council anathematized all who should reject it.

Soon after his favorable edict Justinian was moved by an exposure of the secret machinations of the Monophysites, under the patronage of the empress, to attempt once more a policy of repression and persecution. This only led to renewed trouble, and finally to the revolt of the Monophysite province of Armenia to the Persians. The effect was to bring back the emperor to his plan of reconciliation, and not long after began the famous controversy of "the Three Chapters," the most important movement in the present stage of our subject since it led to the Fifth General Council and constituted its subject-matter.

It was Justinian's personal ambition to go to the heart of the whole matter and settle it by a theological treatise of his own which should convince the Monophysites by answering all their objections to the Council of Chalcedon. But although ambitious of being an authority and disposed to be a despot in spiritual as well as temporal matters, the emperor was open to influence, sometimes in opposite directions, if judiciously applied. He was now persuaded that what was needed and would be efficacious to reconcile the Monophysites was formally to complete the church's condemnation of Nestorianism; and this could only be accomplished by condemning Theodore of Mopsuestia and at least such of the works of Theodoret and Ibas as were directed against Cyril, who with the Monophysites stood even above Athanasius as the defender and representative of the faith. Theodoret and Ibas, who had charged Cyril with Apollinarianism, had themselves been acquitted of all charges of heresy by the Council of Chalcedon. A condemnation would be equally acceptable as against them and as a blow at the authority of the council.

In 544 Justinian issued his edict of the Three Chapters, in which were anathematized the person and the works of Theodore and the particular works but not the persons of Theodoret and Ibas. This act combined in a single policy the emperor, the empress and a certain portion of both parties, the catholics being deterred by that which most commended it to the Monophysites,—the fact namely that to a certain extent it contravened the action of Chalcedon. Like its predecessors it proved to be a measure of compulsory conciliation, which was more successful, if it was so, only because the influence of Justinian was more compelling. The Eastern patriarchs were brought by bribery and intimidation to yield an unwilling subscription to the edict. The chief opposition came from North Africa, Illyria and Dalmatia where the bishops refused to damn the dead or to put a slight upon the decisions of Chalcedon. But the most remarkable feature in the controversy of the Three Chapters was the relation to it of the Pope Vigilius. Vigilius had secured the papal chair through the influence of Theodora at the price of his coöperation with the Monophysite leaders in opposition to the Chalcedonian Decrees. He had put in writing his substantial agreement with them, had rejected the doctrine of the two natures after the union, and had anathematized those who, with Leo, distributed the acts and sufferings of our Lord between his deity and his humanity. When firmly established in his seat however he had changed his tone. Before subscribing the edict, he submitted it to the Western theologian Fulgentius Ferrandus, whose decision was adverse,— mainly upon the grounds already taken by others, (1) that it was unwise to unsettle the action of general councils, and (2) that deceased brethren were beyond the reach of human judgment. Vigilius, vacillating between what he felt to be the sentiment of the Western Church, his past compromises with the Monophysites, and the pressure of the emperor, was in 547 summoned by the latter to Constantinople where he was detained seven years by the emperor's persistent determination to conciliate the church in despite of itself. More than once Vigilius consented to the condemnation of the Three Chapters and then bending before the storm of opposition from the West, that proceeded in one instance even to the point of his excommunication by the church of North Africa, retracted his condemnation. In 551 he begged the emperor to convene a general council, pending which he might withhold his final decision. The emperor consented upon the condition that he should bind himself by an oath not to recede from the condemnation of the Three Chapters. In 553 the Fifth General Council, the Second of Constantinople, met and finally with much delay and trouble extorted a judgment from Vigilius. He had now Western theologians by his side and for once decided firmly and adversely. He would not (1) condemn in the person of Theodore a writer who had died in the communion of the church, nor (2) pronounce heretical the works of Theodoret and Ibas which had received the sanction of Chalcedon. Thereupon the emperor and the council broke off all communion with Vigilius and proceeded to act without him. The edict of the Three Chapters was adopted as it stood; Theodore was anathematized in his person and works and the particular writings of the others were condemned. Then the opposition of Vigilius broke down; he accepted the authority and subscribed the decisions of the council. There was great dissatisfaction in the West, resulting in a schism of many bishops for many years. But there was nothing for Vigilius's successors to do but to accept and sustain his action. And so in the West as in the East the council was recognized as the Fifth Ecumenical.

But the great body of the more zealous and sincere Monophysites was not conciliated. Under the successors of Justinian, Justin II. and Tiberius, repressive measures were once more resorted to, and of course once more failed. The Monophysite communities retain ecclesiastical organizations to this day in Syria, Armenia, Egypt and Abyssinia.

In tracing, as we shall now endeavor to do, the inner, intellectual and spiritual movement of Monophysitism between the Fourth and Fifth General Councils, we may limit ourselves to just those elements that are of permanent and present interest and value, passing over many details of tentative and temporary thought that distracted and divided the party within itself.

The general and characteristic principle of Monophysitism, that of the μιὰ or μόνη φύσις, the one or single nature of the incarnate Lord, is this: that while he combined two natures in himself he so combined them that in him they were not merely morally or gnomically but physically or naturally one. It was not a unity of two, either persons or natures, acting as one, but of one, both person and nature, incapable of acting as two. He was not only one only subject of action but exerted one only kind or mode of activity (ἐνέργεια). He did not act as both God and man or, as Leo represented it, now as God and now as man, but always as the one person that he was. This unity of action or operation, as will be readily felt, might be conceived in several different ways, but as a matter of fact the Monophysite conception was that as our Lord's person was only divine so his whole being and activity even in the flesh was determined only after the divine mode. It was as God that he not merely assumed humanity, taught the truth, worked miracles and destroyed sin and death, but also was humanly born, hungered, suffered and died. What then and where was the human nature that he assumed? It was by the physical act and fact of union with the divine so deified as to lose its own proper ἐνέργεια, and to become a mere veil, garment or mode of visibility of the activity of the divine. Or rather, more than a mere means of visibility, the humanity of our Lord is that in which and by means of which the deity renders itself capable of a kind of activity of which it is incapable in itself; the capacity that is to suffer with and for us. But the whole significance of the human nature of our Lord is that it is that in which God may act, and may be capable of acting, in a certain way. There is no room for any human action, nor indeed any need or demand for any. The whole activity of the incarnation is a purely divine and not a human activity. According to the extremest view, our Lord's very body was so deified by natural conjunction with deity that it was no longer subject to its natural functions and laws. If it hungered, was weary, suffered or died, it was not because it need have done so or indeed did so but only because our divine Lord willed to experience and endure these things in it. If he performed any even the most natural and automatic act in the body it was not an involuntary action of his body but a voluntary act of himself, because we cannot conceive of God as being for a moment really subject to the laws or conditions of matter. There was every gradation of view from this up to a merely imperceptible difference from the position of the church; indeed there were Monophysites who held a truer humanity of the Lord than the current doctrine of catholics. The lower and higher views came thus to divide, as they still divide, the Monophysites into the sects of the Julianists and the Severians. But in the highest view of Severus himself, who approached most nearly to the church and was the greatest of the Monophysites, while there was a disposition and an effort to recognize the continuance in the incarnation of a real humanity, it was only a humanity in its lowest and least distinctively human attributes and activities. According to him the body of Christ was really a human body, but was the mind, were the affections, was the will, were the moral and spiritual functions and dispositions, actions and character of our Lord human also? But it is all these things that constitute a real manhood, a really human nature, activity and life. If our Lord was indeed a man in all respects like unto us, then how can we except any of these things in which our manhood consists? But Severus excepts them every one and leaves after the union not one single attribute or activity distinctive of an actual humanity. He is wholly unwilling to concede to the human soul that reality which he concedes to the human body. Our Lord, e.g., has but one consciousness, one knowledge, and that the divine. From the moment of the union of the natures, i.e. from the moment of the conception in the womb, the consciousness of Jesus was that of the divine Logos; his knowledge was omniscience. The growth in wisdom was only apparent; there was never any limitation and therefore could be no increase or progress. He only gradually revealed or exhibited outwardly that which inwardly was complete and perfect in him from the first. So our Lord had only one, and that the infinitely and eternally perfect divine will. He was no more capable of moral than of mental progress and growth. It could not have been in any actual sense, for himself, that he learned obedience or was made perfect by the things he suffered. The cry, "Not as I will but as thou wilt!" represents no real conflict or struggle of wills. It was not uttered out of any human exigency or need of his own. His natural utterances of ignorance or of weakness are only to be heard by us; he utters them not for himself but for us, for our example and instruction.

The difficulty within Monophysitism itself and the impossibility at the time of any answer to it from the church were due to two main causes, one scientific, the other religious. The scientific difficulty was that neither party, and the church less than the Monophysites, knew exactly what it meant by the terms "nature" and "person," upon which the whole controversy hinged. The Monophysites were convinced that to attribute to our Lord a complete human nature, a humanity in which nothing is lacking that is human, would necessarily be to make him a human as well as divine person, and this seemed to them equivalent to making him two persons. They saw indeed that the church itself whatever it might avow in theory did not hold in practice the opposite truths which it had imposed upon the faith of the world by the authority of Chalcedon. Men either did not hold the one personality or else they did not hold the totality of both natures. Even Leo neither successfully conceived our Lord as one person nor wholly conceded to him the two natures. What was needed to refute Monophysitism was the fuller truth, which was then still in the future, not that our Lord was God and man in the sense that he was sometimes and in some things God and at other times and in other things man, but that his entire incarnate activity was at once that of a divine and that of a human person, and yet not that of two but of only one person both divine and human. What was still lacking to render this conception practically and scientifically as well as theoretically and mystically possible we shall endeavor to show later.

The religious difficulty was in effect an even greater one, since in relation to it the church was scarcely less Monophysite than the Monophysites. The principle of the one incarnate nature is, as we have seen, that the whole change in the humanity of our Lord through the incarnation is the immediate, instantaneous, physical or natural and necessary result of its assumption by deity. The man Jesus is holy not γνώμῃ but φύσει, by fact and necessity of nature, i.e. of his divine nature, and not through any choice, freedom or will of his human nature. There is no room for and there is no conception of a spiritual and moral as distinguished from a physical and necessary incarnation. The humanity in no sense incarnates divinity; it is wholly the divinity which incarnates itself in the humanity. There is no real significance in the human holiness, obedience and self-sacrifice of our Lord; the whole meaning and value of it is that God thus suffers in us and for us. The truth that God is incarnate in a humanity which *itself* in him dies to sin and lives to God, which is the truth of the New Testament, is not yet that of the church. There is a one-sided mystical piety which is willing that God shall be everything in us and is not willing that we shall, by consequence, be everything in God, whereas the whole truth of Jesus Christ is that in him not only God became human but man also became divine.

CHAPTER XIV.

THE MONOTHELITES AND THE THIRD COUNCIL OF CONSTANTINOPLE.

ONOPHYSITISM having under its successive defeats and persecutions withdrawn to the distant confines of the empire, the church was left for a season at peace. But the elements of the unsolved problem were still in a state of ferment, and the controversy soon broke out anew under the altered form of Monothelitism. The successive issues as they were raised and discussed may be briefly stated as follows:

By the suppression or expulsion of the revolt against the Council of Chalcedon the question of the single or double nature was, in terms at least, settled in favor of the latter. That being conceded, shall we say that there were in our Lord not only two complete natures but two complete ἐνέργειαι, or developed activities, of the natures? No, it was answered; for though there are two natures there is only one person who acts in both; and consequently there can be but one operation or activity. It is as much the divine Logos incarnate who performs all the acts that we call human as who performs those that are divine. It will be seen at once that this was giving back to the Monophysites all that had been taken away from them. They had never meant to deny to our Lord a potential but only an actual human nature; such a humanity as this, devoid of its ἰδικὴ ἐνέργεια, its proper functions and activities, they could never have hesitated to concede to him. It will not surprise us to learn that by this seemingly slight concession to them on the part of the church very many Monophysites, even in Egypt their stronghold, were won over and reconciled. But there were also those who protested at once and bitterly that to concede that was to concede everything; that the doctrine of the single functioning or activity of the natures was all that Monophysitism claimed in the single nature. And the church awoke in time to the danger and repudiated the concession.

The next issue to be raised was this: Conceding both the double nature and the double activity in the incarnation, how then are we to assume or assure the unity of the personal life of our Lord? The answer was undertaken to be given in Monothelitism. In the single personality is involved the necessity of a single will. Our Lord could not have had two wills for then he would have been two persons. He had two natures and two corresponding modes of action but it was one and the same will that acted through both and consequently though different in outward form his acts are identical in source and internal character. To this there were many objections and replies. (1) There can no more be a human activity without a human will than a human nature without a human activity. The will is the essence of the ἐνέργεια as the latter is but the actuality and activity of the nature; if one is human all three must be. (2) This involved the psychological question whether the will is a part of the person or a part of the nature, the church practically deciding in favor of the latter. (3) The Lord himself consistently represents his own will as human, "I seek not my own will, but his that sent me," "Not as I will but as thou wilt;" and the Monothelites are forced to be always explaining away his words in an unnatural sense.

This point secured, yet another issue remained to be met. What then was there to secure the accord and unity of the two wills, and was there not a possibility of the human will falling away from the divine? Unfortunately, as we shall see, the church which in the next general council with a sure instinct settled as far as the third point was unprepared as yet to meet the fourth. The double natures, the double functions and the double wills were now affirmed, but with regard to the problem of our Lord's human freedom the matter was left in a suspense that was to operate for a very long time against not only any further progress of the truth but even the securing and applying what had been attained. The ablest of the theologians who had gone so far and done so much to vindicate the now almost complete construction of our Lord's manhood faltered at the last step. For the nature they demanded a true actuality or activity and for the activity a true human will, but to the will they hesitated and declined to attribute a real freedom. But is not freedom as essential to will as will to action, or action to the nature of which it is the proper function?

The ablest of the anti-Monothelite theologians of the church was Maximus, who did much to reëstablish and preserve the truth of a not merely corporeal but intellectual, moral and spiritual humanity in our Lord. He rises very far above the idea that the human nature was only something to be acted in and through by an invisible divine agent, the Logos. Has the Logos, he asks, annihilated the will and activity of the human soul in which he is incarnate? What are our Lord's faith and love and other virtues if they are not realized by the free will and independent activity of his human soul? If he does not possess all the attributes that constitute our nature, especially the proper will and activity of the soul, then his humanity is on a level with the irrational creatures. Especially what shall we say of the holy and righteous obedience of our Lord unto death? How could he say, "I am come not to do my own will, but that I may accomplish the work and keep his commands"? Was it all the obedience of the Logos to God or the obedience of his humanity? The former view makes the divine nature of our Lord a subject and a servant, after the manner of Arius. We must assume the existence of a human will distinct from that of the Logos (Maximus, as quoted by Dorner).

Thus Maximus not only asserts for our Lord a true human will, but secures to it a relative independence from the overpowering and effacing activity of the Logos in and through it. But the freedom which he thus preserves in one connection he surrenders in another. In order to insure the certainty of his human obedience, he attributes to our Lord not that truly human holiness which is the result of freedom and choice and of an actual human development and growth, but a holiness necessary and complete from the first and incapable of progress or change. It is a holiness φύσει, though not by his divine but by his human nature. It is the effect of his virgin birth by the power of the Holy Ghost that his humanity is ἄτρεπτος, incapable of moral change. Thus his humanity is not only not ours which is fallen but it is not that of Adam which was capable of falling; it is a third kind which was neither. And a holiness by necessity of nature and not by act of will is no more a human holiness because the nature is a so-called human one that cannot sin than if it were the divine nature.

It will be seen that there seemed to be two possible ways to provide for the unchangeableness of our Lord's human holiness and obedience. One was the Monophysitic one of so subordinating and subjecting the human to the divine as to leave it no freedom or activity of its own. The other was to ascribe to the human an independence from the divine but to ascribe to it in its own nature, by some foregone action upon it usually associated with the miraculous birth, an impossibility of sinning. Dorner has clearly proved that the last general council, at Constantinople, under the opposite influences operating upon it combined these two contradictory safeguards in a manner so vacillating and inconsistent as to constitute a serious charge against its ecumenicity.

But a council is catholic so far as it is so and no further, and the Sixth General Council did add material elements to the construction of the doctrine of our Lord's person. Its contribution was the assertion of the proper humanity not only of the incarnate nature of our Lord, as decided at Chalcedon, but as essential constituents of it of his activity and will within the nature. So far it was catholic, and not as regards the still unsolved question of the freedom of the human will.

We must now briefly sketch the progress of events from the origin of the Monothelite agitation to its close in what is known as the Sixth and last Ecumenical Council. The philosophical connection of the movement with the physical and mystical speculations of the author known as the Pseudo-Dionysius Areopagitica we need only allude to. The system of Dionysius, which at this time and afterward exerted a great influence upon the theology of the church, was a pantheistic, Neoplatonic appropriation and application of the Christian doctrine of the incarnation to the explanation of the immanent relation of God to nature and to man. Many of its ideas and much of its phraseology, partly derived from Christianity, easily returned to their source and were incorporated into later Christian speculations, mainly of a Monophysitic tendency. Thus was derived the characteristic phrase of this stage of the Monothelite movement, as descriptive of our Lord's incarnate activity, $\mu\iota\grave{a}$ $\theta\epsilon a\nu\delta\rho\iota\kappa\grave{\eta}$ $\grave{\epsilon}\nu\acute{\epsilon}\rho\gamma\epsilon\iota a$, "one theandric or divine-human activity." The beginning of the discussion, as we have said, was as follows: Conceding the two natures

x

in our Lord, are we to concede also two series of activities or only a single either divine or divine-human activity? Here we must discriminate two different kinds of unity, an essential and an actual or practical unity. Of course every one must and even the Nestorians did most of all affirm the practical unity of our Lord's will and activity. However truly the wills and activities in him were two in nature they were certainly one in operation; they were so in accord and harmony in their every movement that while physically and potentially two they were actually one. This gnomic unity, as it was called, is relative; it is a unity in difference, an accord or harmony or concurrence of two or more. Now the real danger perhaps and certainly constant fear of such a gnomic unity was that it would end, even though it did not begin, in a Nestorian duality of persons in our Lord. The church itself largely shared the Monophysitic disposition to ascribe not a gnomic or moral but an essential or necessary unity if not to our Lord's nature yet to his activity in the natures. They said, it is not the nature that acts but the person in the nature. Consequently if our Lord is one person though in two natures his activity is essentially one, although in two modes or through two series of external conditions.

There were political as well as religious reasons why such a compromise with Monophysitism should commend itself just at this time. In the face of the Mohammedan invasions the Emperor Heraclius was anxious to unite the empire and especially to bring about peace among the Christians of Egypt. The patriarch Cyrus of Alexandria was his personal friend and agent, appointed there with this especial end in view. And this doctrinal concession had enabled Cyrus to reconcile the Monophysites by thousands. While the work of conciliation was thus going on in Egypt it suddenly encountered a violent opposition in the person of a monk Sophronius, who soon after became patriarch of Jerusalem. This interruption led to a reference by Cyrus of the question of the μιὰ ἐνέργεια, to which Sophronius had taken exception, to the patriarch Sergius of Constantinople. Sergius after a careful examination of the matter expressed himself as of one mind with Cyrus but counselled him, for the sake not only of the truth but of the work of peace he was accomplishing, to avoid the use of both phrases, the μιὰ ἐνέργεια and the δυὸ ἐνέργειαι. The first, he said, was new and might by some be identified with Monophysitism; the second was clearly false, since it would lead to two wills, sometimes opposed, which was impossible in one person; it would involve therefore a Nestorian separation of the humanity from the deity. "The doctrine of the God-taught fathers is that the humanity of the Lord never acts by itself or in opposition to the suggestions of the Logos hypostatically united with it, but merely when, as and in the measure in which God the Logos willed it. As our body is governed by the soul, so was the entire human life system of Christ always and in all things impelled by God." Much depends of course in language like this upon whether it is meant that the deity acts spiritually and morally upon the humanity and influences it through the human will and free activity, or whether the meaning is that it acts upon it physically and necessarily; in the latter case the activity is essentially and not morally one, which denies to our Lord any possibility of a human holiness or obedience and makes his entire spiritual and moral activity that of God alone and not of man at all.

Sergius had at first prevailed upon both Cyrus and Sophronius to forbear discussion and dispute in view of the interests at stake. But subsequently foreseeing that Sophronius, as patriarch of Jerusalem, would not continue to maintain silence, he submitted the whole matter in a full account of it to Honorius, bishop of Rome. Honorius gave it the most thorough consideration and in a very careful and clear analysis of the point at issue carried, for the first time, the whole question back from that of two natures or two operations to that of two wills in our Lord. The unity of the two natures, he maintained, was to be secured by the principle not of a *una operatio* but of a *unus operator*. It lay neither in the natures nor in the functions or activities of the natures, but in the person. Our Lord being one person possessed one will which acted in two modes of operation. Thus Honorius, bishop of Rome, was the first to give systematic statement to the doctrine of the one will in our Lord, and was the true originator of Monothelitism.

Meanwhile the Emperor Heraclius was impatient for a basis upon which to settle the disturbance created by Sophronius and to resume the work of conciliation. In A.D. 638 he issued his Ἔκθεσις πίστεως, or exposition of the faith, taking substantially the position of Honorius, forbidding any further discussion of the single or double activity and enforcing the doctrine of the one will. But quite apart from the inherent difficulties in this new solution of the problem of our Lord's unity in duality, what was much more practically to the point was the fact that this doctrine of Honorius's was in direct contradiction to the point of view of Leo and the Epistle to Flavian, to say nothing of the formula of Chalcedon. The consequence was that after Honorius's death in 638 his successors at once reversed the attitude of the Roman see and entered upon a war to the death with Monothelitism. The new emperor Constans adjusted himself to the change in the situation to the extent of substituting for the Ἔκθεσις of his predecessor his own Τύπος τῆς πίστεως, in which all discussion was forbidden not only of the one or two operations but of the one or two wills. But this was equally inadequate, and the Lateran Council of 649, under Pope Martin I., condemned the Τύπος for undertaking to suppress the truth of the two wills. In this stage of the controversy the most prominent and ablest of the theologians of the church was Maximus, of whom we have already spoken. The position of Maximus was substantially in the line of Leo and his Tome. He vindicated the position of the will as a constituent element in the idea of a rational being and therefore in the nature and operation of our Lord's humanity if it is real. "He was even as a man essentially a voluntary being. The saying of the fathers that Christ moulded our will does not mean that the Logos determined the will of Christ; but that he as a man subjected humanity in himself and through himself to God the Father, thus setting us an example of a perfect kind that we also may voluntarily submit ourselves" (Dorner). Here almost for the first time in this Christological discussion we have something like an adequate recognition of the full significance of our Lord's human activity in the work of our redemption and completion. The whole truth of Christ is twofold and requires the totality of both sides, as Leo said better than he either knew or meant in the *totus in suis, totus in nostris*. Not only does it not consist solely in something which God became or did as God in the nature of man, something which deity suffered or accomplished by suffering, but even the divine part in the incarnation is most properly manifested in what man does and becomes. The truth as it is in Jesus is humanity's death to sin and life to God. It is an act at once of God in humanity and equally of humanity in God. The human Jesus by the way of the cross brings man into at-one-ment with God and redemption from sin and death. As Maximus expresses it, he as a man subjected humanity in himself and through himself to God the Father. A human activity that is thus the redemption and completion of humanity must have been in itself not only the activity of a very real and actual humanity but a very human activity of it. It must have been quite as really an activity of manhood as it was of Godhead.

This Maximus saw and attempted to secure; if he still fell short in one or more respects it was only because the spiritual science of his day was still incomplete. A brief reference to the defects of his thought will prepare us to see wherein it needed to be completed.

In the first place the real cause and we may almost say justification of the great Monothelitic revolt from the church lay in the fact that the predominant mind of the latter as represented by Leo and now even by Maximus did not offer to it any real unity of the natures in Christ. One personal subject lived and acted in both, and they were thus united in him but they were not united in themselves. In him they remained distinct and apart and he acted now in one of them and now in the other. The Monothelites could not see any difference of consequence or value between this and the dual personality of Nestorianism. The two natures, they said with much truth, are never truly combined in your one Christ but remain forever outside and alongside of each other. Their only unity is that the personal subject of both is the divine Logos, who in the divine nature acts in accordance with what is proper to it and in the human nature acts in and through what is distinctive and constitutive of it, e.g. through a human will and activity. This is no real unity but only a juxtaposition and concord of two forever separate and different things. If such an activity in two distinct natures were really carried out through the totality of the functions of both it would necessarily result in two personalities as well as personal activities. It only does not, if indeed it does not, because the church does not really allow to our Lord, what it professes to do, a complete and actual human will, activity, or nature. This was a very real objection, the explanation of which lay in the fact that even Maximus had not yet outgrown the old and well-nigh universal conception that the divine and human natures are two essentially different and mutually exclusive things, which may be brought into juxtaposition and accord with each other but into no closer relation of unity. The church needed to feel more deeply and truly that it is the very nature of the divine Logos of humanity to become human as it is also the nature of humanity to become divine. So little is either changed from itself or into the other by becoming it, as the church feared, that it only truly becomes itself in becoming the other. God as Logos of man only fulfils himself as and in man, and man as son and image of God only realizes and becomes himself in God. Both of these ends are revealed as accomplished in Jesus Christ.

In the second place, we have already seen how Maximus, in his praiseworthy effort to secure the humanity of our Lord from a mere absorption and loss of itself or of all that is prope ly distinctive of itself in the divinity, attempts to preserve the immutability of his holy obedience by the alternative device of ascribing to his very humanity, through the action of the Holy Ghost in his miraculous birth, a character that not only separates it from ours which is fallen but from Adam's which was capable of falling. The difficulty is that that at once renders our Lord's holy obedience in our nature unlike that of any really human being whether unfallen or fallen. A holiness φύσει, by necessity of nature either human or divine, is not a human holiness. The true operation of the Holy Ghost in our Lord was not to make the nature physically and necessarily holy in him but to make him as a man (as Maximus himself had said) spiritually and morally holy in the nature.

The dyothelite reaction in Rome after Honorius had seriously interfered with if it had not defeated the emperor's scheme of conciliation, as it led at last to another schism between Rome and Constantinople. The emperor resorted to persecution and at intervals of six or seven years, Martin I., Maximus and other leaders of the catholic opponents of Monothelitism died as martyrs in exile and under the most inhuman treatment. In 678 Constantine Pogonatus ended the unhappy strife by entering into negotiations with Domnus, Bishop of Rome, to summon a general council. The Sixth General Council assembled in Constantinople A.D. 680. A circular letter from Agatho, who in the meantime had succeeded Domnus, was destined to perform somewhat the same part in its decisions that Leo's had done at Chalcedon. And the doctrinal position of Agatho was little more than a reproduction of that of Leo, with only such further development of statement as was necessitated by over two centuries' further progress of thought. He affirms the two natures, two natural wills and two activities. And then, quite in the line of Leo, but with much more fulness and elaborateness, he illustrates from the Scriptures the long contrast of distinctly human and distinctly divine acts performed by our Lord, concluding with the affirmation that " scriptural passages must in general be understood to refer now to the humanity, now to the divinity of Christ." The symbol of the council was in substantial accord with the views of Agatho, so that its proceedings may be correctly characterized as supplementary to those of Chalcedon.

Apart from the doctrinal symbol adopted by the council, the points of interest connected with it are the following. The Emperor Constantine Pogonatus opened the proceedings in person, attended by thirteen officers of the court. On his left hand were ranged the Roman legates, the archbishop of Ravenna and "the remaining bishops subject to Rome"; on his right hand were the patriarchs of Constantinople, Antioch, and a representative of the patriarch of Alexandria, and "the remaining bishops subject to Constantinople." Thus the relative positions of primacy accorded to the two capital cities of the world, Old and New Rome, were duly observed. Early in the council complaints were received from the legates of Agatho of the novel teaching of Cyrus of Alexandria and Sergius of Constantinople and his three successors with regard to the one activity and will of our Lord. Nothing was said of Honorius who had developed their opinions into the Monothelitism which the council was assembled to condemn. In the twelfth and thirteenth actions the whole correspondence of Cyrus, Sergius and Honorius to which reference was made in the historical sketch was read before the council. Whereupon these three with the three successors of Sergius were cast out of the church as heretics and betrayers of the truth.

The definition signed by all present at the close, in

the presence of the emperor, consisted of (1) a declaration of agreement with the five previous general councils of the church, (2) the recital and acceptance of the two creeds of Nicæa and Constantinople in their original forms, (3) its own definition, to which was appended the anathema against those by name, including Honorius, who had been condemned for Monothelitism. Agatho having died about the time of the close of the council, the proceedings were transmitted by the emperor to his successor Leo II., who promptly returned his acceptance of all the acts of the council, including the excommunication of Honorius as a traitor to the faith.

In the middle of the following century (about A.D. 750) the long course of theological and Christological thought that constituted the conciliar period of the church came to a close in the person of John of Damascus, who sums up and completes the dogmatical contribution of the Greek Church to the Christian faith. His principal work, "Concerning the Orthodox Faith," covers all the results of the great councils. But he treats in a separate work the question of the two wills, activities and remaining natural attributes of Christ. "The same Lord Jesus Christ," he says, "we acknowledge to be perfect God and perfect man. He had all that the Father had with the exception of aseity [i.e. the Son is from the Father while the Father is *a se*, from himself alone]; and all that the first Adam had with the exception of sin. Whatever naturally pertained to the two natures of which he was constituted was also his,—two natural wills, the divine and the human; two natural activities; a double natural freedom of will, a divine and a human; and twofold wisdom and twofold knowledge. These are the natural attributes without which the natures cannot subsist" (Dorner). It will be seen that John of Damascus presses to the utmost the conclusions of the councils. But beyond clearer statements and fuller arguments he makes no further advance, if any such remained to be made, in the science of Christology. After a brief interval the conciliar period was to be succeeded by the scholastic.

CHAPTER XV.

ADOPTIONISM.

ITH John of Damascus the long-sustained movement of thought that had been the life of the conciliar period came to a close without completing its immediate task. Maximus, the Sixth General Council and the general summation of Christological results so far attained left the picture of the person of Christ lacking, by just one crowning trait, organic and logical completion. And the final step had of necessity to be taken somewhere, unless the mind of the church were to cease to perform its living function.

The step was taken or attempted in an unexpected quarter and under new and strange conditions, but that the effort was a direct continuation of the process of Christological construction which we have been tracing will appear of itself. That Adoptionism like Nestorianism—with which though at a much later stage and with distinct differences and improvements it in general agreed—merited and needed decisive correction if not the summary condemnation it received, we shall endeavor to show. But we shall also endeavor to show that the church, whose action in the matter is happily not to be received as universal or final, by its indiscriminate and unqualified practical extinction of Adoptionism inflicted upon itself an almost irreparable loss and regression. It has been affirmed or admitted much more widely than by Dr. Dorner that the extirpation of Adoptionism had the practical effect of wiping out the gain of the later general councils and putting back the mind of the church to the stage of Cyril and the period preceding the decrees of Chalcedon. In order to judge of the justice of this charge let us briefly trace the doctrinal origin, development and fate of Adoptionism.

It will be remembered that the action of Chalcedon and of the Sixth and last General Council, the Third of Constantinople, was gradually to develop the doctrine of the real humanity of our Lord. Let us recall the terms in which John of Damascus had summed up the result of two and a half centuries of controversy upon this one point: "Whatever pertained to the two natures of which our Lord was constituted was also his,—two natural wills, the divine and the human; two natural activities; a double natural freedom of will, a divine and a human; and twofold wisdom and twofold knowledge. These are the natural attributes without which the natures cannot exist." It is unnecessary to attempt to trace the chain of circumstances by which at the close of the eighth century, a hundred years after the termination of Greek Christology, the problem should be taken up just where it had been broken off by the German or Gothic mind of the farthest West, now for the first time speculatively awakened. But so it was: Elipandus, archbishop of Toledo and primate of Spain, Felix of

Urgellis, and perhaps the great body of the Spanish church, then found themselves attempting to carry out to its logical conclusion the unfinished task of the last general council in the East.

The conclusion that forced itself on their mind was somewhat as follows: to attribute to our Lord (1) two natures, (2) two activities proper or characteristic of the natures, (3) two wills or volitional centres, and (4) a twofold consciousness and freedom, is already to have conceded to him a twofold personality. Herein appeared at last the consequence that had all along been so much dreaded and its appearance developed at once not only a blind and indiscriminating opposition but also a practical retraction and abandonment of the whole process that had so logically led up to it,—that is, all the dyophysitic and dyothelitic gains of the last three councils.

Let us endeavor more comprehensively and dispassionately to discover what the Adoptionists really meant and what was the truth of our Lord that sought utterance through them. Very much though by no means all of the misunderstanding arose from a merely verbal ambiguity that now reached its culmination, from which we ourselves are not yet free: the use of the terms "person" and "personality." At one time we mean by "person" simply and identically what is meant by an ego, a subject of spiritual activities. At other times we mean not the ego merely as such but certain qualities or characteristics, a certain *nature* of the ego. Thus we define personality and say that a person is one who possesses self-consciousness, reason and freedom. Now the whole catholic contention against the dangerous tendencies of Nestorianism and Adoptionism means that there must be no risk of thinking or representing two egos or subjects, a divine and a human, in our Lord. Each indeed loudly disclaimed the two egos or double personalities, but it by no means followed from that that they were not logically involved in their teaching, and the church did what it could to have it understood once for all that any system of thought that by remotest consequence involved them stood thereby condemned.

Adoptionism never for an instant intentionally or consciously implied two egos or subjects in our Lord. It held that the Logos was the one subject equally of his humanity and his divinity. When it would ascribe to him a human as well as a divine personality it used the word in quite the other sense, arriving at its conclusion somewhat in the following way: if one define personality to consist in or to be self-consciousness, reason and freedom, and if one ascribe to our Lord with John of Damascus, representing the mind of the church, a distinctively and properly human consciousness, reason and freedom—how can one deny him human personality? Not that our Lord is two egos or persons in that sense, but that the one Lord in his divine consciousness, reason, freedom, character and activity is a divine person, and in his human consciousness, reason, freedom, character and activity is a human person. He is not *alius et alius* but he is *aliter et aliter;* he is not two persons but in the sense in which we have defined the terms he possesses two personalities or modes of personal consciousness, thought, volition and action. He is as truly a man, which means a human person, as he is God, which means a divine person. Adoptionism claimed to be equally in agreement with the church in affirming the one person of the Lord and in holding with the decrees of 451 and 680 his twofold personal consciousness, will and activity. What was the meaning, it asked, of all that affirmation of a proper human nature, will, activity, consciousness, reason and freedom in our Lord, but that the Son of God was incarnate not in an irrational, involuntary and impersonal but in a rational, free and personal human nature and life?

The motive and meaning of Adoptionism will better appear, however, if we begin with the proper starting-point from which it took its name. Because of the ambiguity that has been pointed out it wisely did not take its stand upon the claim of a twofold personality but upon that of the twofold *Sonship* of our Lord.

The personal designations of the incarnate Lord we know were two, Logos or Word and Son of God. Of these the first designates him properly only in his deity but the second may describe him in both his divine and human natures. Both as God and as man our Lord is Son of God. His divine, proper or natural Sonship by eternal generation from the substance of the Father had been thoroughly developed and defined and was universally understood and accepted through the Trinitarian theology of the church. All were equally willing to accept the truth expressed in the term "Theotocos" and in Theopaschitism,—the Son of Mary is Son of God, and God suffered for us. What is true of our Lord in one nature may be pred-

Y

icated of him in the other, or whatever is true of either nature is true of him who is the personality of both.

But Adoptionism while accepting these truths attempted, with what success we shall see, to proceed to another: that of our Lord's not divine but human Sonship to God. In the spirit in which Maximus in vindication of the human activity of Christ had said, "He as a man subjected humanity to God"—i.e. brought it back into unity with the divine nature and life,—in precisely the same spirit and sense, though further developed, the Adoptionists taught that Jesus Christ as man had brought humanity in his person into a new relationship of sonship to God. The Sonship thus predicated of our Lord and first realized by him in humanity is distinctively human and not divine, of grace and not by nature; whereas in his eternal and divine nature he is υἱὸς ἴδιος, proper or essential Son of God, in his human nature or as man he is υἱὸς θετός, constituted or adopted Son of God.

Truth in itself and scriptural value underlay this point of view to a degree not apprehended by the catholic mind of the church, and for the time being that mind rejected it. As it has come up again and will continue to come up for rehearing and a fairer judgment it may be well to glance in passing at its New Testament basis.

In the Epistle to the Ephesians St. Paul describes humanity as having been eternally predestined to υἱοθεσία, or the relation to God of a υἱὸς θετός. Translated into ordinary language this means that man is constituted by his spiritual nature to enter or be taken into such a participation in the divine nature and life as to become son of God. The New Testament point of view is that sonship in this sense is not natural but to be acquired. In our Lord himself in whom it is first humanly realized it does not result from the fact of his human nature but from the act of his human life. He as man *made* humanity son of God.

There is indeed a sense in which even man may be called son of God by nature. If God is the father of spirits and finite spirits are not mere products of nature but children of God there is a natural and essential kinship or sonship of every human soul to God. But it is evident that though this be so and be presupposed, the point of view of the New Testament is at most that this is only a potential sonship and has to be actualized in the case of every individual soul by an act of divine grace on one side and of human faith on the other. As a matter of fact it may be correct to say that the grace and faith in each case only condition and bring to actuality an already existent sonship. But as a matter of actual usage the language of the New Testament is that the grace and the faith originate and constitute the sonship. They have made humanity in Christ son of God and they enable every human being in Christ to become son of God. The sonship is not by generation but by regeneration. Man is indeed constituted by his nature to become son of God but he becomes so only by an act of the personal Godhead and of his own personal manhood. To as many as receive him does the Son of God give power to become sons of God.

There is however no real contradiction between those who contend that the act of grace and faith only brings to actuality the fact of sonship and those who contend that it creates it if each will but recognize the difference of point of view and of the sense in which terms are used. Sonship could not be imparted to one whose nature it was not to be and who was not therefore potentially already a son, and mere potential sonship is nothing until it becomes actual.

Without going further into these questions, the teaching of St. Paul and we may say that of all the epistles of the New Testament is that it is the natural predestination of human nature to find its complement and completion in a participation in the divine nature, human life in the divine life. And this υἱοθεσία was to be attained "through Jesus Christ" (Eph. i. 5). In the man Christ Jesus humanity attained the adoption of sons, was made and became son of God.

Similarly in Romans viii. 29: in the divine foreknowledge men are predestinated to be conformed to the image of God's Son, who is thus to be "first-begotten or first-born among many brethren." Here we do not wish to deny that the Son spoken of is υἱὸς ἴδιος, the divine and eternal personal archetype in heaven of all human sonship upon earth. But that he was "first-born among many brethren," when taken in connection with the general analogy of the New Testament teaching, can only mean that our Lord as man first realized in his humanity that divine Sonship into participation in which he was to bring many brethren. Thus he who was in his deity essential or proper Son of God in his humanity was constituted or became through his holy obedience and self-sacrifice Son of God by grace and adoption. He was (Rom. i. 3) κατὰ πνεῦμα ἁγιωσύνης, through his offering of himself by the eternal Spirit without spot to God, constituted and instituted Son of God in power by his resurrection from the dead.

The whole argument of the Epistle to the Hebrews illustrates this truth. The essential and eternal Sonship, it can easily be proved, is everywhere presupposed, but the Sonship actually treated of is that human one first realized in the person of the man Christ Jesus. He who was before all things and by whom all things exist and consist was as man, through self-fulfilment in nature and grace, to become heir of all things, to be himself the crown of his own creation (i. 2). When he had in our nature made purgation of our sins, he sat down at the right hand of the Majesty on high, having lifted humanity in his person to its destiny above the angels (i. 3). We see not yet humanity as a whole but we do see it already in him through death crowned with glory and honor. It was necessary that God in bringing many sons to glory should first perfect the great leader and captain of their salvation through suffering. Already in him has humanity been sanctified through the destruction of sin and death and him who through these had had the dominion over it (ii. 8, etc.). We are partakers with Christ in all that he has wrought and become for us if we hold fast our faith in him (iii. 14). We have not in him one unlike or incapable of sympathizing with us, but one who tempted in all points like as we are was yet without sin (iv. 14). Having learned obedience by the things he suffered and having been himself perfected he became the author of the eternal salvation of us all (v. 9). Thus he as our forerunner has entered for us within the veil. He has brought us in him into unity with the divine nature and life (vi. 20). The law made men high priests who were still sinful and imperfect but the true high priest of humanity is υἱὸς εἰς τὸν αἰῶνα τετελειωμένος, one who has been perfected forever as Son or who has attained and entered into a forever perfected and complete relation of Sonship to God (vii. 28). We might go thus through every chapter and show how Jesus Christ was not only the perfect divine grace but also the perfect human faith and obedience which together constitute the υἱοθεσία, the human sonship of which as man he was the author.

Such a Sonship by grace the Adoptionists predicated of our Lord in his humanity without at all impugning the proper and essential Sonship of his divinity. It is questioned by some who would impute obscurity and uncertainty to their views whether they meant to associate the divine adoption of humanity in Christ with his birth, baptism or resurrection. Their meaning is clear enough and is true.

In the first place it was just the true principle at the root of the whole movement that the change wrought in humanity by the incarnation was not the immediate, physical and necessary result of the *assumption* but the free, spiritual and personal result of an *adoption*. Humanity became son of God not by the mere fact, *ipso facto*, of God becoming man but by the consequent and complementary act of man becoming partaker of the nature and life of God. The human sonship represented by Jesus Christ was not by fact of his deity alone but by act of his humanity also. It was therefore not the result of the mere birth of deity into humanity.

In the second place there are stronger appearances of an Adoptionist connection of our Lord's adoption or becoming Son of God with his baptism. In an outward way we may say that he became Son of God not by the physical act of being born but by the spiritual act of being baptized and filled with the Holy Ghost. In this way he is not physically but spiritually Son of God. We know that at his baptism the heavens were opened, the Holy Ghost descended upon him, and in that fulness of the Spirit which was his anointing and constituted him the Christ the voice of the Father proclaimed him the beloved Son in whom he was well pleased. There was a profound truth in this, in that it represents the Sonship as not natural and necessary but spiritual and free.

But in the third place the human sonship attained for us by our Lord is as little in all its reality constituted by his anointing with the Holy Ghost as it was by his birth into the world. Both of these were precedent conditions but in itself it consisted in the spiritual act by which in consequence of them humanity became actually something new and divine. By such an act of his whole life as truly and completely human as it was divine, finished upon Calvary and consummated and crowned at the right hand of God, he was himself constituted and constituted humanity in himself Son of God. This act was in and of itself a literal and real atonement or reconciliation, redemption and resurrection of us all. As in Adam all were dead so in Christ all were risen. He destroyed death and brought life and immortality to light as previously he had in the likeness of our sinful flesh condemned and destroyed sin in our flesh and raised the spirit in us to holiness and God. As he died to sin and lived to God so we are to account ourselves through him dead to sin and alive to God. It was in perfect consistency with such representations that the Adoptionists dated the realization of the human sonship to God of which Jesus Christ was the author not from the act of natural birth and only symbolically or sacramentally from that of his baptism with the Holy Ghost but really and finally from the moment of the resurrection of humanity in his person from sin and death. In the flesh of the first Adam our Lord was born of the seed of David but in the spirit or spiritual manhood of the second Adam into which humanity was raised in him he was constituted and instituted Son of God in power by his resurrection from the dead (Rom. i. 4).

The truth then of the human becoming Son of God of our Lord himself in our nature is strictly scriptural. And it is just as truly catholic in the sense that the true meaning and function of our Lord's humanity in deity will not come to organic completeness without it.

There was however a limitation in the view of the Adoptionists that not only prevented success in carrying out the truth for which they stood but also brought them into a collision with the church as hurtful to it as it was fatal to them. Dwelling upon the personally human agency of our Lord in the life and work of the incarnation and so upon his true and complete manhood, they formed to themselves a conception of the man Christ Jesus as needlessly as it was unwarrantably inadequate. Our Lord was indeed very man, more truly even because more wholly and completely man than we ourselves, but that does not mean that he is only a single or particular human being precisely in the sense in which one of us is so. The Nestorians with all their endeavor had found it impossible to rise above that limited notion of our Lord's personal manhood, and of the Adoptionists it must be confessed that, however theoretically they might protest to the contrary, practically they represented him in a manner difficult to reconcile with the personal identity of the human Jesus with the eternal divine Word. They did not successfully attain the point of seeing how the personal human Jesus could be himself the personal divine Logos. Thus they contended that the *man* Christ Jesus, he who was son of Mary, son of David, son of Adam, could not be properly or essentially Son of God. He could be so called nuncupatively by reason of his identification with the eternal Son or Logos, but in himself humanly he was Son of man only and not Son of God. We are told in the Scriptures that God was in Christ but not that he was Christ or that Christ was God. This is very like the Nestorian explaining away " the Logos became man " into " the Logos united himself with man or with a man." On the whole there can be little doubt that the Adoptionist representation of the man Christ Jesus as a limited and individual human being like one of us did justify the charge of their great antagonist Alcuin that though they did not mean it their position led practically to a Nestorian twofold personality of the Lord.

It would have been infinitely better if the church instead of extirpating Adoptionism for its incompleteness had taken it up and carried it on into a true catholic completion. What was needed to do this was a truer and fuller construction of our Lord's humanity than had yet been attained. What the Adoptionists failed to see needed to be shown, that it was possible to ascribe to our Lord a true personal humanity that was in itself also true and proper personal deity instead of being only united or associated with it. In order to appreciate this it is necessary to reflect upon the peculiar predicates applied and applicable to our Lord's manhood alone among men. Of whom else beside him can it be said that he recapitulates and includes humanity in himself and is the head of it? or that he is not a single and limited human individual but universal humanity, all men and every man? And let it be specially observed, he not only possesses the nature of every man but is the personality of every man. Every human being may say and ought to say "Not I but Christ." The universal and everlasting relation of every man to the personal manhood of Jesus Christ at once differentiates him as man from every other man and that without impairing in the least the propriety or reality of his manhood.

Let us attempt a construction of what might truly be called our Lord's personal humanity which instead of being compelled with the Adoptionists to deny its proper divinity shall feel itself compelled to include it. And we shall appeal not to the scientific definitions but to the intuitive faith and practical experience of the church from the beginning with regard to the human person of its Lord. The human Christ is the same to every human soul that knows him or is so just in proportion as it knows him really and truly. He is the same not only "yesterday, to-day and forever" but also universally or to every actual knowledge or experience of him.

Now how shall we describe just what our Lord is in his humanity to every human being? There is in every finite spirit of man by virtue of his kinship to the Father of spirits an element and aspect of infinitude. That is to say, while there is in him what is particular or individual there is that in him also which is universal. Every one who reflects is more or less conscious that every folly or fault of which he is guilty is an offence against an absolute standard of wisdom, righteousness and goodness which is the only true measure of himself. Sin is the transgression of the particular against the universal or absolute in us. Now Jesus Christ is the personal human perfection of every human person. It is the end of every man to become Christ. When we speak of the inner, truer, ideal man that is in every man we appeal from the particular to the universal, from the limited to the absolute, from the human to the divine in him. To say that Christ is our wisdom is to say that he is our reason or understanding in its absolute form; to say that he is our righteousness is to say that he is the absolute freedom of our wills, our spiritual and moral activities; to say that he is our life is to say that he is not only our nature but ourselves raised above all limitation or contradiction of sin and death and brought into participation in the absolute and eternal life of God.

All this is contained in the single consciousness which is distinctive of Christianity, " not I but Christ." Christ instead of the ego to a man does not mean to him the loss but the gain of his personality. It means the substitution for his outer, particular and separate self of his inner, universal and divine self. Let any one reflect upon all that it means to pass out of one's self into Christ and it will be realized that it is only that losing which is the true finding one's self.

We realize that that faculty which we call reason is in us both a faculty or organ of the infinite and itself an infinite faculty. There is no limit whatever to man's possible conception of truth, beauty and goodness. In the same way there is no natural limit to the possibility of a true freedom or liberty of the human will; there is no perfect freedom for us short of the infinite or absolute one of unity with the will of God. "Be ye perfect as your Father in heaven is perfect" is the only limit and measure of our own wisdom and righteousness. Now as wisdom, true freedom or righteousness and in general what we may call character is an infinite or absolute thing, so that human personality which is the subject of all these is in itself also an infinite, eternal and absolute thing. The French philosopher Janet has laid down the principle that in every man we must distinguish between his individuality and his personality. The individuality is that in him which is particular; it is the accidents that differentiate him from other individuals of the same genus or species. The personality is that in him which is essential and universal. As the man loses in individuality through the unity of the common reason and freedom, especially through that of the common spirit and life of charity or love, he gains in personality, so that when every man's personality becomes perfect or absolute all men will become one, and yet so that while each man then shall be all he will only then also be perfectly himself.

We might say then that as each man's universal or absolute reason is the divine reason, his freedom or righteousness the divine freedom and his character the divine character, so the absolute personality of every man, which is compounded of rational consciousness, moral freedom and spiritual character, is not something apart from God but is rather God himself personally realized and fulfilled in us. In this way the divine Logos and Christ, the divine man who is our Lord, is eternal and absolute humanity. "Not I but Christ" does not mean "not I but the Logos or the Second Person in the Trinity": it means "not I but my essential and true self or personality" which while it is in the truest sense "I" is also God.

The conclusions thus reached with regard to our Lord's personal humanity are drawn inductively not only from the predicates that are by common consent applied to him but also from the actual relations that all men spiritually bear to him. It is an actual matter of fact to all those who make experience of it that he is our universal and eternal selves. No individual or particular man could be that to us, while that he can be and is so is with us a matter of spiritual verification and knowledge. This is in a sense arguing from ourselves to our Lord, from the particular in ourselves to the general or universal in him, but it is in accord with the somewhat more a priori speculative conclusions of the church. As Christ is our eternal or divine so are we his temporal and human image or expression. It is he who was from the first intended or predestined to be expressed or to express himself in humanity. A perfect work of art combines in itself two elements; it is not only the perfect material expression of an idea but it is also the idea perfectly expressed in the material. In a much truer and higher sense perfected manhood is not merely humanity imaging the divine Logos: it is the Logos himself imaged, embodied, incarnated in humanity. The essential truth of humanity is God himself in it, not some thought or idea of his as in the case of the human artist but his personal reason, freedom and activity, his wisdom, righteousness and life freely and personally made and become those of men. It was thus the nature of the Logos to become man as it was that of man to be the incarnation of the Logos. Neither is changed or converted from itself in becoming the other but only realizes and fulfils itself.

If the Adoptionists could but have seen the personal humanity of our Lord in this light they would not have felt themselves necessitated to deny even of his manhood but on the contrary would have been compelled to predicate of it with the church a proper and essential divine Sonship. They would have been able to reconcile the apparently exclusive and incompatible truths that Jesus Christ was in his humanity both proper and adoptive Son of God. He was both the truth to be realized and the human realization of the truth of man's divine sonship. The Sonship that was his in his deity *became* his in his humanity and that not by the fact in itself of his becoming man nor yet by the mere fact of his baptism from above with the fulness of the Holy Ghost but by that spiritual and moral transformation which by its grace he actually wrought in humanity through death to sin and resurrection to God.

Adoptionism however failed to rise to the true conception of our Lord's manhood. Desiring to see in him a humanity in all points like our own it made him only a particular and limited human being like ourselves and not that universal and divine man whom we have endeavored to describe. To the former could only pertain as they described it a nuncupative or nominal and not the essential and proper divine Sonship that belonged to the latter.

In a series of local councils between the years 790 and 800, of which the most notable was that of Frankfort in 794, Adoptionism was progressively more and more condemned and reprobated and in a few years became extinct.

CHAPTER XVI.

THE CHRISTOLOGICAL GOAL.

HE goal of all true Christological thought is to arrive at such a construction of the doctrine of the person and work of Jesus Christ as shall be (3) catholic, (2) scriptural and (1) true in itself. This assumes that there is a person and work of Christ which is for us the objective as it is to be the subjective, absolute truth of God, the universe and ourselves; that the elements of that truth were revealed through the facts of our Lord's human life and are sufficiently contained in their scriptural representation and interpretation; and that while the truth of Christ is in one aspect absolute it is also in another sense relative to us and is to find its ultimate verification in the universal testimony of human reason and experience. The imperfect experience and knowledge of our Lord which has been attained by his church as representing the spiritual consciousness and life of humanity is nevertheless sufficient to have established a certitude that will never be lost from its true and inmost mind and heart,—the certitude that in him is realized and contained the whole truth of God in his relation to man

and the whole truth of man in his relation to God. To apprehend and state this scientifically, in terms that will embrace all the conditions and elements that enter into so complex and comprehensive a fact, may have baffled the speculative or reflective mind of Christendom. No one mind can simultaneously and equally appreciate all that is involved in the whole truth of the incarnation. The collective mind of the church which sooner or later excludes what is spiritually false and includes what is spiritually true has not yet and in this world never will wholly comprehend or express it. But the efforts, errors and corrections of the past and the confirmations, agreements and certitudes that have been attained through them have at least had the effect of fixing forever the conviction that however imperfectly it understands there is yet a perfect truth which it imperfectly understands, and that if it will but be true to that truth it will continue to grow as it has grown in knowledge and understanding. There is such a thing as a catholic mind; there are already results that have finally approved themselves and will nevermore be shaken. Every real individual or conciliar contribution to such a sum of results has been or will sooner or later be accepted as catholic, and additions will continue to be made to the end of time.

But we must carefully discriminate between the fact of Christ in the world and the science of Christ in the world. The fact of God in Christ reconciling the world to himself and men in Christ reconciled to God and so redeemed from sin and raised out of death has existed continuously from the beginning and will continue to the end, right through and despite the speculative doubts and questionings and even the practical mistakes and perversions of actual Christianity. The faithlessness of man will not bring to naught the faith of God. He will be true though every man be a liar. God in one man and one man in God is proof of what ought to be the truth of God in every man and every man in God. And though there be not even one such man, still God is true and Jesus Christ is his truth.

If we would criticise the singularly subtle, strong and philosophical as well as theological mind of the Greek world and church of the conciliar period, we should say that its primary lack was that of the as yet undeveloped capacity to apply to its facts a proper scientific or inductive method. It was not of course that the fathers did not know the Scriptures, —they were full of their letter, spirit and life,—but they knew them as the Greeks knew nature, which was certainly not as modern science knows it. Jesus Christ is to be known from the Old and New Testaments taken together as science is to be learned from nature. It makes no difference that one is to be apprehended spiritually and the other physically. To elicit the conception of the one Christ as he reveals himself in his own words and deeds, as he is faithfully portrayed by the synoptics, as he interiorly manifests himself to St. Peter, St. Paul, St. John and the other writers of the New Testament, is just as much an act of induction and requires the same training and qualities as the process by which the truths, laws and unity of nature are scientifically determined. As there are a priori and deductive conclusions with regard to the natural world that however logical, consistent or beautiful in themselves are not drawn from and consequently are not true to the facts of the world as it is, so we must say that very much of the theology and Christology of the fathers is a priori or deductive in its character and is neither derived from nor consistent with the full and exact mind of the Scriptures as a whole. While catholic life was full of the fact of God in Christ catholic thought was not as able as it is now to see Jesus exactly as he is in himself, as he appeared objectively to the earlier and subjectively to the later observation and knowledge of his New Testament witnesses. Before but especially during the conciliar period the divinity of our Lord shone too brightly for all to be able to see and appreciate the completeness in its every detail of his humanity; and the earlier and dominant Christology, constructed wholly from that side, presented sometimes a picture of it as unlike the actual and scriptural Jesus as the extremest a priori physical theory of nature is to its actual facts and phenomena. With whatever prepossession or freedom from prepossession we undertake it, the effect of an exact spiritual study of the mind of the New Testament, after that of any later movement of Christian thought, is surprise and wondering admiration. It is as true to the truth of the spirit as nature itself is to natural truth and in the same way. In the first place it is a unity but a unity in diversity, and as it requires a whole mind to see the absolute unity of nature in its infinite diversity so also does it to see the one and whole Christ in his every trait and aspect in the New Testament. And in the second place while all the materials are given no induction is made for us from them but it is left to the spiritual science of humanity to construct for itself the Christ as it is to physical science to arrive for itself at the unity and wholeness of natural knowledge. In this way we arrive a posteriori at a sort of natural conviction, that confirms the instinct of the church, of a divinity in Holy Scripture similar to that in nature.

With the New Testament, all Christology must begin with the fact and facts, precisely as they are, of the human personality and personal life of Jesus Christ. The historical Jesus is human through and through, and who can wish to limit or be willing not to sound and experience all the blessed consequences of that great fact? Nothing can be truly said on that side of the truth that one ought not to be glad to accept. At the same time the Jesus of history is humanity raised to the power of God. It is a humanity free from sin and alive from death; a humanity that has rent from top to bottom the veil of flesh and entered in the spirit into the holy of holies of the divine nature and life. Humanity as our Lord received it was not what it is as he has made it. His conquest in it of sin and death, his own human death to sin and life to God have constituted it at least actually what it was before only potentially, son of God through personal participation in the divine nature, character and life. All this in him was strictly a human act and was only what it was the nature and destination of humanity in and through him to do and become. It is what is meant by man's eternal predestination to υἱοθεσία or the adoption of sons through Jesus Christ unto God. Our Lord became Son of God through the process, his whole human life of love and self-sacrifice was itself indeed the process, by which alone humanity becomes or can become son of God. He is the way; no man comes to the Father but by him. And the new and living way he has opened is through his flesh, through that supreme conquest and crucifixion of his flesh in which he by the eternal Spirit offered himself without spot to God. He is the ἀρχηγὸς καὶ τελειωτὴς, the human author and perfecter of that faith, obedience and self-sacrifice by means of which as symbolized by his cross man becomes his own divine and spiritual instead of his only natural and carnal self. Thus atonement, redemption and resurrection are all processes wrought in humanity bringing it back to God, holiness and life, and they were all wrought out in and through the human life, death and life again out of death of our Lord Jesus Christ. Thus Jesus Christ as man is not only υἱὸς θετὸς, he is the very υἱοθεσία of humanity. Human sonship to God in its actuality at least as distinguished from its potentiality was constituted and consummated by his human life, death and resurrection; he became and was instated Son of God with power according to the spirit of holiness out of and through his resurrection from the dead.

Recognizing thus as a matter of fact the essential and complete humanity of our Lord the Adoptionists, as we saw, thought it a contradiction and neutralization of it to say that Jesus Christ, our Lord in his humanity, as man, was proper or essential Son of God. As divine, they said, as eternal Logos he is υἱὸς ἴδιος but as man he is υἱὸς θετός. Thus they were in danger of thinking and representing two sonships and sons in our Lord, both of course personal, which would make him two persons. But now let us think for a moment of just this human Sonship and personality of our Lord. The most characteristic fact in the New Testament, next after the truth of our Lord's essential and complete humanity, is its peculiar position and relation to all the rest of humanity. There can be no question that our Lord felt himself to be something as man to every man, the truth, righteousness and life of all men. Why should he bid us all: "In the world ye shall have tribulation: but be of good cheer; I have overcome the world"? Why should all men be baptized into him? Why is it the end of every man to be not himself but Christ? Why is he nearer to every man than himself—the inner man within the outer men that we are? We have already suggested the answer. Jesus Christ not only assumed the common nature of us all but is also the common or universal personality of all of us. He is the universal reason or wisdom, the universal will or freedom and righteousness, and so the universal personality of every finite person in the world. The end of man to Godward is to become God so far as his nature qualifies and predestinates him to become partaker of the divine nature and life, and this he has done in the person of Jesus Christ, who is not only the Head but the life also of the whole body of spiritual humanity. This we say every man has done so far as he is potentially in Christ; this every man does so far as he realizes that he is no longer himself but Christ, no longer his individual and particular but his universal and divine self.

But if it is the end of man to Godward to become God, that is because it is the end of God to manward to become man. The divine Logos is the Logos of God and of all things, not only of man. But in so far as he is the Logos of man, so far as he is that which or he who is to be expressed in man, his predestination could not have been otherwise fulfilled than in what we know as the incarnation. The difference between Jesus Christ and other men is that while he is universal or divine humanity incarnate in a particular man, they in him are particular men who have realized or attained their universal and divine manhood through him. Our Lord was a particular man and as such everything may be predicated of him that is proper to man, more than can be predicated of any other man because he alone has realized all the potentialities of manhood. Our Lord was also universal humanity and so every human being may predicate of himself and realize in himself all that is true of him; he may in Christ be not himself but Christ.

Why then should we hesitate as the Adoptionists did to call even the human Jesus not only adopted but also essential and proper Son of God? It was because in their vindication of his particular manhood and his adopted Sonship they lost sight too far of his universal manhood and in that of his essential divine Sonship. If they had seen that more clearly and fully they would have been more willing to call even the human Christ proper as well as adopted Son of God. As against Nestorians and Adoptionists we affirm that the Logos *became* man and then as man *became* Son of God,—and that neither by conversion of deity into humanity nor of humanity into deity. For it was the nature and self-fulfilment of the Logos to become man and of man through him to become partaker of the divine nature and life, which is to become son of God. Each did not cease to be but truly became himself through the act of the other.

In discovering the truth it is necessary to proceed from outward facts to inward principles, but in stating it we may reverse the order, and we have now arrived at a point where we may sum up the conclusions of the catholic doctrine of the person of our Lord, reviewing it from within outward. The Trinitarian discussion terminated with the assertion of living relations and movements within the nature of the Godhead. It affirmed an interior and essential function of the Logos in the personal life of God himself. But he who is Logos of God is Logos of all else; he exerts a cosmical function as reason, will and energy of the whole creation. All things come into being through him; and without him, apart from or outside of him, nothing is that is. He is the rational or ideal world of which all things are but outward appearances or phenomena. Whatever there is rational or free, spiritual or moral—in a word, personal—in the universe is he. Whatever is not is at least symbol, sensible expression or $\varphi\alpha\iota\nu\acute{o}\mu\varepsilon\nu o\nu$ of him. The only thing in the universe that in its inner essence or universal form is not he is the possible and actual free activity of finite personal spirits that are made to be free images of himself, of his personality, but that are free also to distort and destroy that image. The only thing in the world that is not in a sense God is sin.

Further, the Logos of God and the cosmos is the Logos of man. That is of man not as mere product and part of nature but as spiritual and personal son of God. Every man who so realizes and becomes himself does so in him and does so as the result of a double act,—an act of the divine personality becoming the man and another of the man becoming not himself but Christ—forsaking his particular, that is, for his universal and divine personality. So every man is predestined to incarnate the Logos as the Logos to incarnate himself in every man.

Now we must remember that the incarnation is part of a universal process. It is the nature of him who is the universal reason and principle of things to be the mediator, the bond of union or element of unity between God and things. He is God in the universe and the universe in God. The universe in fulfilling him fulfils both God and itself. As he was the beginning so he is to be the end in which or whom all things will return to God and he and they shall be one. This however becomes plainest when we limit it to the incarnation itself. The very essence and truth of the incarnation is its both-sidedness. What we might call the generic incarnation is the whole act in the history and destination of humanity, as of every man, by which God personally fulfils himself in it and it fulfils itself in God. Then all men will be Christ, will be taken up into the universal divine personal humanity of Christ and all will be one, losing in individual differences all they have gained in personal comprehension and agreement. Now the meaning and truth to be realized in the generic incarnation must have been realized in what we might call the particular incarnation of our Lord. We see not yet man but we see Jesus, exalted and crowned with glory and honor; we see the process revealed in him which is to be realized in us. And what is of most consequence in what is revealed in him is not how God may be human but how man may become divine. The former is God's part which we may safely leave to him, the latter is ours and it behooves us to know and perform it. What we need to know is how God in leading many sons to glory first made the great human captain and exemplar of our salvation perfect through suffering. We learn in him " the way " in which men become sons of God; the new and living way that he has opened and consecrated for us through the rent veil of the flesh into the holy of holies of the spirit. One thing by true inner instinct the church through all the aberrations of its outward science always kept faithfully, and that was the general assertion of the very manhood equally with the very Godhead of our Lord. The Christological meaning and value of this is the double truth of the incarnation, according to which on the one hand God becomes man without ceasing to be himself and on the other hand equally man becomes God or one with God without in any faculty or function ceasing to be himself. The incarnation being the true and in the higher sense natural and predestined unity of God and man must necessarily be equally God graciously fulfilling himself in humanity and humanity through faith, obedience and self-sacrificing love fulfilling God in itself and itself in God. Therefore in what we have called the particular incarnation we see in our Lord first in all that it can possibly mean the Logos become man, and secondly a man who in the way of man and as the very truth and revelation of the way of man becomes God or Son of God. With regard to this man we can only repeat what we have said of him, that he in no wise differs from other men save that he is the universal and the divine become particular and human while we who are particular and human become in him universal and divine, or in other words he is primarily divine and secondarily human while we are primarily human and secondarily and only in him divine. He is both proper and adopted Son of God while we are only adopted and not proper sons of God.

It will help us in following out the bearings and consequences of the incarnation to remember that when we speak or think of it as a self-emptying, contracting or humbling of the Godhead, we are thinking of God only in his physical, not his spiritual, moral and truly personal qualities. God like man and man like God is greatest and most himself as love. All his natural or physical properties, as his omniscience or his omnipotence, are but the servants of that central quality which is himself. Our human Lord was greatest and most himself when in weakness and shame he was led as a sheep to the slaughter and, as a lamb before her shearers is dumb, opened not his mouth. And God in all his relations to us in this infinite universe of wisdom and power is most God, most divine and most great in the mystery of his grace toward us in the person of Jesus Christ. The incarnation and the cross are God not at his lowest but at his highest.

Again we need to remember that the incarnation is an incarnation not of the physical properties but of the spiritual, moral and strictly personal qualities of God. It is God in man in the sense and manner in which it was the nature of God and man to be one in the other. It was not the nature of man to share the natural or physical but only the spiritual and personal qualities of God. "Be ye perfect as your Father in heaven is perfect" does not mean, be omniscient or omnipotent. It means, love as God, give and forgive as God, die for one another as God has died for you, have the character and live the life of God, be your divine and not your earthly, sensual, devilish self. When our Lord said "He that hath seen me hath seen the Father" he did not mean that we had seen in him the divine omnipotence or omniscience. We saw something better and higher than that, even the divine love that is not any property of God but God himself, and that we saw raised to its highest power in the incarnation and the cross. That can be in man and was in man and only makes him infinitely more man. But omniscience or omnipotence cannot be in him and he remain man. All the personal, spiritual, moral qualities can incarnate themselves but the physical or natural properties of God cannot be incarnate because it is not the nature or within the potentiality of man to contain or possess them. An omnipotent or omniscient man is an impossibility. The spirit, character and life of God in us will indeed expand indefinitely our human faculty for knowledge and our human power of action but they will always remain human. It is not that in us which becomes divine in Christ. What does so become is our spiritual and personal qualities, not our physical or natural properties. And vice versa what of God becomes human in us is his spiritual, not his physical attributes, his love, not his knowledge or his power.

If Jesus Christ then is what we might call the natural truth of the incarnation, we see God in him spiritually and not physically. His love is God, his holiness is God, his character and life are God, but then they are all equally man. Just those things were incarnate in him that *could* become man, not those that could not. The Logos was incarnate in him just in the way and to the extent in which it was the nature and the purpose of the Logos to be incarnate in man. It is absurd therefore to speak of the omniscience or omnipotence of our incarnate Lord as though they were a part of the incarnation. Even now in his ascended and exalted humanity, however our Lord might and does " share in " the omniscience and omnipotence of the Logos, he is not humanly omniscient or omnipotent, and he certainly was not so on earth before the completion and exaltation of his human faculties and powers.

With regard to the modes in which Christian thought has tried to conceive and represent the " becoming-man" of God, those are without question to be finally rejected which are based upon the principle of an absolute self-depotentiation of the Logos. It is impossible to entertain the idea of any suspension of those functions of the eternal second person of the Trinity which are a part of the internal and essential life of God. It is equally impossible to think of any interruption of the cosmic functions of the eternal reason, will and energy of the universe. Yet we may and must think of that same mind, will and heart of God made flesh in Christ, crucified for us upon Calvary, and become the inner personality and divine self of every man who can say "Not I but he!" Since the revelation and experience of that truth in the person of Jesus Christ the human soul can never again be satisfied with anything less either for itself or from God. His nature as well as ours requires that it should complete itself, at least to usward, in that lowest act which is also its highest. God like us only truly finds himself as he has truly lost himself in love. It is he then who is in God and is God, who is in the cosmos and is its living principle and essential life, who is also our incarnate Lord. He is one and the same in all, and yet assuredly the Logos in the man and humanity is not the Logos as he is in God or the cosmos. Neither does he in his incarnation discharge those larger functions nor does his incarnation suspend or interrupt them. We can only say that he so far only incarnates himself or becomes man as it is the meaning and end of the incarnation that he should do so. And it would not only be an impossibility and a contradiction in itself but would wholly annul the whole truth and value of the incarnation if the deity of our Lord should import into the human faculties and functions of his manhood natural properties and powers which not only do not belong to it but which would neutralize it or convert it into something else. God can spiritually and ethically become man and thereby only fulfil and exalt the manhood because the spiritual and ethical nature of God and man are the same; man as well as God is essentially spirit, truth and love. But God cannot physically become man or man God because the physical properties and characteristics of deity and humanity are inconvertible. Therefore we say that in all spiritual qualities, faculties and functions the Logos was so man that the man was also the Logos. It was the nature and distinction of the Logos, his function to manward, to be the universal personal truth of every man as every man is the particular personal truth or image of him. But the physical natures, properties and functions of our Lord remain forever two. Omniscience and omnipotence no more pertain to him as man than bodily parts and functions belong to him as God. They may be intimately conjoined, now especially in our Lord's exaltation the humanity may in him in some way above our comprehension " share " the omniscience, omnipotence and even omnipresence of his deity. But the human Jesus was man; no man saw God in him save as Godhead may be expressed in manhood, as God and man are capable of being one. He loved as God; so far as his death was the act of his love he died as God; but he ate, slept, walked as man and so far as his knowledge was natural knowledge and his acts produced physical effects he knew as man and acted as man. That does not mean that he had not supernatural knowledge and did not work miracles but that even in these he was man and both knew and worked as man. And he himself affirms, " Verily, verily, I say unto you, He that believeth on me, the works that I do shall he do also, and greater works than these shall he do." It may not be possible for us to explain how the omniscient, omnipotent and omnipresent Logos entered personally into humanity without bringing with him into it all these properties but we have not to give a natural explanation of the mystery of the incarnation. To say that the Logos became man is in itself to say that the Infinite entered into limitations. Omniscience, omnipotence and omnipresence cannot so enter but Love can. They would be diminished and annihilated by it but he is only magnified and fulfilled by it. Whatever self-emptyings or humiliations were involved in the incarnation we know only enough about them to know that they are to the greatness and glory of that in God which makes him most himself. Our incarnate Lord is personal God, personal love, personal holiness, truth and life. It is not only that he has shared our nature and imparts his to us; he takes not ours but ourselves and gives us himself, not merely his. St. Paul does not say " Not my nature but Christ's " but " Not I but Christ!" In every man the eternal Logos finds and becomes himself, as every man for the first time truly finds and becomes himself in him.

With regard to the other theory which discarding

the notion of an absolute self-depotentiation of the Logos or of any limitation or contraction in himself holds to a gradual or progressive incarnation or self-communication of the Logos to humanity, this much in it at least may win our sympathy and interest. In the first place its motive is to provide for what is an indispensable necessity to the truth and purpose of the incarnation, a true human development in every respect of our Lord's humanity from its conception to its exaltation. But secondly and even more its aim is to provide for a spiritual and moral in distinction from a merely physical and necessary incarnation. The Logos is incarnate in the whole Christ and preeminently in a human spirit and life and not merely a human flesh or nature. The character of Jesus, the fact of his human holiness from sin and human life out of death, is infinitely more the incarnation than the actuality of his natural flesh and blood. In fact his natural manhood is only the condition, not the essence or reality of the incarnation. He became man σαρκὶ, in the flesh, in order that he might as man become the incarnation of God πνεύματι, in the spirit. In a word it is spiritual and not natural manhood in Jesus Christ that is the true and completed incarnation. However difficult it is for us to conceive or represent both sides of such a double truth, it is necessary for us to see in our Lord not only the Logos personally present and expressed in manhood but also a manhood which by the spiritual and personal act of its whole life incarnates and expresses the Logos. This requires an extension of the act of incarnation over the whole human life of our Lord and makes only the resurrection and ascension the completion and consummation of it.

The general result of the foregoing reflections is to bring us to the following conclusion with regard to the unity of our Lord's person in the duality of his divine and human natures. To begin with we must discriminate between physical and spiritual natures both in God and ourselves. In spiritual or personal nature there is no essential difference or mutual exclusion between God and man. The same love that is the nature of God is the nature of man; the divine reason, will and character may become ours also and must become ours if we are truly to become ourselves. He is our only holiness, righteousness and life.

Yet while there is no spiritual difference in kind there is an infinite physical or natural difference between God and us that can never be transcended. The physical or natural properties and qualities of God can never become man's or those of man God's. In the nature of things the Logos cannot cease to be nor can humanity become omnipresent, omnipotent or omniscient. Our incarnate Lord then is personal Godhead and personal manhood in the unity and totality of that spiritual nature in which it is their constitution and predestination to become one. But physically or naturally Godhead and manhood do not become one and the same in him. The Logos remains omnipresent, omnipotent and omniscient, the manhood never acquires any of these divine properties. Even now in his exaltation our Lord as human in some ineffable way may and must "share" or "participate in" the omnipresence and omniscience of the

Logos but he is not humanly omnipresent or omniscient. And the time is past when we can ascribe to the humanly developing and incomplete manhood of our Lord on earth any act of immediate and non-human omnipotence or omniscience. Though the catholic doctors did not always mean it, the catholic doctrine of the distinctness of the natures in the unity of the person meant that the physical properties of one nature did not pass over into the other nature. Against this fundamental truth the great Leo himself and many able theologians then and now offend when they represent the human Jesus as now manifesting the properties of man and now those of God. On the contrary what consciousness our Lord more and more acquired of even his own higher and eternal nature and preëxistence came to him humanly through his own spiritual intuitions and revelations to him from the Father, as in a lower way we come to know our sonship to God partly through instinct born of the fact that we are sons and partly through self-revelations to us from God. Our interest in this view is only secondarily that from a scientific point of view it is the true and only possible one. It is very much more that from the religious point of view it is the only one that is consistent with a true incarnation and with a true view of the meaning, operation and results of the incarnation. In no other way does God really fulfil himself in man and man in God, as is first the case for us in the divine and the human person of our Lord.

The most serious criticism of the practically predominant tendency of patristic and still more of later

Christological thought is that a one-sided view of our Lord's person led to a much more one-sided view of his work. A Christology in which the human is unduly subordinated to the divine leads to a soteriology in which the human part is still more unduly lost in the divine. In the dominant theology every distinctive term descriptive of human salvation has come to be interpreted almost wholly as an act of God and hardly at all as an act even in man, much less of man. Thus for example with regard to the acts which we designate atonement and redemption it might almost be said that if God could in himself and without becoming man at all have died instead of men it would have answered all the purposes of the popular theology as an expiation from the guilt and a deliverance from the penalty of our sins. The human nature was only assumed as that in which it should be possible for God so to suffer for or instead of us. Or at the most, from that point of view, it would be that the Godhead became incarnate in the likeness of our sinful flesh in order that there might be the likeness of a condemnation of sin in the flesh, or in other words a representation of man's dying for and from his sins and being made alive to God. Of course atonement and redemption are acts of God but they are real for us only as they are acts performed in man and not outside of him. If the essence of the atonement is found where it lies, in the fact that humanity taken into God itself dies to and from the sin that separates it from him and lives in the holiness in which it is one with him, we shall see at once that the atonement could not have been an act of God performed for humanity externally because it is essentially an act performed for humanity internally. God's atonement is *our* reconciliation and reunion with him; his redemption is our freedom from sin and death. The atonement was accomplished when humanity in Jesus Christ was made one with God by the spiritual and moral act of the cross; the redemption was finished when in him men overcame sin and destroyed death. The whole spiritual science of the New Testament is to show us in Jesus Christ how the divine humanity was realized for us and is to be realized in and by us. Our Lord himself expressed it in that one word, the cross; the cross which is the eternal symbol of self-sacrificing love; love, in which God lost and found himself in us and in which we lose and find ourselves in God.

INDEX.

Acacius of Bercœa, 230, 231.
Acacius of Constantinople, 272, excommunicated, 272, 273.
Adoptionism, 60, rejection, 68, 301 sq., New Testament basis, 306 sq., truth, 310, limitations, 312 sq., similarity to Nestorianism, 313, 314, catholic view, 314 sq., 326 sq., error recapitulated, 325 sq.
"Æons," 62, 70.
Aëtius, 159.
Agatho, 297.
Alcuin, 314.
Alexander, bishop of Alexandria, 59, 91, 95, letter from Constantine, 111, 116, 117, at Nicæa, 124, 141, death, 151.
Alexander of Hierapolis, 232, imperial pressure, 238.
Alexandria, in early centuries, 60 sq. See Greek Thought.
Alexandria, Council of, under Athanasius, 157.
Alexandria, school of, stand for divinity of Christ, 192, 198, 202, 217; support of Rome, 246.
Alexandria, see of, letter from Constantine, 133.
"All, always, everywhere," 44, 45.
Anastasius, 213.
Anastasius, Emperor, 273.
Anatolius, 250.
Anomœans, 159.
"Anthropotocos," 211.
Antioch, Council of, repudiates use of word "homoöusion," 144, 153, 154.
Antioch, Council of, under John, 229.
Antioch, patriarchate, 95.
Antioch, school of, 58, 116, stand for human aspect of Christ, 192, 202 sq., 217, against Cyril, 227 sq., 231 sq., 235 sq.
Antioch, synods of, condemn Ebionism, 57.
Apollinaris, Apollinarianism, 66, 67, rejected, 68, 69, 177, 180 sq., Docetism, 188 sq., catholic view, per contra, 189 sq., relations to Arianism and Nestorianism, 192, 201, opposes dualism, 193, catholic view, 194, forerunner of Monophysitism, 195.
Arians, Arianism, 58, connection with Samosatenism, 59, with Nestorianism, 59, 60, condemned, 68, 70; difference from other heresies, 90, 91, not Christological but theological, 95 sq., tenets, 96 sq., true value negative, 100, catholic doctrine, 100 sq., relations to Constantine, 105, relations of conservatives to, 141, 142, after Nicene Council, 148 sq., charges against Athanasius, 151, under Constantius, etc., 153 sq., character of doctrine, 158 sq., 168, dissolution, 171 sq., expulsion under Nestorius, 213.
Ariminum, Council of, 156.

Aristotle, definition of "rational," 34.

Arius, 58, 91, 95, letter to Eusebius, 96, position, 96 sq., letter from Constantine, 111, 116, relations to Constantine, 112, his following, 119, at Nicæa, 119, 120, contrasted with Athanasius, 124, character, 125, banished, 132, restored, 150, pronounced orthodox, 152, death, 152. See Arians.

Arles, Council of, 112, 114, 155.

Artemas, 59.

Artemon, 56, 57, 71, 91.

"Aseity," 102, 299.

Athanasius, 92, 95, relation to Constantine, 112, 115, life and character, 123 sq., regrets necessity of definitions, 129, argument at Nicæa, 131 sq., after Nicæa, 139 sq., vs. Eusebius, 142, disobeys summons of emperor, 142, estimate of homoousion, 145 sq., attacks of Arians, 149, 150, banished, 150, 152, succeeds to patriarchate of Alexandria, 151, charges against, 151; in various councils, 152, restored to see, 153, second banishment, 153, declared innocent at Rome, 154, at Sardica, 154; return, 155, condemnation at Arles and Milan, 155, romance of career, 156, banished by Julian, 157, restored by Jovian, 157, Council of Alexandria, 157, subsequent life, 158, policy toward Semi-Arians, 159, 160, at Second General Council, 163 sq., teaches "natural unity" of divine and human in Christ, 196, silence in regard to analysis of Christ's humanity, 204.

Atonement, 37, according to Cyril, 237, true view, 294, 325, 340, 341.

Attila, 248.

Augustine, 114, 176.

Aurelius, Marcus, 5.

Baptism, 166.

Basil, 163, 164, 173, quoted, 175, 176.

"Begotten," 103, 104.

Callistus, 71.

Canon of Scripture, 25–27.

Carthage, 12.

Catholic truth, 40 sq., in infant church, 48, 49. See Church.

Celestine, 220, 221, 231.

Chalcedon, Council of. See Fourth General Council.

Chalcedonian Decrees, 253, 255; confirmed, 270.

Christ, the Logos of all creation, 83, universality of his humanity, 82 sq. See Apollinaris, Christology.

Christianity, what it is, 26, double problem involved, 30 sq., full claim concerning Christ, 35 sq., vs. Gnosticism, 62 sq., averse to speculation, 79, state religion, 134 sq., course between Arianism and Sabellianism, 168 sq., essential principle, 172, two aspects, 199. See Christology.

Christology, of the New Testament, 1 sq., moral and religious ideal primarily in Christ, not in his teaching, 5, 6, Christ more than ideal of humanity, 7, 8, 11 sq., his relation to Old Testament, 8 sq., agreement of synoptics with St. John, 14, 15, 22 sq., complete union of divine and human, 15 sq., depth of question, 69 sq., universality of his humanity, 82, the Logos of all creation, 83, after Nicean Council, 124 sq., 180 sq., full doctrine regarding Christ's humanity, 182 sq., relation of Nestorianism to, 202 sq., "Tome

of St. Leo," 260 sq., goal, 320 sq., general defects of early, summed up, 322 sq., true inductive method, 322, full doctrine as against Adoptionism, 314 sq., summary, 326 sq., 338 sq. See Adoptionism, Antioch, Apollinarianism, Christianity, Councils, Cyril, Docetism, Ebionism, Logos, Monophysitism, Monothelitism, Nestorianism, etc.
"Christotocos," 211.
Chrysaphius, 243, 245, 249.
Chrysostom, 210, deacon, 211, bishop of Constantinople, 211, characteristics, 212, exile, 212, 215.
Church, catholic, 18, 22, 24, 28, birthday, 31, authority, 32, interpretation of Scriptures, 40 sq., relation to councils, 45, 46, first Trinitarian, 77 sq. See Adoptionism, Apollinarianism, Arianism, Dualism, Logos, etc.
Clement of Alexandria, 28, 79, 202.
Conservatives, after Nicean Council, 141 sq.
Constans, 153–155, 293.
Constantia, 149.
Constantine, character, 105 sq., letter to Alexander and Arius, 111, 116, Council of Arles, 112, of Nicæa, 112, 116 sq., relations to Arius, 112, to Athanasius and Eusebius, 113, calls Nicean Council, 114, proposes "homoousion," 126, writes to Alexandria, 133, after Nicean Council, 138, affected by Eusebius, etc., 149, associated with Arians, 150 sq., death, 153.
Constantine II., 153, 154.
Constantine Pogonatus, 297, 298.
Constantinople, councils of. See Councils.
Constantius, 109, 153, 155, 156, death, 156.

Cosmology, and Cosmogony, 61, 62, 167.
Council, First General, Ebionism condemned, 68, 80; charge against Arius, 98, 109, 112, called by Constantine, 114, work, 114 sq., creed of conservatives, 121, of Nicæa, 127 sq., result of council, 132, relation to church, 135 sq., peculiar value, 135, reaction, 138.
Council, Second General, condemns Apollinarianism, 67, Docetism, 68, 162 sq., value, 170 sq., 177, canon regarding ranks of bishops of Constantinople and Rome, 179, 265.
Council, Third General, Ebionism condemned, 68, issue, 214, at Ephesus, 223 sq., briberies, 224, confusion, 228.
Council, Fourth General, Ebionism condemned, 67, 232, 235, 251 sq., value, 252 sq., Chalcedonian decree, 255, result, 255, effects disappointing, 256 sq., Rome vs. Constantinople, 266.
Council, Fifth General, Ebionism condemned, 68, 271, 274, 275, 277, 278.
Council, Sixth General, Docetism condemned, 68, 262, Dorner's view, 288, why catholic, 289, 297 sq.
Councils, Alexandria, 157. Antioch, see Antioch. Ariminum, 156. Arles, see Arles. Cæsarea, 150, 152. Chalcedon, see Council, Fourth General. Ephesus, see Council, Third General. Ephesus, under Dioscorus, 245, 247, 248. Frankfort, 319. Jerusalem, 150, 152. Lateran, 293. Milan, 155. Nicene, see Council, First General. Philippopolis, 154. Rimini, 156. Robber, 245, 247, 248. Rome, 154. Sardica, see Sardica. Tarsus, 229. Tyre, 150, 152.

Councils, Constantinople, First, see Council, Second General. Third, see Council, Sixth General. Conservative, 150, 152. Local (A.D. 448), 242, 245.
Councils, the one primary question at issue, 1 sq., accident, not essence, 45, imperial pressure, 80, 127.
Creed, of conservatives at Nicæa, 121, opposition, 122, 123, Nicean, 127, expansion of, at Constantinople, 163 sq., exact nature, 177 sq., indorsed by Antiochians, 229.
Crispus, 106.
Cyril, 215 sq., 218, treatise, 219, issue with Nestorius, 219, 220, correspondence with Celestine, 221, letter to Nestorius, 222, lack of caution, 222, 227, advantage over Nestorius, 223, deposed by Antiochians, 228, vindication, 229, reconciliation with John, 230, Christological position, 233 sq., faults, 235 sq., attacks works of Theodore, 239, death and character, 239, 240, contributions to doctrine, 240, synodical letters received at Chalcedon, 253.
Cyrus of Alexandria, 291, 292, 298.

Decrees, Chalcedonian, 253, 255, confirmed, 270.
Deism, 167.
Diodorus of Tarsus, 192, 203, 211, 212.
Dionysius, 289.
Dionysius of Alexandria, 92, relations to Arians, 93.
Dioscorus, 243 sq., president of Robber Council, 245, folly, 247, opposition of Leo, 248, excommunicates Leo, 250, at Chalcedon, 251, overthrow, 252.
Docetism, 60, 63 sq., rejected, 68, 95, pantheism of, 168, of Apollinaris, 188 sq., new forms, 256, 258.
Domnus, 297.
Donatists, 112, 118.
Dorner, quoted, 137, 197, 254, 256, 287, 294, 299, 302.
Dualism, 70, opposed by Apollinaris, 193, catholic view, 194.

Easter, 116, 133.
Ebion, 54, 59. See Ebionism.
Ebionism, 50, 54 sq., condemned, 68, 70, not speculative, 79, source of Arianism, 91, 104, outcome of wrong use of "homoousion," 145, deism, 168, new forms, 256, 258.
Ebionitic Monarchianism, 70. See Ebionism.
Ecumenical. See Council.
Elipandus, 302.
Elustathius of Antioch, 117.
"Ἐνέργεια," 279, 284.
"Ἕνωσις," 218.
Ephesus, Council of. See Council, Third General.
Ephesus, Council of, under Dioscorus, 245, 247, 248.
Epictetus, 5.
Essence. See "Ousia."
Eternal generation, 101, 104.
Eunomius, Eunomians, 159.
Eusebius of Cæsarea, 115, 117–120, creed, 121, 126, character, 142, vs. Athanasius, 142, relations to Constantine, 149.
Eusebius of Dorylæum, 242, 245, 252.
Eusebius of Nicomedia, 96, 113, 119, 120, relations to Constantine, 149, 150, translated to Constantinople, 153, 156.
Eustathius, 150.
Eustathius of Antioch, 117.
Eutyches, Eutychianism, 67, rejected, 68, 242, condemned, 243, 253 sq., decision reversed, 245, appeal to Leo, 246, condemned

Index.

and excommunicated at Chalcedon, 252.

Fathers, early, 29.
Felix of Urgellis, 303.
Felix III., 272.
Flavian, 242, 243, 245, 246, letter from Leo, 247.
Frankfort, Council of, 319.
Fulgentius Ferrandus, 276.

Genseric, 249.
George of Cappadocia, 153, 156.
Gnosticism, 62, 63, 70.
God, knowledge of, 32 sq.
Golden Church, 153.
Gospel, primitive, 10 sq.
Greek thought and theology, contrast with Latin, 60, tendency, 64, criticism of, 322, 323.
Gregory of Cappadocia, 155.
Gregory of Nazianzus, 163, 164, 173, 176.
Gregory of Neo-Cæsarea, 92.
Gregory of Nyssa, 163, 164, 173.

"Henoticon," 272.
Heraclius, 290, 292.
"Heteroöusion," 159.
Hilary, Pope, 248.
Hilary of Poictiers, 163, quoted, 174.
Holy Ghost, 178.
"Homoiousion," 147, 157, 160.
"Homoöusion," 92, 118, proposed by Constantine, 126, 128, 129, 130, 140, objections to, 143 sq., estimate of Athanasius, 145 sq., 163, Six Articles, 234.
Honorius, 292, opposed to Chalcedon, 293, condemned by Sixth General Council, 299.
Hormisidas, 274.
Hosius, of Cordova, 116, 117, 118, 126, 156.
"Humanitarianism," revival of Ebionism, 60.
Hypatia, 216.
Hypostasis, 146, 164, 165, defect in Leo's teaching, 257 sq.; 268, 303, 304.

Ibas, works anathematized by Justinian, 275, 277.
Immanence, 73, 74.
Incarnation, 31, 37, difficulties, 86 sq., position taken at Fourth General Council, 255, Tome of St. Leo, 260 sq., part of a universal process, 329, not physical but spiritual, 332. See Antioch, Apollinarianism, Christology, Cyril, Logos, Nestorianism, etc.
Inspiration, 32, 39, 40.
Irenæus, 29, 79, 196, 217.

Janet, quoted, 316.
Jerome, summary of Council of Rimini, 156.
Jerusalem, church of, 48.
Jerusalem, Council of, 150, 152.
Jesus. See Christ.
John, St., Gospel of, 22 sq.; vs. Docetism, 64.
John I., Pope, 274.
John of Antioch, 222, 225, name attached to letter to Nestorius, 226, delay in reaching Ephesus, 227, after Third General Council, 229 sq., reconciliation with Cyril, 230, imperial pressure, 238.
John of Damascus, 268, 299, 302, 304.
Jovian, 157.
Judaism, 19, 20, in early church, 49 sq., mission, 51 sq., influence of, in Samosatenism and Arianism, 58.
Julian, 107, 125, 156, 157.
Julianists, 280.
Julius, bishop of Rome, 153, 154.
Justin, Emperor, 273.
Justin II., 278.
Justinian, 273 sq., anathematizations, 275, Fifth General Council, 277.

348   Index.

Kant, 20.

"Labarum," 109, 110.
Lateran Council, 293.
Latrocinium, 245, 247, 248.
Law and gospel, 19, 20.
Leo the Great, 245, judgment on Eutyches, 246, correspondence with Flavian and Theodoret, 246, the Tome, 247, 254, analysis of, 260 sq., letters disregarded by Dioscorus, 260, activity against Dioscorus, 248, greatness, 248, 249, part in Fourth General Council, 251 sq., intellectual limitations, 257 sq., supremacy of Rome, 263, 266, regarded in East as latent Nestorian, 274.
Leo I., Emperor, 270.
Leo II., 299.
Libanius, 211.
Liberius of Rome, 156.
Licinius, 105, 110.
Logos, 82, sq., θεὸς, but not ὁ θεός, 88, Arian views, 96 sq., catholic doctrine, 100 sq., revealed in creation, 167, 184 sq.; Nestorian views, 204 sq., 218, catholic doctrine, 317 sq., 325 sq. See Adoptionism, Incarnation, Monophysitism, Monothelitism, etc.
Lucian, 58, 91, 117, 119.

Macedonius, Macedonians, 178, 213.
Macrina, 176.
Magnentius, 155.
Marcellus of Ancyra, 140, 144, 150, pronounced orthodox at Rome, 154, 168.
Marcian, 250, 252, 253, 263, 264.
Martin I., 293, 297.
Mary. See Theotocos.
Maximian, 224, 229.
Maximus, 287, 288, 293 sq., death, 297, quoted, 306.
Meletian schism, 116, 133.
Memnon, 223, deposed by Antiochians, 228.

Milan, Council of, 155.
Miracles, 13, none in nature, 85.
"Monarchia," 70 sq., 91.
Monarchianism, Ebionitic, 70. Patripassian, see Patripassian Monarchianism. Sabellian, see Sabellian Monarchianism.
Mongus, Peter, 272.
Monica, 176.
Monophysitism, 67, rejected, 68, 195, 196, 269 sq., liturgical additions, 270, 273, 274, revolt, 274, Fifth General Council, 277, present force, 278, principles, 278 sq., difficulties, 281 sq., attempted conciliation, 290, 291; real cause of revolt, 295.
Monothelitism, 67, rejected, 68, 284 sq., Honorius originator, 292, later popes, 293.

Nature, divine principle in, 84 sq., no miracles in, 85.
Neale, quoted, 58.
Nestorianism, condemned, 68, 192, 201 sq., charges against, 217 sq., summed up, 232 sq., not dead with Nestorius, 238, 256. See Nestorius.
Nestorius, 201, personality, 213, 216, 218, attacked by Cyril, 219, 220, letter to Celestine, 220, condemned at Rome, 221, the twelve anathematizations, 222, counter-anathematizations, 222, weakness, 223, deposed and banished, 224, 226, 228, letter from Antioch, 226, firmness, 227, John of Antioch joins in condemnation, 230, in retirement, 231, faith in his innocence, 231, 232.
New Testament, 24, 25. See Christianity.
Newman, "Arians of the Fourth Century," quoted, 58.
Nicean Council. See Council, First General.
Noetus, 71.

Index. 349

Nonna, 176.
Novatians, 213.

Old Testament, 8, 10. See Christianity.
Origen, 79, relation to Arians, 92, 93, 101, 144, 202.
"Ousia," 94, 127, 129, 146 sq., 163, 164, not revealed in creation, 167.

Pantheism, 73 sq., 167.
Paschal controversy, 116, 133.
Patripassian Monarchianism, 71 sq., 76, accepts incarnation, 79, contrasted with Arianism, 91 sq.; 95, 104; reviewed, 270.
Paul, St., opposition to other apostles, 17 sq., 49; mission, 21, 22; vs. Docetism, 64.
Paul of Constantinople, 153.
Paul of Emesa, 230, 231.
Paul of Samosata, 57 sq., 91, condemned at Antioch, 144, 145.
Pelagius, 40.
Person, Persona. See Hypostasis.
Peter Mongus, 272.
Peter the Fuller, 270.
Philippopolis, Council of, 154.
Photius, 144.
Pogonatus, Constantine, 297, 298.
Praxeas, 71.
Proclus, 238.
"Prosopon," 165.
Pseudo-Dionysius Areopagitica, 289.
Pulcheria, 249, accession, 250, 253.

Quartodecimans, 213.

Redemption, 37. See Atonement.
Religion and morality identical in Christ, 6.
Rimini, Council of, 156.
Robber Council, 245, 247, 248.
Rome, Council of, 154.
Rome, supremacy of, 179; supports Alexandria, 246, under Leo, 263, 264, Chalcedonian canon, 265.

Sabellian Monarchianism, 71 sq., 76, accepts incarnation, 79, contrasted with Arianism, 91 sq., 95; economic Trinity, 104. See Sabellianism.
Sabellianism, use of homoöusion, 144, doctrine, 168. See Sabellian Monarchianism.
Sabellius, 71.
Samosatenism, 57, 58, connection with Arianism, 59.
Sardica, Council of, 154, canon of regarding supremacy of Rome, 179.
Scriptures. See Canon, Inspiration, Christology, Christianity, etc.
Semi-Arians, 147, 157, 158, 159, 172.
Sergius of Constantinople, 291, 292, 298.
Severians, 280.
Severus, 280.
Six Articles, the, 229, 230, 234.
Sixtus III., 231.
Socrates, 60, 64.
Son of God, views of Adoptionism, 305 sq. See Logos, Incarnation, Church, etc.
Sophronius, 291, 292.
Substance, Substantia, 165. See "Ousia."
"Συνάφεια," 209, 218.

Tarsus, Council of, 229.
Tertullian, 129, 144, 196.
Theodora, 273, 276.
Theodore of Mopsuestia, 203, 204 sq., exegetical, 210, friend of Chrysostom, 210 sq., 214, 220, error speculative, 224, venerated, 226, works studied, 238, influence after death, 239, anathematized by Justinian, 275.
Theodoret, 212, 222, 225, 226, reputed author of letter to Nes-

torius, 226; quarrel with Cyril, 231, 232, Six Articles, 234, attacked by Dioscorus, 244, deposed, 244, excluded from Robber Council, 245, sympathy with Leo, 247, at Chalcedon, 251, works anathematized by Justinian, 275, 277.

Theodosius II., 222, 228, 244, 249, death, 250.

Theodosius the Great, 162, 172.

Theodotus, 56, 57, 71, 91.

Theopaschitism, 270.

Theophilus of Alexandria, 215, 219.

Theotocos, 210, 211, 213, 214, 219, 234.

"Three Chapters," 275 sq.

Tiberius, 278.

Tome of St. Leo, 247, 253, 257, 259, analysis, 260 sq.

Trinity, doctrine of, 69 sq., refutes pantheism, 73 sq., one solution of difficulties, 76, a fact not a doctrine, 76, primitive thought, 81 sq., estimate of Athanasius, 146, review of thought to Second General Council, 166 sq., position taken by Fourth General Council, 252, termination of discussion, 328. See Athanasius, Christology, Christianity, Council, First General, Hypostasis, etc.

Truth and reason, 32 sq. See Church.

Tyre, Council of, 150, 152.

Ulfilas, 171.

Valens, 157.

Valentinian, 157.

Valentinian III., 249.

Victor, 57, 71.

Vigilius, 276 sq.

Virgin. See Theotocos.

Whitsunday, 31.

Zeno, 5.

Zeno, Emperor, 271, 272, 273.

Zenobia, 58.

Zephyrinus, 57, 71.

INDEX TO INTRODUCTION.

Abyssinia, under Monophysite influence, lxv.
Acacians, xxxiii.
Acacius of Cæsarea, xxxiii.
Achillas, xxi, xxii.
Adiaphorites, lxiv.
Adoptionists, liii.
Aëtians, xxx, xxxiii.
Aëtius, xxx.
Aëtius, general, xlii.
Agapetus, lxii.
Agatho, bishop of Rome, lxix.
Agnoëtae, lxiv.
Alaric, xlii.
Alexander of Alexandria, xxii; calls council against Arian heresy, xxiii, xxiv; at Nicæa, xxv; death, xxviii.
Alexander of Antioch, xlviii.
Alexander of Constantinople, xxix.
Alexandria, Council of, condemns Arius, xxiii.
Alexandria, Synod of, xxxv.
Ambrose, xxxvi, xxxvii, xlii, xliii.
Anastasius, chaplain of Nestorius, xlviii.
Anastasius, Emperor, lxii.
Ancyra, Council of, xxxiii.
Anegray, lxvii.
Anomœans, xxx, xxxiii.
Antioch, Council of, xxx.
Aphthartodocetics, lxiv.
Apollinaris, Apollinarians, xxxv, xxxvii, xxxviii, xxxix, xl, xlix, liv.
Arcadius, xlii.
Arians, Arianism, xxi sq.; at Nicæa, xxv; relations to Athanasius, xxx; supremacy and divisions, xxxiii, xxxvii; condemned by Second General Council, xli; relations to Origen, xlv; philosophical weakness, liv; Spain redeemed, lxv, lxvi.
Ariminum, Council of, xxxiii.
Arius, life and character, xxi sq.; heresy defined, xxii; condemned, xxiii; afterward, xxiv; at Nicæa, xxvii; conflict reopened, xxviii; restoration ordered, xxix; death, xxix.
Arles, Council of, xx, xxi.
Armenian Church, becomes Monophysitic, lxv.
Askidas, Theodorus, lxii.
Athanasius, xxiii; at Nicæa, xxv sq.; bishop, xxviii; relations to Constantine, xxviii, xxix; banished, xxix; restored, xxx; driven out, xxx; Council of Antioch, xxx; innocency confirmed by Julius, xxxi; by Council of Sardica, xxxi; condemned by Council of Philippopolis, xxxii; returns to Alexandria, xxxii; synods of Arles and Milan, xxxii; banished, xxxiii; approach of Semi-Arians, xxxiv; return to Alexandria, xxxiv; Synod of Alexandria, xxxv; flight and return, xxxvi; death and character, xxxvi; against Apollinaris, xxxviii; canonical books, xli; regard for Origen, xliv.

352 Index.

Attila, xlii.
Augustine, xlii, xliii; "Confessions," xliv; death, li.
Augustine, missionary, lxvii.
Bangor, monastery, lxvii.
"Banquet" of Arius, xxiv.
Baptism, Council of Arles on, xxi.
Barsumas of Nisibis, liii.
Basil of Cæsarea, xxxvi, xxxvii, xxxviii.
Basilicus, lxi.
Benedict, lxvii.
Benedictine Order, lxvii.
Bobbio, monastery, lxvii.
Boniface, general, xlii.
Bright, on Athanasius, xxxvi.
Cæcilianus, xx, xxi.
Canonical books, xli.
Canons of Nicæa, xxvii; of Second General Council, xli; of Fourth, lxi; of Quinisext, lxxi.
C. nons and Decrees, Collection of, lxvi.
Cappadocians, xxxvii.
Cassino, Monte, lxvii.
Cathari, xx.
Catholics, xxv. See under different councils and names of leaders.
Celestine of Rome, l, lii.
Chalcedon, Council of, xli, lviii, lix sq.
Charlemagne, lxvi.
Christotocos, xlix.
Chrysaphius, lvii.
Chrysostom, xlii, xlv; persecution and death, xlvi.
Columba, lxvii.
Columbanus, lxvii.
"Communicatio idiomatum," lv.
Constans, xxix, xxxi, xxxii; death, xxxii.
Constans II., lxix.
Constantia, xxiv, xxviii.
Constantine, Edict of Milan, xix, xx; appeal of Donatists, xxi; sole emperor, xxiv; on the Arians, xxiv sq.; Council of Nicæa, xxv sq.; relations to Athanasius, xxviii, xxix; death, xxix.

Constantine II., xxix; restores Athanasius, xxx; slain, xxx.
Constantine IV., lxix.
Constantinople, Council of, xxxiii; Second General Council at, xxxix sq.; rank of see, xli; council at, A.D. 448, lvi; synod at, A.D. 545, lxiii; Fifth General Council at, lxiii; Sixth General Council at, lxix; councils at, A.D. 553–680, lxxii; Quinisext at, lxxi.
Constantius, xxix, xxxi, xxxii; relations to Eusebius, xxx.
Constantius Chlorus, xix.
"Constitutum," lxiii.
Copts, descendants of Monophysites, lxv.
Council, at Rome, condemning Donatists, xx; of Arles, xx, xxi; of Alexandria, condemning Arius, xxiii; of Nicæa, xxv sq.; of Tyre, xxix, xxx; of Antioch, xxx; of Sardica, xxxi; of Philippopolis, xxxi, xxxii; of Milan, xxxii; of Sirmium, xxxiii; of Ancyra, xxxiii; of Ariminum, xxxiii; of Seleucia, xxxiii; of Constantinople, A.D. 360, xxxiii; at Rome, against Apollinaris, etc., xxxviii; Second General, xxxix sq.; of Chalcedon (Fourth General), xli, lviii, lix sq.; of Laodicea, xli; of Hippo, xli; of Rome, condemning Nestorius, l; Third General, li; of Constantinople, A.D. 448, lvi; "Robbers'," lviii, lix, lx; Fifth General, lxiii; Third of Toledo, lxv; Sixth General, lxix; at Constantinople, A.D. 553–680, lxxi; Quinisext, lxxi.
Cyril of Alexandria, xlviii; challenges Nestorius, li; at Ephesus, li, lii; death and character, liii, liv.
Cyril of Jerusalem, xxxix.
Cyrus, patriarch of Alexandria, lxviii.
Damasus, xxxviii.

"Deipara," lvi.
Diodorus, xlvi.
Dionysius Areopagitica, lxxi.
Dionysius Exiguus, lxvi.
Dionysius of Milan, xxxii.
Dioscorus, lvii, lviii, lix; at Chalcedon, lx.
Dogma, right view of, lxxii.
Donatists, xx, xxi, xliii.
Donatus, xx.
Easter, date fixed, xxi, xxvii.
Ecthesis, lxix.
Ephesus, Third General Council at, li; Robbers' Council at, lviii, lix.
Eudoxia, xlv, xlvi.
Eunomians, xxx, xxxiii.
Eunomius, xxx.
Eusebians, xxvi, xxx; withdraw from Council of Sardica, xxxi; Long-lined Formula, xxxii; Council of Sirmium, xxxiii, xxxiv.
Eusebius of Cæsarea, quoted, xix; timidity, xxiii.
Eusebius of Dorylæum, xlviii, xlix, lvi; deposed, lviii.
Eusebius of Nicomedia, xxiii, xxiv; Council of Nicæa, xxvi, xxvii; banishment, xxviii; reopens Arian controversy, xxviii; charges against Athanasius, xxix; baptizes Constantine, xxix; bishop of Constantinople, xxx; death, xxxi.
Eusebius of Vercelli, xxxii.
Eustathians, xxxiv.
Eustathius of Antioch, xxv, xxviii, xxxiv, xlviii.
Eutropius of Hadrianople, xxviii.
Eutyches, Eutychianism, lvi, lvii; Robbers' Council, lviii, lix; at Chalcedon, lx, lxiv.
Euzoius, xxxiv.
Exukontians, xxxiii.
Felix III., lxii.
Felix of Aptunga, xx.
"Fighters against the Spirit," xxxviii.
Filioque, lxvi.

Flavian, xl.
Flavian of Constantinople, lvi, lvii, lviii, lix; at Chalcedon, lx.
Flavian of Thessalonica, li.
Fontaines, lxvii.
Formula, Long-lined, xxxii.
Formula Makrostichos, xxxii.
Frumentius, xxviii.
Gaudentius of Naissus, xxxi.
"Genetrix Dei," lvi.
Genseric, xlii.
George of Alexandria, xxxiv.
Gnosticism, similarity to Apollinarianism, liv.
"Golden Church," xxx.
Goths, xlii.
Gratian, xxxvii.
Gregory I., lxvii.
Gregory of Alexandria, xxxii.
Gregory of Nazianzus, xxxvi, xxxvii; at Second General Council, xxxix, xl; death, xliii.
Gregory of Nyssa, xxxvi, xxxvii, xxxviii, xxxix; death, xliii.
Gregory the Illuminator, lxv.
Helena, xix.
"Henoticon," lxi, lxv.
Heraclius, lxviii, lxix.
Hermogenes, xxxi.
Heterousiasts, xxv, xxx, xxxiii.
Hilary, legate to the Latrocinium, lix.
Hilary of Poitiers, xxxii, xxxvi.
Hippo, Council of, xli.
Holy Ghost, xxxv, xxxviii.
Homœans, xxixii.
Homoiousians, xxvi, xxxiii, xxxiv.
Homoöusion, xxvi, xxxv.
Honorius, emperor, xlii.
Honorius, Pope, lxviii; anathematized, lxx.
Hormisdas, lxii.
Hosius of Cordova, xxiv, xxv, xxxi, xxxii, xxxiii.
Huns, xlii.
Hy, lxvii.
Hypatia, liii.
Hypostatic union, lv, lx, lxi.
Ibas, liii, lxi, lxiii.

Iona, lxvii.
Jacobites, lxv.
Jacobus Baradæus, lxiv.
Jerome, xlii, xliv.
John, Count, lii.
John of Antioch, xlviii, li, lii; reconciliation with Cyril, liii.
Johannes Scholasticus, lxvi.
"Judicatum," lxiii.
Julian, xxxiv, xxxvi.
Julian of Halicarnassus, lxiv.
Julius of Rome, xxx, xxxi, xxxii.
Justin, lxii.
Justina, xliii.
Justinian, lxii; repudiates Three Chapters, lxii; summons general council, lxiii; confirms election to Papacy, lxiv; influence, lxvi.
Juvenal of Jerusalem, li.
Khosroes, King of Persia, lxviii.
Kyrion, lxv.
Laodicea, Council of, xli.
Lateran Synod, First, lxix.
Latrocinium, lviii, lix, lx.
Leo I., lvii, lviii.
Leo III., lxvi.
Leovigild, lxv.
Libanius, xlvi.
Liberius of Rome, xxxii, xxxiii.
Licinius, xix, xx, xxi, xxiv.
Lombards, lxvii.
"Long Brothers," xlv.
Long-lined Formula, xxxii.
Lucifer of Cagliari, xxxii, xxxv.
Luxeuil, lxvii.
Macarius of Antioch, lxix.
Macedonians, xxxviii, xl.
Macedonius, xxxi, xxxv, xl.
Makrostichos, xxxii.
Marcellus of Ancyra, xxxi, xxxii.
Marcian, lix, lxi.
Maris the Persian, lxiii.
Martin I., lxix, lxxi.
Mary, xxxix, xlviii, lv.
"Mater Dei," lvi.
Maurice, emperor, lxv.
Maxentius, xix.
Maximus, bishop of Constantinople, xxxix.

Maximus, the anti-Monothelite, lxx, lxxi.
Melchiades, xx.
Melchites, lxv.
Meletians, xxix, xxxiv.
Meletius, bishop of Lycopolis, xx, xxvii, xxxiv, xxxix, xl.
Memnon of Ephesus, li, lii.
Mennas, lxviii.
Milan, Council of, xxxii.
Milan, Edict of, xix, xx.
Milvian Bridge, battle of, xix.
Mohammed, lxviii.
Möhler, on Athanasius, xxxvi.
Monasticism, lxvii.
Monophysites, lxi; divisions, lxiv, lxv, lxviii.
Monothelites, lxviii, lxx sq.
Monte Cassino, lxvii.
Mother of God, xxxix, xlviii, lvi.
Neander, opinion of Arius, xxii.
Nectarius, xl.
Nestorianism, xxxviii, liii; its subtlety, liv; its errors, liv sq.
Nestorius, xlv, xlviii, l; sentenced, li, lii; character, liii.
Nicæa, Council of, xxv sq.
Nicene Creed, xxvi, xl, lii, lxvi.
Nisibis, liii.
"Oak, The," xlvi.
Onesiphorus, lix.
Origen, xliv, xlv, lxii.
Ostrogoths, xlii.
Papal Supremacy, xxvii, xxxi, xxxii, xli.
Paul of Constantinople, A.D. 342, xxxi.
Paul of Constantinople, A.D. 646, lxix.
Paulinus, xxxii, xxxvi, xxxix, xl.
Pelagians, Pelagianism, xliii, xlvii, lii.
Pelagius, Pope, lxiv.
Peter Mongus, lxii.
Peter of Alexandria, xx, xxi.
Peter the Fuller, lxi.
Phantasiasts, lxiv.
Philippopolis, Council of, xxxi, xxxii.

Index. 355

Photinus, xxxii.
Photius, l.
Placidia, xlii.
Pneumatomachi, xxxviii.
Pogonatus, lxix.
Proclus, xlix.
Pulcheria, xlii, lix.
Pyrrhus of Constantinople, lxx.
Quartodecimans, xxvii.
Radagaisus, xlii.
Reccared, lxv, lxvi.
"Robbers' Council," lviii, lix, lx.
Rome, Council of, condemning Donatists, xx; condemning Nestorius, l; synod at, A.D. 810, lxvi.
Rufinus, xliv.
Sabellians, Sabellianism, xxvi, xxxiv, xxxv; condemned by Second General Council, xli.
Sardica, Council of, xxxi.
Scotland, lxvii.
Scotus Erigena, lxxi.
Seleucia, Council of, xxxiii.
Semi-Arians, xxx, xxxiii, xxxiv.
Sergius, lxviii, lxix.
Severians, lxiv, lxviii.
Severus, lxiv.
Sirmium, Council of, xxxiii.
Sirmium, Synod of, xxxii.
Sophronius, lxviii.
Sotades, xxiv.
Spain redeemed from Arianism, lxv.
Stanley, opinion of Arius, xxii.
Suevi, xlii.
Synod of Sirmium, xxxii; of Arles, xxxii; of Milan, xxxii; of Alexandria, xxxv; at Constantinople, A.D. 545, lxiii; at Rome, A.D. 810, lxvi; First Lateran, lxix.
"Thalia" of Arius, xxiv.
Theodelinda, lxvii.
Theodochos, xlix.
Theodora, lxii.
Theodore of Mopsuestia, teaching, xlvi, xlvii, xlix, lxii, lxiii.
Theodore of Pharan, lxviii.
Theodore of Rome, lxix.
Theodoret, xlvii, li, lvi, lviii, lxi, lxiii.
Theodorus Askidas, lxii.
Theodosius, xxxvii, xxxix, xlii, xliii.
Theodosius II., xlii, li; Third General Council, lii, liii; death, lix.
Theodosius, monk, lxi.
Theodotus, xlviii.
Theophilus of Alexandria, xlv, l.
Theotocos, xxxix, xlviii, liv, lvi.
Three Chapters, lxii, lxiii, lxiv.
Timotheus Ælurus, lxi.
Tiridates, lxv.
Toledo, Third Council of, lxv.
"Trullus," lxix, lxxi.
"Typos," lxix, lxxi.
Tyre, Council of, xxix, xxxi.
Ulphilas, xlii.
Valens, xxxvi, xxxvii, xlii.
Valentinian III., xlii, lviii.
Vandals, xlii.
Vigilius, lxii, lxiii, lxiv.
Virgin Mary, xxxix, xlviii, lvi.
Visigoths, xlii.
Wagemann, quoted, lxxi.
Zeno, lxi, lxv.

New Volume Now Ready. **Price 12s.**

The International Critical Commentary

Editors—Canon DRIVER, Dr. PLUMMER and Dr. BRIGGS.

Just published, in post 8vo (pp. 678), price 12s.,

A

CRITICAL AND EXEGETICAL COMMENTARY

ON THE

GOSPEL ACCORDING TO S. LUKE

BY THE

Rev. ALFRED PLUMMER, M.A., D.D.

MASTER OF UNIVERSITY COLLEGE, DURHAM
FORMERLY FELLOW AND SENIOR TUTOR OF TRINITY COLLEGE, OXFORD

FIVE VOLUMES OF THE SERIES ARE NOW READY—*See also following pages.*

'We can sincerely congratulate the authors and the publishers upon producing one of the most epoch-making theological series of the day.'—*Church Bells.*

'The International Critical Commentary promises to be one of the most successful enterprises of an enterprising age. . . . So far as it has gone it satisfies the highest expectations and requirements.'—*The Bookman.*

'This series seems likely to surpass all previous enterprises of the kind in Great Britain and America.'—*Methodist Times.*

THE INTERNATIONAL CRITICAL COMMENTARY

In post 8vo (pp. 530), price 12s.,

DEUTERONOMY

BY THE

Rev. S. R. DRIVER, D.D.,

REGIUS PROFESSOR OF HEBREW, AND CANON OF CHRIST CHURCH, OXFORD.

Professor G. A. SMITH (in *The Critical Review*) says: 'The series could have had no better introduction than this volume from its Old Testament editor. . . . Dr. Driver has achieved a commentary of rare learning and still more rare candour and sobriety of judgment. . . . It is everywhere based on an independent study of the text and history . . . it has a large number of new details: its treatment of the religious value of the book is beyond praise. We find, in short, all those virtues which are conspicuous in the author's previous works, with a warmer and more interesting style of expression.'

'There is plenty of room for such a comprehensive commentary as that which we are now promised, and if the subsequent volumes of the series come up to the standard of excellence set in the work that now lies before us, the series will supply a real want in our literature. . . . The Introduction is a masterly piece of work, and here the Oxford Professor of Hebrew is at his best. It gives by far the best and fairest discussion that we have ever seen of the critical problems connected with the book.'—*Guardian*.

'We have said enough, we hope, to send the student to this commentary. . . . To the diligent miner there is a wealth of gold and precious stones awaiting his toil and industry.'—*Church Bells*.

'The commentary on the text of Deuteronomy is characterised by the highest learning and fulness of research, and will be of great value, not only to the ordinary student, but to the mature scholar.'—*Record*.

'The work will be not less a treasure to the English student than a credit to English scholarship.'—*Christian World*.

In post 8vo (pp. 526), price 12s.,

JUDGES

BY THE

Rev. GEORGE F. MOORE, D.D.,

PROFESSOR OF HEBREW IN ANDOVER THEOLOGICAL SEMINARY, MASS.

Professor H. E. RYLE, D.D., says: 'I think it may safely be averred that so full and scientific a commentary upon the text and subject-matter of the Book of Judges has never been produced in the English language.'

'Dr. Moore's "Judges" will come as a deep surprise to many in this country. It is not in any respect, so far as we have been able to judge, of lighter weight than the two great volumes of the series which appeared before it.'—*The Expository Times*.

'It is unquestionably the best commentary that has hitherto been published on the Book of Judges.'—*London Quarterly Review*.

'Professor Moore of Andover follows up Canon Driver's volume on Deuteronomy with a commentary on "Judges," marked by as great learning—it could not be greater —and perhaps by somewhat more freedom of expression. . . . He has examined every word, every letter, of the original text under the microscope.'—*Academy*.

EDINBURGH: T. & T. CLARK, 38 GEORGE STREET.

THE INTERNATIONAL CRITICAL COMMENTARY

In post 8vo (pp. 375), price 10s. 6d.,

ST. MARK'S GOSPEL

BY THE
Rev. EZRA P. GOULD, S.T.D.,

PROFESSOR OF THE NEW TESTAMENT LITERATURE AND LANGUAGE,
DIVINITY SCHOOL OF THE PROTESTANT EPISCOPAL CHURCH, PHILADELPHIA.

'This commentary is written with ability and judgment; it contains much valuable material, and it carries the reader satisfactorily through the Gospel. Great care has been spent upon the text.'—*The Expositor.*

'Everything relating to the department of criticism on these points is more thoroughly explained and illustrated here than has ever been done before in an English commentary.'—*Methodist Times.*

In post 8vo (pp. 562), price 12s.,

ROMANS

BY THE
Rev. WILLIAM SANDAY, D.D., LL.D.,

LADY MARGARET PROFESSOR OF DIVINITY, AND
CANON OF CHRIST CHURCH, OXFORD;

AND THE
Rev. ARTHUR C. HEADLAM, B.D.,

FELLOW OF ALL SOULS' COLLEGE, OXFORD.

Principal F. H. CHASE, D.D., Cambridge, says: 'We welcome it as an epoch-making contribution to the study of St. Paul.'

'This is an excellent commentary, scholarly, clear, doctrinal, reverent, and learned. . . . It is a volume which will bring credit to English scholarship, and while it is the crown of much good work on the part of the older editor, it gives promise of equally good work in the future from both.'—*Guardian.*

'A most valuable gift to the student of Romans. . . . It is the fullest and freshest in learning, the most patient, the most willing to be intelligible, and to make the Apostle so; and it need not be added, in any work of Dr. Sanday, that in textual criticism it will be a standard authority.'—*British Weekly.*

'Will at once take its place in the front rank of similar works. Its rich fulness of learning, its careful and dispassionate statement of difficulties, and its candour, which will not affect an undue positiveness, call upon us to give it a very hearty welcome.'—*The Record.*

'It stands easily at the head of English commentaries. It has qualities, especially in what concerns the text, in which it is superior to the best works of Continental scholars.'—*The Critical Review.*

EDINBURGH: T. & T. CLARK, 38 GEORGE STREET.

SPECIMEN PAGE

DEUTERONOMY

XXIX.–XXX. *Moses' Third Discourse. Israel formally called upon to enter into the Deuteronomic Covenant.*

The Deuteronomic Code ends with c. 28. C. 29–30 is of the nature of a supplement, insisting afresh upon the fundamental principle of the Code, viz. devotion to Jehovah, and calling upon Israel to yield loyal allegiance to it. The discourse falls naturally into three parts. In the first, Moses, after referring to what Jehovah has done for Israel ($29^{1-8\,(2-9)}$), reminds them that the purpose for which they are now assembled together is that they may enter solemnly into covenant with Him, and warns them afresh of the disastrous consequences, including national ruin and exile, which a lapse into idolatry will inevitably entail ($29^{9-28\,(10-29)}$); in the second, imagining the threatened exile to have taken place, he promises that even then, if Israel sincerely repents, Jehovah will again receive it into His favour, and restore it to the land of promise (30^{1-10}); in the third, he sums up, in brief but forcible words, the two alternatives placed before Israel, life and happiness on the one side, death and misfortune on the other, and adjures the nation to choose wisely between them (30^{11-20}).

In these chapters, the connection is sometimes imperfect, esp. between 30^{1-10} and 30^{11-20} (see on 30^{11}); several words and phrases occur, not otherwise found in Dt. (Dillm. notes השכיל $29^{8\,(9)}$, אלה *oath, imprecation,* $29^{11.\,13.\,14.\,19.\,20\,(12.\,14.\,19.\,20.\,21)}$ 30^7, *idol-blocks* and *detestations* $29^{16\,(17)}$, פן יש $29^{17\,(18)}$, שרירות *stubbornness* $29^{18\,(19)}$, עשן אף and סלח $29^{19\,(20)}$, לרעה *unto evil* $29^{20\,(21)}$, תחלואים *sicknesses* $29^{21\,(22)}$, *forsake the covenant* $29^{24\,(25)}$, נתש *pluck up* $29^{27\,(28)}$, הריח *drive away* $30^{1.\,4}$; and the phrases $29^{5\,(6)b.\,17\,(18)b\,L.\,18\,(19)b}$); and the points of contact with Jeremiah are more numerous than usual. A question thus arises, whether the text is throughout in its original order, and whether it is entirely by the same hand as the body of Dt.: see the Introduction, § 4.

XXIX. 1–8 (2–9). Moses reminds the Israelites of all that Jehovah has wrought for them, from the time of their deliverance from Egypt, founding upon it a renewed exhortation to obey the words of the covenant.—The paragraph is a recapitulation of the substance of earlier parts of Dt., stated largely in the same phraseology.—**1 (2).** *And Moses called unto all Israel* (1^1), *and said unto them*] exactly as 5^1.—*Ye* (emph.) *have*

238   THE GOSPEL ACCORDING TO S. LUKE   [VIII. 54, 55.

This laying hold of her hand and the raised voice (ἐφώνησεν) are consonant with waking one out of sleep, and the two may be regarded as the means of the miracle. Comp. and contrast throughout Acts ix. 36–42.

Ἡ παῖς, ἔγειρε. "Arise, get up," not "awake." Mt. omits the command; Mk. gives the exact words, *Talitha cumi*. For the nom. with the art. as voc. see on x. 21, xviii. 11, 13. For ἐφώνησεν comp. ver. 8, xvi. 24.

55. ἐπέστρεψεν τὸ πνεῦμα αὐτῆς. There can be no doubt that the Evangelist uses the phrase of the spirit returning to a dead body, which is the accurate use of the phrase. Only the beloved physician makes this statement. In LXX it is twice used of a living man's strength reviving; of the fainting Samson (Judg. xv. 19), and of the starving Egyptian (1 Sam. xxx. 12). Note that Lk. has his favourite παραχρῆμα, where Mk. has his favourite εὐθύς; and comp. ver. 44, v. 25, xviii. 43, xxii. 60.

διέταξεν αὐτῇ δοθῆναι φαγεῖν. This care of Jesus in commanding food after the child's long exhaustion would be of special interest to Lk. In their joy and excitement the parents might have forgotten it. The charge is somewhat parallel to ἔδωκεν αὐτὸν τῇ μητρὶ αὐτοῦ (vii. 15) of the widow's son at Nain. In each case He intimates that nature is to resume its usual course: the old ties and the old responsibilities are to begin again.

ὁ δὲ παρήγγειλεν αὐτοῖς μηδενὶ εἰπεῖν τὸ γεγονός. The command has been rejected as an unintelligible addition to the narrative. No such command was given at Nain or at Bethany. The object of it cannot have been to keep the miracle a secret. Many were outside expecting the funeral, and they would have to be told why no funeral was to take place. It can hardly have been Christ's intention in this way to prevent the multitude from making a bad use of the miracle. This command to the parents would not have attained such an object. It was given more probably for the parents' sake, to keep them from letting the effect of this great blessing evaporate in vainglorious gossip. To thank God for it at home would be far more profitable than talking about it abroad.

IX. 1–50. *To the Departure for Jerusalem.*

This is the last of the four sections into which the Ministry in Galilee (iv. 14–ix. 50) was divided. It contains the Mission of the Twelve (1–9), the Feeding of the Five Thousand (10–17), the Transfiguration (28–36), the Healing of the Demoniac Boy (37–43), and two Predictions of the Passion (18–27, 43–50).

1–9. The Mission of the Twelve and the Fears of Herod. Mt. x. 1–15; Mk. vi. 7–11. Mt. is the most full. Lk. gives no note

THE INTERNATIONAL CRITICAL COMMENTARY.

The following eminent Scholars have contributed, or are engaged upon, the Volumes named below :—

THE OLD TESTAMENT.

Genesis.	The Rev. T. K. CHEYNE, D.D., Oriel Professor of the Interpretation of Holy Scripture, Oxford.
Exodus.	The Rev. A. R. S. KENNEDY, D.D., Professor of Hebrew, University of Edinburgh.
Leviticus.	The Rev. H. A. WHITE, M.A., Fellow of New College, Oxford.
Numbers.	G. BUCHANAN GRAY, M.A., Lecturer in Hebrew, Mansfield College, Oxford.
Deuteronomy.	The Rev. S. R. DRIVER, D.D., Regius Professor of Hebrew, Oxford. [*Ready*, 12s.
Joshua.	The Rev. GEORGE ADAM SMITH, D.D., Professor of Hebrew, Free Church College, Glasgow.
Judges.	The Rev. GEORGE MOORE, D.D., Professor of Hebrew, Andover Theological Seminary, Andover, Mass. [*Ready*, 12s.
Samuel.	The Rev. H. P. SMITH, D.D., late Professor of Hebrew, Lane Theological Seminary, Cincinnati, Ohio.
Kings.	The Rev. FRANCIS BROWN, D.D., Professor of Hebrew and Cognate Languages, Union Theological Seminary, New York City.
Isaiah.	The Rev. A. B. DAVIDSON, D.D., LL.D., Professor of Hebrew, Free Church College, Edinburgh.
Jeremiah.	The Rev. A. F. KIRKPATRICK, D.D., Regius Professor of Hebrew, and Fellow of Trinity College, Cambridge.
Minor Prophets.	W. R. HARPER, Ph.D., President of the University of Chicago, Illinois.
Psalms.	The Rev. CHARLES A. BRIGGS, D.D., Edward Robinson Professor of Biblical Theology, Union Theological Seminary, New York.
Proverbs.	The Rev. C. H. TOY, D.D., Professor of Hebrew, Harvard University, Cambridge, Massachusetts.
Job.	The Rev. S. R. DRIVER, D.D., Regius Professor of Hebrew, Oxford.
Daniel.	The Rev. JOHN P. PETERS, Ph.D., late Professor of Hebrew, P. E. Divinity School, Philadelphia, now Rector of St. Michael's Church, New York City.
Ezra and Nehemiah.	The Rev. L. W. BATTEN, Ph.D., Professor of Hebrew, P. E. Divinity School, Philadelphia.
Chronicles.	The Rev. EDWARD L. CURTIS, D.D., Professor of Hebrew, Yale University, New Haven, Conn.

THE INTERNATIONAL CRITICAL COMMENTARY—continued.

THE NEW TESTAMENT.

Mark.	The Rev. E. P. GOULD, D.D., Professor of New Testament Exegesis, P. E. Divinity School, Philadelphia. [*Ready*, 10s. 6d.
Luke.	The Rev. ALFRED PLUMMER, D.D., Master of University College, Durham. [*Ready*, 12s.
Acts.	The Rev. FREDERICK H. CHASE, D.D., Fellow of Christ's College, Cambridge.
Romans.	The Rev. WILLIAM SANDAY, D.D., Lady Margaret Professor of Divinity, and Canon of Christ Church, Oxford; and the Rev. A. C. HEADLAM, B.D., Fellow of All Souls' College, Oxford. [*Ready*, 12s.
Corinthians.	The Rev. ARCH. ROBERTSON, D.D., Principal of Bishop Hatfield's Hall, Durham.
Galatians.	The Rev. ERNEST D. BURTON, A.B., Professor of New Testament Literature, University of Chicago.
Ephesians and Colossians.	The Rev. T. K. ABBOTT, B.D., D.Lit., formerly Professor of Biblical Greek, Trinity College, Dublin.
Philippians and Philemon.	The Rev. MARVIN R. VINCENT, D.D., Professor of Biblical Literature, Union Theological Seminary, New York City.
The Pastoral Epistles.	The Rev. WALTER LOCK, M.A., Dean Ireland's Professor of Exegesis, Oxford.
Hebrews.	The Rev. T. C. EDWARDS, D.D., Principal of the Theological College, Bala; late Principal of University College of Wales, Aberystwyth.
James.	The Rev. JAMES H. ROPES, A.B., Instructor in New Testament Criticism in Harvard University.
Peter and Jude.	The Rev. CHARLES BIGG, D.D., Rector of Fenny Compton, Leamington; Bampton Lecturer, 1886.
Revelation.	The Rev. ROBERT H. CHARLES, M.A., Trinity College, Dublin, and Exeter College, Oxford.

Other engagements will be announced shortly.

EDINBURGH: T. & T. CLARK, 38 GEORGE STREET.
LONDON: SIMPKIN, MARSHALL, HAMILTON, KENT, & CO. LTD.

The International Theological Library

EDITED BY

PROFESSORS S. D. F. SALMOND, D.D., AND C. A. BRIGGS, D.D.

This Library is designed to cover the whole field of Christian Theology. Each volume is to be complete in itself, while, at the same time, it will form part of a carefully planned whole. It is intended to form a Series of Text-Books for Students of Theology. The Authors will be scholars of recognised reputation in the several branches of study assigned to them. They will be associated with each other and with the Editors in the effort to provide a series of volumes which may adequately represent the present condition of investigation.

'The "International Theological Library," to which we have already learned to look for the best and most recent in the historical, literary, and linguistic study of the Bible.'—President W. R. HARPER, of Chicago University, in *The Biblical World*.

The First Four Volumes of the Series are now ready, viz. :—

An Introduction to the Literature of the Old Testament. By S. R. DRIVER, D.D., Regius Professor of Hebrew, and Canon of Christ Church, Oxford. Fifth Edition, with Appendix. Post 8vo, price 12s.

Christian Ethics. By NEWMAN SMYTH, D.D., Author of 'Old Faiths in New Light,' etc. Third Edition. Post 8vo, 10s. 6d.

Apologetics; or, Christianity Defensively Stated. By A. B. BRUCE, D.D., Professor of Apologetics and New Testament Exegesis, Free Church College, Glasgow. Third Edition. Post 8vo, 10s. 6d.

History of Christian Doctrine. By G. P. FISHER, D.D., LL.D., Professor of Ecclesiastical History, Yale College, New Haven, U.S.A. Post 8vo, 12s. *Just Published.*

(1) Of Professor DRIVER'S 'INTRODUCTION,' *The Times* says :—'The service which Canon Driver's book will render in the present confusion of mind on this great subject, can scarcely be overestimated.'

The Guardian says :—'By far the best account of the great critical problems connected with the Old Testament that has yet been written. . . . It is a perfect marvel of compression and lucidity combined. A monument of learning and well-balanced judgment.'

(2) Of Dr. NEWMAN SMYTH'S 'CHRISTIAN ETHICS,' *The Bookman* says :—'There is not a dead, dull, conventional line in the volume. It is the work of a wise, well-informed, independent, and thoroughly competent writer. It removes a reproach from our indigenous theology, fills a glaring blank in our literature, and is sure to become *the* text-book in Christian Ethics.'

(3) Of Professor BRUCE'S 'APOLOGETICS,' *The Expository Times* says : — 'The force and the freshness of all the writings that Dr. Bruce has hitherto published have doubtless led many to look forward with eager hope to this work; and there need not be any fear of disappointment. It has all the characteristics of the author's personality. . . . It will render an inestimable service.'

(4) Of Professor FISHER'S 'CHRISTIAN DOCTRINE,' *The Critical Review* says :— 'A clear, readable, well-proportioned, and, regarding it as a whole, remarkably just and accurate account of what the course and development of doctrine throughout the ages, and in different countries, has been.'

*** *A Prospectus giving full details of the Series, with list of Contributors, sent free on application to the Publishers, Messrs. T. & T. Clark, 38 George Street, Edinburgh.*

www.ingramcontent.com/pod-product-compliance
Lightning Source LLC
Chambersburg PA
CBHW020526300426
44111CB00008B/556